HMSO On Subs

GH01017991

The Effects of Acid Depos
Terrestrial Environment in
United Kingdom

INFORMATION ROOM CENTRAL LIBRARY

BARNSLEY LIBRARIES

3 8059 00040 9146

The Effects of Acid Deposition on the Terrestrial Environment in the United Kingdom

United Kingdom Terrestrial Effects Review Group

First Report

Prepared at the request of the Department of the Environment

LONDON : HER MAJESTY'S STATIONERY OFFICE

© Crown Copyright 1988
First published 1988
ISBN 0 11 752029 2

United Kingdom
Terrestrial Effects Review Group

M.H. Unsworth *Chairman*	Institute of Terrestrial Ecology (until August 1987) University of Nottingham
J.N.B. Bell	Imperial College of Science and Technology
V.J. Black	Loughborough University of Technology
M.S. Cresser	University of Aberdeen
N.M. Darrall	Central Electricity Research Laboratories
A.W. Davison	University of Newcastle
P.H. Freer-Smith	University of Ulster (until August 1987) Forestry Commission
P. Ineson	Institute of Terrestrial Ecology (Natural Environment Research Council)
J.A. Lee	University of Manchester
F.T. Last	Chairman 1985–86 Institute of Terrestrial Ecology (Natural Environment Research Council) (retired 1986) University of Newcastle
T.A. Mansfield	University of Lancaster
M.H. Martin	University of Bristol
H.G. Miller	University of Aberdeen
T.M. Roberts	Central Electricity Research Laboratories
C.E.R. Pitcairn *Technical Secretary*	Department of the Environment
R.B. Wilson *Executive Secretary*	Department of the Environment

The authors accept responsibility for the contents of this report but the views expressed are their own and not necessarily those of the organisations to which they belong or the Department of the Environment.

CONTENTS

EXECUTIVE SUMMARY

1. The Terrestrial Effects Review Group (TERG) was set up to review the effects of acid deposition and its related pollutants on crops, trees and natural vegetation in the United Kingdom. Expert subgroups reviewed different aspects of this extremely broad topic, taking into account relevant evidence from other countries in Europe and from North America. This report is the first compilation of their findings.

2. To the layman, acidity reaching soils and plants is often thought to arise only from 'acid rain'. In fact acidity is also associated with pollutant gases and particles, and can be generated naturally. The review group has used the term 'acid deposition' to describe all the mechanisms by which acidity can reach the surface. The group has also considered effects of the pollutant gas ozone, because it is frequently associated with acid deposition.

3. Gaseous and particulate pollutants occur in the atmosphere in mixtures and may be primary (produced directly by industry, transport and from man's domestic and agricultural activities) or secondary (created in the atmosphere by chemical reactions involving some of the primary pollutants). The major *primary pollutants* are sulphur dioxide, oxides of nitrogen, ammonia and hydrocarbons. Emission sources for sulphur dioxide are almost entirely non-mobile, whereas those for oxides of nitrogen and hydrocarbons are both mobile and non-mobile and both industrial and rural sources of ammonia exist. The major *secondary pollutants* are ozone and acid rain. *Particulate pollutants* include soot, metallic particles and aerosols such as ammonium sulphate and ammonium nitrate.

4. Gases and particles may be deposited directly onto vegetation, soil and other surfaces, a process known as *dry deposition* or they may be incorporated in cloud, rain drops or snowflakes and transferred by gravitational settling to surfaces, (*wet deposition*) or turbulent transfer and impaction as with mists (*occult precipitation*).

5. The mixtures of pollutants in the atmosphere differ from place to place not only because of differences in emissions, but also because of factors such as weather and topography. Consequently, a number of distinctive pollution climates exist in the UK. The review group felt the concept of pollution climates to be useful in assessing the impact of air pollutants on vegetation. They identified a need for a better data base to define pollution climates so that impacts in different areas of the UK can be analysed and intercomparisons can be made with pollution response research in other countries. Even with the present limited data, it is clear that major vegetation types are exposed to different pollution climates. For example, arable crops in southern England may be exposed to larger concentrations of gaseous pollutants than plantation forests in the uplands of Scotland where occult precipitation may be a significant input.

6. Pollution research in the UK until the 1970s concentrated on effects of gaseous pollutants on crops and grasslands. In the UK and Germany, sulphur dioxide was the main focus of research, whereas in North America concern centred mainly on effects of ozone. As research intensified, it was realised that:

i) pollutants could affect plant growth and crop yields without visible blemishes;

ii) exposure to mixtures of pollutants could be more damaging than exposure to single pollutants;

iii) significant interactions occur between pollutants and other stresses;

iv) pollutants could influence plant growth *indirectly* by soil-mediated effects.

7. Two environmental problems altered the emphasis of research into air pollution effects. Acidification of fresh waters in Scandinavia was increasingly recognised as being associated with acid deposition and a previously unidentified type of forest damage was identified in a number of European countries. There has been a considerable expansion of research on effects of air pollutants on trees to attempt to explain forest damage and there has also been expanded effort on soil acidification processes. These topics and existing and continuing research on other plant species formed the basis of this review.

8. Agricultural soils are not normally at risk from acidification because agricultural practices, particularly liming, are designed to counteract acidity. Any large scale changes in agricultural land use and practices may however require a re-assessment of this conclusion. For example, since 1976 there has been a seven fold reduction in the amount of lime applied to a Cumbrian catchment and certain fields have received no lime since the liming subsidy ceased. A recent assessment of the state of the environment in the European Community reported that the application of lime to agricultural soils had decreased by 15–20% in the United Kingdom.

9. Forest soils can become acidified because pollutants are efficiently trapped on tree foliage and are subsequently washed from leaves and stems by rain. Some trees also tend to acidify soils in the absence of pollutants and attempts must be made to separate the effects of trees on soils from those of pollutants. The effects on soils of pollutant trapping by heather and bracken, which can give extensive ground cover, are as yet virtually unknown.

10. There are indications that acidification affects the biological activity of soils, reduces rates of litter decomposition and restricts consequent nutrient release. Soil acidification will also affect the mycorrhizal relationships between certain fungi and the fine roots of forest trees

that facilitate tree nutrition. The significance of these effects is not fully established and this is an important research area for the future.

11. The group reviewed the pollution sensitivity of the major types of vegetation in the UK: grasslands (including permanent pasture and rough grazing); arable crops; woodlands; and semi-natural ecosystems. Different land uses are often accompanied by different pollution climates, for example gaseous pollutants predominate in arable farming areas of central England whereas acid rain is an important input to upland areas where forestry is currently practiced. However, land-use in the UK may change markedly in the future as a result of changes in agricultural policy. There would be advantages for assessing future impacts of air pollutants in drawing together information on the distribution of vegetation in the UK with the results of the new rural air pollution monitoring networks.

12. There is no evidence that grasslands or arable crops in the UK are damaged directly by acid rain but there is considerable evidence from research in UK and elsewhere that these crops are sensitive to gaseous pollutants.

13. Concentrations of gaseous pollutants tend to be largest in urban/urban fringe areas and experiments to determine whether plant growth in these areas is affected by current air quality have produced apparently conflicting results. Yield increases as well as decreases have been reported. These differences may be the result of different pollutant mixtures at different sites and in different years, or may reflect interactions between pollutant and climatic stresses.

14. In rural areas of south east England air quality reduced the yield of experimental plots of a range of crop species such as peas, beans and spinach in most summers; the effect seems to be related to atmospheric ozone concentrations. Recent evidence also suggests that the combined effects of ozone, sulphur dioxide and oxides of nitrogen may explain why pea yields decreased progressively along a transect from rural areas into London.

15. Experiments in which cereals in the field and laboratory were exposed to controlled concentrations of gaseous pollutants have shown that yields are reduced without visible damage by exposure to sulphur dioxide alone and in mixtures with nitrogen dioxide at concentrations above 40 parts per billion. Although these concentrations are higher than mean annual rural values, they may be equalled or exceeded at many sites for periods of very short duration (episodes).

16. Knowledge of the basic mechanisms by which pollutants damage plants is vital for the understanding of plant responses. The effect of single pollutants and more importantly, pollutant mixtures on biochemical and physiological processes taking place in grasses and crop plants are becoming better understood. Considerable progress is being made in understanding how pollutants at realistic concentrations affect stomatal responses, biochemical reactions, photosynthesis and assimilation. At present, knowledge is mainly limited to effects on leaves and further research is needed on effects on root growth, flowering, fruit production and crop quality.

17. While there has been substantial research in the UK and elsewhere into sensitivity of crops to pollutants, much less is known of the sensitivity of trees. Due to the longevity, size and genetic variation of trees, pollution research on them is technically demanding and must of necessity be long term. Progress is being made in investigating the effects on trees of sulphur dioxide, nitrogen dioxide and ozone singly and in mixtures. The effects of acid mists and ozone in combination and the interaction of pollutants with other stresses such as drought and frost are also being investigated. Evidence of direct damage to trees by acid rain alone is inconclusive at present.

18. During the late 1970s, concern initially grew in Germany over the health of silver fir, Norway spruce and later Scots pine, beech and oak. Surveys in several countries of central Europe have confirmed that forest decline is occurring. Few of the symptoms of forest decline are unique or specific and it has proved impossible to determine the causes of decline from an examination of these alone. Many hypotheses have been proposed to explain the decline, some of which are not pollution-related. It is still not clear what role, if any, acid deposition plays in forest decline but three major hypotheses involving acid deposition have been proposed:

i) acidification of soils leading to loss of nutrients, aluminium mobilisation and root damage,

ii) exposure of foliage to pollutant gases and acid mist or rain,

iii) interactions between pollutant stress and other stresses.

At the present time it is not possible to decide conclusively whether any one or more of these hypotheses is the true cause of decline.

19. Surveys of the health of forest plantations (Sitka spruce, Norway spruce and Scots pine) in the UK have been made by the Forestry Commission since 1984. The 1986 and 1987 survey suggested a significant reduction in crown density in all three species but, as in other parts of Europe, causal links have not been established with pollution or with any other stress. Surveys of beech since 1985 have not shown any increasing damage symptoms, or a trend of declining tree health. However, this species is not in good health and pollution cannot be excluded as a contributing stress.

20. It is doubtful whether surveys of tree health alone will ever establish causes of damage. Consequently, there is a need for controlled exposure experiments and specific tests to identify air pollution damage. A number of physical, physiological and biochemical tests indicative of air pollution stress are being developed. A multinational pilot study led by the UK has shown that some of these can identify significant differences between trees growing in different pollution climates. Experiments are now required to apply such tests to trees which have been exposed to controlled concentrations of pollutants.

21. The impact of acid deposition on natural vegetation has received little attention. This vegetation consists mainly of moorland, mire and heathland composed of heather, bracken, grasses and mosses. In the north and west of Britain, natural communities occur mainly in upland areas where growth may be limited by availability of nitrogen. Man-made emissions of nitrogen oxides have increased in recent decades and there is evidence of increasing nitrate concentrations in rainfall and a greater contribution of nitrogen oxides to total acidity of rainfall.

22. Blanket bogs of the southern Pennines have been damaged by the sulphur and nitrogen deposition which has occurred since the onset of the Industrial Revolution, but little is known about the effects of increased deposition of nitrogen compounds, including ammonia, on the wider array of species present in upland communities.

23. It has only recently been recognised, particularly from long term research in Sweden, that naturally acidic soils may be vulnerable to acid depositions. Some soils in the UK (eg. podzols of North West Wales) have already become saturated with sulphate, and further deposition of sulphate leads to increases in acidity and aluminium concentrations in drainage waters. The importance of sulphate input from acid deposition, superimposed upon already substantial maritime-derived sulphate inputs at some sites needs to be established.

24. Plants are subject to a wide range of natural stresses which may not only influence plant growth directly but may also modify plant response to pollutants. For example, some species are more sensitive to pollutants in winter than at other times and there is good evidence that pollutants reduce frost resistance and winter hardiness in cereals and trees. Interactions between pollutants and water stress also occur. Exposure to pollutants can result in enhanced water loss in some plants and also reduces root growth, leading to increased sensitivity to water stress in times of drought and a reduced potential for regrowth following grazing, mowing, and trampling. Some fungal diseases are increased and others decreased by pollutants. Recently the growth rates of certain plant pests such as aphids have been shown to be stimulated by pollutants.

25. Many scientists believe there might be significant climatic changes from man-made pollution. In addition to considering the direct consequences of climatic change, the responses of terrestrial systems to pollutants such as acid deposition might differ in the changed climates of the future.

26. The review group concludes that

i) Major agricultural crops in the UK are unlikely to be damaged directly by current rural concentrations of sulphur dioxide and nitrogen oxides. However, in most summers, concentrations of ozone occurring in some areas of south-east England are likely to reduce yields of sensitive crops. Recent evidence suggests that interactions between pollutant stresses and other stresses such as pests, may be extremely important in influencing crop yields. However on the basis of present information, it is not possible to make precise assessments of effects of pollutants on national crop yields.

ii) There is as yet no direct proof of pollution-related forest decline in the UK, but some forests are subjected to pollution climates which may be expected to cause stress. Isolated trees in hedgerows and urban areas may also be at risk. On the basis of this circumstantial evidence, it is recommended that surveys be maintained and more specific diagnostic tests for pollution damage be developed.

iii) Few data exist on the impact of air pollutants on natural vegetation. Blanket bogs have been damaged by deposition of sulphur and nitrogen. In view of the amenity value of the relatively large areas of other natural vegetation such as moorlands and heath in the UK, there is a need to extend air pollution research in this field.

iv) It has become increasingly evident that acid deposition is accelerating acidification of some soils, and that changes in soil biology may result. Such changes are likely to alter plant nutrition and to change the chemistry and biology of freshwaters (streams and lakes). Consequently this should be a high priority area for future UK research.

v) The responses of plants to pollutants are complex and are likely to be influenced by other stresses. To interpret these responses in the field, it is essential that research, aimed at understanding basic mechanisms by which pollutants affect plants, is maintained and that such research should complement more applied projects on evaluating systems at risk.

vi) Information from the recently expanded pollution monitoring networks should be drawn together with land use surveys as an aid in identifying areas where vegetation and soils may be at risk from air pollution and to help in assessing potential impacts of pollution on changed land uses.

vii) If predictions of future climate change are substantiated, there will be a need to reassess the responses of terrestrial systems to pollutants such as acid deposition in the light of the changed climatic conditions.

List of Plates

List of Tables

List of Figures

INTRODUCTION

1.1 BACKGROUND

In the past, emissions from domestic fires and industry polluted our towns and cities, blackening buildings, killing vegetation, and endangering health. At that time smoke and sulphur dioxide (SO_2) were considered to be the main damaging agents, but it gradually became apparent that the polluted atmosphere almost always contains mixtures of pollutants.

The Clean Air Acts of the 1950s required domestic, commercial and industrial users to burn fuel in a more efficient manner. The combination of the Acts, modernisation and changes in fuel resulted in a trend towards taller stacks which effectively dispersed pollutant emissions from industrial centres. However tall stacks also increased the already important long range transport of SO_2 and oxides of nitrogen (NO_x). Thus, from the mid 1950s while the air in urban areas of the UK became cleaner, at about the same time, there was also recognition that there could be long range transport of air pollution.

Changes in rainfall acidity were observed in northern Europe and Scandinavia in the 1960s and evidence began to accumulate that areas receiving rain of high acidity coincided with areas where fish numbers in rivers and lakes were reducing. The Swedish submission to the United Nations Conference on the Human Environment in 1972 also pointed out possible deleterious effects of pollutant deposition on arable land, forests and soils.

Detrimental effects of acid precipitation were recognised in freshwater systems in the late 1970s. Although forests were considered by some to be at risk from acid precipitation, no obvious signs of visible damage were observed until the 1980s. Forest damage was identified during the 1980s in many countries of central Europe, but symptoms vary from region to region. At about the same time, similar forest damage was reported in eastern North America, particularly at high elevations. There is still however considerable uncertainty regarding the causes of this damage.

In the 1970s, research in industrialised countries into the effects of air pollution concentrated largely on the effects of gaseous pollutants on crops and grasslands. In the UK and West Germany, SO_2 was the main focus of interest, whereas in North America concern was centred on the effects of ozone.

As research intensified it was recognised that, contrary to some previous assertions, many air pollutants could restrict plant growth without causing visible blemishes. Interactions which could not have been predicted previously were shown to occur between individual pollutants and also between pollutants and other stresses.

In response to the disturbing reports of damage to forests and freshwaters in central Europe, Scandinavia, and North America, concern began to be expressed in the early 1980s over the risks to forests and freshwaters in Britain. The House of Lords Select Committee on the European Communities (Twenty-Second Report, *Air Pollution*, 1984) and the House of Commons Environment Committee (Fourth Report, *Acid Rain*, 1984) both reviewed the acid rain situation and made a number of recommendations. In response to the general public concern and to these reports, research by Government Departments, Research Councils and industry was expanded, new monitoring programmes were begun and a series of review groups were set up by the Department of the Environment to assess available information and to advise on research needs in relation to 'acid rain' and its effects.

This report has been produced by the Terrestrial Effects Review Group (TERG), which was established to review the direct and indirect effects of acidic deposition and its associated pollutants on crops, forests and natural vegetation in the UK. The first chapters review in detail some fundamental aspects of exposure to acid deposition – definition of the inputs of air pollutants to various ecosystems, effects of those pollutants on soils and the mechanisms by which plants respond to pollutants. Subsequent chapters consider the responses of specific plant systems and review the interaction of pollutants with naturally occurring stresses. Reports of other DOE review groups are listed in Appendix 4.

1.2 'ACID RAIN' OR 'ACID DEPOSITION'

The **primary pollutants** responsible for acid rain are SO_2 (mainly from coal combustion), nitric oxide (NO), and hydrocarbons (both from motor vehicles and other combustion processes). These gases may be directly deposited onto surfaces by the process of **dry deposition** or alternatively they may be incorporated in rain drops or snow flakes and transferred to surfaces indirectly as **wet deposition**. Wind-blown cloud or fog droplets may be directly captured by vegetation, a transfer pathway known as **occult deposition** (occult = hidden) because the droplets concerned are too small to be adequately captured by conventional wet deposition collectors.

Secondary pollutants such as nitrogen dioxide (NO_2) and ozone (which is formed in the lower atmosphere by the photochemical action of sunlight on primary pollutants) also contribute towards acidity. The primary pollutant gases can be transformed in the atmosphere to sulphate and nitrate by chemical reactions involving ozone and related compounds. These reactions provide most of the acids responsible for acidifying precipitation.

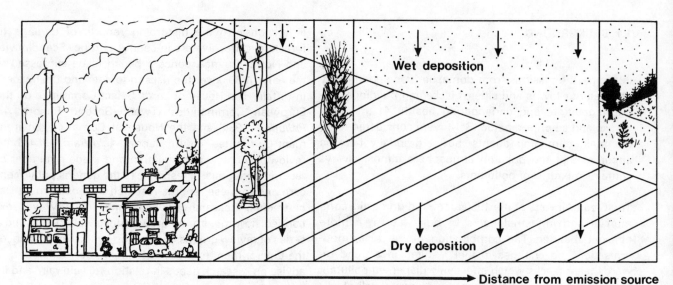

Wet deposition

Dry deposition

→ **Distance from emission source**

1.1   Schematic relationships between pollution sources, deposition processes and land use.

Pollutants may be transported over great distances, often being deposited many miles from source. The longer the pollutants are retained in the atmosphere, the greater the chance of chemical reactions and of subsequent deposition in rain or snow. Consequently wet and occult deposition are the main forms of acid deposition in areas remote from sources while dry deposition is greater in urban and rural areas which are close to emission sources. Figure 1.1 illustrates these points schematically. Near to pollution sources where pollutants are predominantly in a gaseous form, land use in the UK is primarily amenity planting, horticulture and arable farming. As distance from the source increases, wet deposition becomes more important and in the UK this situation generally occurs in areas where forests and natural vegetation are the dominant communities.

Although the term 'acid rain' is most commonly used in the popular press, in this review the more accurate term 'acid deposition' will be used. There are separate DOE review groups for acid deposition and photochemical oxidants (see Appendix 4). Chapter 2 draws on these to give a broad introduction into the main features responsible for the pollution climates of the UK ie. the mixtures of pollutants that occur in different parts of the country and that vary on a diurnal and seasonal basis.

1.3   LAND USE AND POLLUTION CLIMATE IN THE UK

In any attempt to quantify the impact of air pollution on vegetation in the UK, it is necessary not only to take into account the distribution and magnitude of phytotoxic air pollutants, but also to relate these to the distribution of species at risk. Information on the distribution of species is available from a number of sources, eg. agricultural census returns, surveys of natural species, and land use surveys. Such data are not always however sufficiently

compatible to allow ready combination of the data-bases to give detailed maps of distribution. More generally, the main rural land uses can be summarised. Cereals occupy about 15% of the UK land area, predominantly in the east; grasslands (30%) and rough grazing (27%) are mainly in the west and the uplands; woodlands cover less than 10% of the land and are currently concentrated in less fertile upland areas.

In several European countries, forests occupy a larger proportion of the land area than in the UK (eg. West Germany – 29%), and forestry and agriculture are intermixed to give a greater mosaic of land use than occurs in the UK. However, the area and distribution of different types of land use in the UK is likely to change markedly in the future as a result of changes in agricultural policy. It is difficult to predict the nature of these changes, but they will need to be taken into account when making future estimates of the impact of air pollution on vegetation.

At the time of this review there are insufficient long term records to reliably establish the pollution climate of large parts of the UK. The newly established rural pollution monitoring networks will provide data to fill this gap in the near future. At such a time it would be useful to draw together the data bases for pollution climate and vegetation distribution as an aid in identifying any areas at risk, and to assist in assessing the potential effects of pollution if there are land use changes. The Review Group therefore recommend that a mechanism for developing such a link should be established.

1.4   EFFECTS OF POLLUTANTS ON PLANTS AND SOILS

Pollutants may effect plants **directly** by absorption through foliage, or **indirectly** by damaging soils and altering nutrient availability.

Direct Effects

Research into the direct effects of pollutants can be approached in several ways. Plants can be grown at field sites along a gradient of pollution concentration eg. from urban to rural areas along a prevailing wind direction. Alternatively plants may be grown in chambers ventilated with ambient air or with air that has been filtered or plants can be exposed in the field or laboratory to carefully controlled concentrations of artificially supplied pollutants. Each of these approaches has strengths and weaknesses for improving understanding of relationships between air pollution and plant response.

Fundamental studies of the effects of pollutants on biochemical and physiological processes in plants (reviewed in Chapter 4) have made considerable progress towards revealing the ways in which pollutant damage occurs. Direct effects of pollutants on plant productivity, particularly crop yield, have received considerable attention and are reviewed in Chapters 5, 6 and 7. Effects on reproduction and survival are also important, especially in natural systems but have been much less studied. Effects on natural systems are reviewed in Chapter 8.

Indirect Effects

Pollutants may alter the acidity of soils, and hence modify biological activity, thus affecting plant growth through changes in nutrient availability. There is considerable variation in the UK in the susceptibility of soils to acidification. Relationships between soil chemistry, soil biology and pollutant deposition are reviewed in Chapter 3.

1.5 INTERACTIONS BETWEEN POLLUTANTS AND OTHER ENVIRONMENTAL FACTORS

Pollutants at low concentrations while insufficient to cause measurable damage on their own may predispose plants to injury from other stresses such as frost or drought, or may interact with co-occurring stresses to cause damage. There is growing recognition of the importance of the modifying effects of factors such as light intensity, temperature and drought on plant responses to pollutants. Considerable importance is also attached to the interactions between pollutants and other stresses, particularly in determining effects on plants in the field. Research in this rapidly expanding area is reviewed in Chapters 9 and 10.

1.6 FOREST DECLINE

Following concern over forest decline in central Europe, there has been pressure to determine the state of forest health in the UK. In Chapter 11 the Review Group assesses the current situation throughout Europe, and discuss the results of UK surveys of various types. The major hypotheses to explain forest decline are reviewed, and the evidence to support them is discussed with respect to conditions in central Europe and in the UK.

1.7 FUTURE PROGRESS

In the course of this extensive review a number of recommendations have been made. These are summarised at the end of the report. This is the first report of the Terrestrial Effects Review Group. There is considerable work in progress on many of the topics discussed here and the Review Group plan to produce supplements to update the various sections as new research results become available.

POLLUTION CLIMATE

2.1 PHYSICAL CLIMATE

The physical climate has primary influence on the terrestrial effects of pollution, because it often determines the amounts of pollutants reaching vegetation and soil. It also has a secondary influence when it introduces other stresses such as cold or drought which may interact with plant responses to pollution. Such interactions are discussed in Chapter 10. The most important aspect of physical climate that relates to acid deposition is rainfall. There is more than a factor of five difference in rainfall between the driest parts of south east England and the wettest parts of north west Scotland. Clearly the amounts of acid and other chemical substances deposited in rain are likely to vary considerably over the country because of the rainfall pattern. Similarly there are substantial differences in snowfall across the country and so the amounts of pollution deposited in snow and the duration of exposure will vary considerably.

A second feature which is important in determining pollution exposure is the mixing of the atmosphere introduced by windspeed. This feature is important for the dispersion of pollutants from their sources and for the transport of the pollution from the atmosphere to the surface. There is a general tendency for the windspeed to increase with distance northwards and westwards in Britain. This means that conditions of stagnant air that are most likely to allow the build-up of pollutants are more common in central and southern England than elsewhere.

The generation of secondary pollutants such as ozone is influenced by durations of bright sunshine and summertime temperatures. These and other aspects of the physical climate such as minimum winter temperatures, frequencies of drought, and variation in humidity, can be found from relevant publications of the Meteorological Office and will be referred to at various stages throughout this report.

The term climate describes the average mixture of weather factors (temperature, rain, wind, sunshine etc.) experienced in a region. The phrase 'pollution climate' is used to describe the mixtures of pollutants that occur on a regional scale. Although these mixtures vary from year to year and with season, pollution climate provides a broad distinction between the pollution exposure in different regions in much the same way that physical climate gives a general insight into the typical weather.

2.2 ATMOSPHERIC CONSTITUENTS

2.2.1 Gaseous Pollutants

Gaseous pollutants can be divided into primary and secondary categories. Primary pollutants are those pro-duced directly from man's industrial and domestic activities. Secondary pollutants are those created in the atmosphere by chemical processes operating on primary pollutants. Many of these pollutant substances also have natural sources, eg. sulphur compounds from oceans and freshwaters, nitrogen oxides from soils, and hydrocarbons from the foliage of trees.

Primary pollutants

The primary pollutants of main interest to this review are SO_2, NO and NO_2, ammonia, hydrogen fluoride and hydrocarbons. SO_2 is produced during the combustion of sulphur-containing fossil fuels and the smelting of sulphur-containing ores. Oxides of nitrogen are formed mainly by oxidation of atmospheric nitrogen at high temperatures in combustion processes, particularly in motor vehicle engines and power stations. The main nitrogen oxide formed in such combustion is NO but small amounts of NO_2 are also produced.

Emissions of ammonia are primarily from agricultural sources although localised industrial emissions can occur, especially around nitrogen fertilizer factories. There are also rural emissions of hydrogen sulphide from anaerobic decomposition of plant material. Hydrogen fluoride is emitted by a limited number of industrial processes, eg. brickmaking, the smelting of aluminium ores and phosphate fertilizer production. Its distribution therefore tends to be most intensively concentrated around a few point sources, although there is also widespread deposition of hydrogen fluoride resulting from coal burning. Hydrocarbons arise from unburned fuel in motor exhausts, emissions from the petrochemical industry and from evaporation of various volatile hydrocarbon based products.

Secondary pollutants

Of the substances generally regarded as secondary pollutants, attention is usually concentrated on ozone, which in the lower atmosphere has at least two sources:

(i) formation in the stratosphere by the action of ultra-violet sunlight on oxygen and transport to the ground

(ii) formation in the lower atmosphere by the action of sunlight on the primary pollutants, oxides of nitrogen and hydrocarbons. This photochemical reaction proceeds most effectively at high air temperatures and in bright sunshine and can also create a number of other compounds, leading in some conditions to photochemical smogs.

Other secondary pollutants generated by photochemical reactions include sulphuric and nitric acids and hydrogen peroxide. Strictly speaking, NO_2 is also a secondary pollutant as it can be formed in the atmosphere by the oxidation of primary emissions of NO.

2.2.2 Particulate pollutants

Particles are emitted from industrial fuel combustion, for example pulverised fuel ash from power generation and domestic coal burning can be a large source of unburnt carbon particles (soot). In urban areas of Britain such particles were a major source of pollution until the Clean Air Act of 1956. Since that time, controls on smoke emissions and changes in types of fuels used have substantially reduced the concentration of particulate pollutants in urban areas.

Particles of metallic compounds are emitted from industrial processes and from motor vehicle exhausts. Large particles fall to the ground relatively close to sources and are not considered within this review. Very small particles such as lead and fuel ash can be transported long distances.

Other particles are generated in the atmosphere by chemical reactions that oxidise SO_2 and NO_2 to sulphuric acid and nitric acid. Some of the particles formed in this way may react with other atmospheric constituents such as ammonia to form more complex compounds. These particles can be very widely distributed in the atmosphere and the resulting haze leads to reduced visibility especially in summertime.

2.3 ANNUAL AVERAGE CONCENTRATIONS

2.3.1 Sulphur dioxide

Annual mean concentrations of SO_2 can be calculated with reasonable accuracy from knowledge of the distribution of emissions from industry and domestic sources and appropriate meteorological information. Figure 2.1 shows annual mean concentrations derived in this way. The largest concentrations occur in the London area and in central England where there are very high densities of emission sources. The range of annual mean concentrations in different parts of Britain is more than a factor of ten.

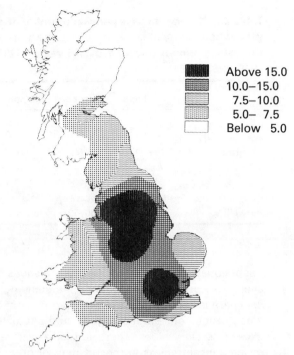

■	Above 15.0
▦	10.0–15.0
▤	7.5–10.0
░	5.0– 7.5
□	Below 5.0

2.1 Average ground-level concentration of SO_2, 1983, (interpolated from model results). (Taken from Perrin, 1987).

2.3.2 Nitrogen oxides

At present it is not possible to construct maps such as Figure 2.1 for NO_x. As a rough generalisation, available monitoring data show that the distribution of annual mean NO_x concentrations in the UK, when expressed in parts per billion (ppb), is probably similar to the distribution of SO_2 in Figure 2.1. Knowledge of the distribution of NO_x concentrations in the UK needs to be improved.

2.3.3 Ozone

Table 2.1 shows annual mean ozone concentrations at a number of sites in the UK. On most occasions the ozone measured at the surface has been produced naturally in the stratosphere, and so annual mean concentrations do

Table 2.1 Annual mean concentrations of ozone for 1978–85 in ppb

	1978	1979	1980	1981	1982	1983	1984	1985
Devilla (Fife)	19	18	*	—	—	—	—	—
Glasgow (Strathclyde)	—	—	—	—	—	21	15	9
Bottesford (Leicestershire)	22	30	27	18	23	21	21	20
Sibton (Suffolk)	31	22	15	24	25	27	23	*
Harwell (Oxfordshire)	—	—	—	—	29	26	26	29

— site not operational

* no data processed

(Data taken from PORG Interim Report 1986)

Table 2.2 Number of days per year (number of hours per year) when hourly mean ozone concentrations exceeded the values shown (meaned over 5 years – 1978, 1979, 1980, 1983, 1984)

	60 ppb	80 ppb	100 ppb	120 ppb
Range of 2 northern sites (Devilla, Glasgow)	6 (27)	1 (4)	1 (1)	0 (0)
Range of 3 southern sites (Bottesford, Sibton and Harwell)	20–50 (120–310)	6–14 (30–70)	2–5 (6–18)	1 (1)

not adequately reflect the occasional episodes of photochemically produced ozone. For understanding plant response, it is important to know the frequency of episodes when ozone concentrations generated photochemically exceed certain values. There are far fewer records of ozone concentrations in the UK than of other gaseous pollutants and the Photochemical Oxidant Review Group has currently reviewed the available information. The limited evidence suggests that ozone episodes are less frequent in northern Britain than in the south. Table 2.2

illustrates this point for sites in central Scotland and in southern England, using data averaged over a number of years when observations were made at all locations. Figure 2.2 shows the number of hours during 1984 when the ozone concentration exceeded 80 ppb at sites in the UK. The table and figure make it clear that ozone episodes are an infrequent occurrence in Britain, but at the lower threshold appear to be more common in the south than in the north. There is evidence from North America and elsewhere that ozone concentrations increase with elevation and show less diurnal variation. Consequently vegetation at mountain sites may be more frequently exposed to phytotoxic concentrations. At present there are only limited UK data on the variation of ozone concentrations with altitude.

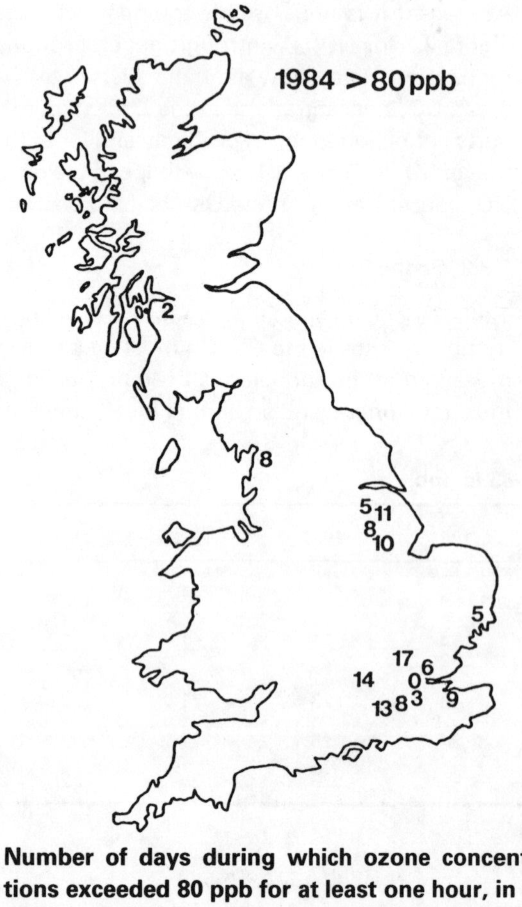

2.3.4 Urban concentrations

The values in Figure 2.1 and Table 2.2 do not give an adequate picture of mean concentrations of gaseous pollutants in urban areas. Because these areas are often major sources of primary pollutants, there can be considerable variation from site to site. Table 2.3 illustrates the range of annual mean concentrations of sulphur and nitrogen oxides based on monitoring at three urban sites. Concentrations of ozone in urban areas are likely to be lower than at rural sites because some of the ozone is destroyed in converting NO to NO_2, and in oxidising SO_2. There are insufficient data to be able to quantify this loss of ozone.

Table 2.3 Range of annual mean urban concentrations of SO_2 and NO_2 (based on Warren Springs Laboratory 1983 data for Central London Laboratory, (a non kerbside site), and Cromwell Road, London and Hope Street, Glasgow, (kerbside sites)

Annual Mean Concentration in ppb		
SO_2	NO_2	NO
17–25	40–70	40–200

2.3.5 Seasonal variation in concentrations

In rural areas, SO_2 concentrations are typically 50% higher than the annual means during the three winter months of the year and consequently 10–20% lower than the annual means in the remaining months of the year. Nitrogen oxides probably have the same type of variation although there are fewer data to support this statement. Episodes of photochemical ozone above the natural background are primarily an occurrence in the warmer months of the year and so are most likely in the period April to September. Ozone from the stratosphere can occasionally reach high concentrations near the ground during certain meteorological conditions in spring.

1984 > 80 ppb

2.2 Number of days during which ozone concentrations exceeded 80 ppb for at least one hour, in the UK, during 1984. (Taken from UK PORG, 1987).

2.3.6 Diurnal variations

Diurnal cycles of pollutant concentrations are influenced more strongly by meteorological factors than by changes in primary emissions. At rural sites, SO_2 and NO_x concentrations vary during the day by $\pm10-20\%$ from their daily mean values, with the lowest concentrations at night and maxima in the early part of the day. In urban situations, where there are sources of SO_2 and NO_x at low elevations, concentrations are likely to be largest at night. Ozone concentrations corresponding to photochemical activity usually peak in the afternoon and decrease to low values at night-time.

Short periods of large concentrations of gaseous pollutants – 'episodes' – may occur if there are nearby sources of primary pollutants or if the weather favours the buildup of secondary pollutants. Similarly, episodes of very acidic rainfall are observed.

2.4 DRY DEPOSITION OF GASES AND PARTICLES

Dry deposition is the direct transfer of gases and particles onto terrestrial surfaces. In principle the responses of vegetation to pollutants must be related to the

*See pH in glossary

amounts of pollutant that are actually absorbed and so knowledge of rates of dry deposition would be useful to understand responses of the terrestrial ecosystem. However, dry deposition depends in a complex manner on the movement of pollutants in the atmosphere and their absorption by leaf and soil surfaces. At present it is not possible to relate the effects of acidic deposition to the amounts of dry deposition, but this remains an objective for future research.

2.5 WET DEPOSITION

Deposition of acidity and related chemical compounds has been reviewed by the Acid Rain Review Group (UK RGAR, 1987). There are two aspects of the regional variability in acidity, first the average concentration of acidity or hydrogen ion concentration $(H^+)^*$ in rain, second the quantity of H^+ that reaches the ground. Figure 2.3(b) shows that the concentration of acidity in rain is not known for large parts of England and Wales, but over northern Britain there is an increase by a factor of about two in concentration moving from the west to the east coast. These regional changes are much smaller than the regional variation in rainfall amount and so when these two features are combined together to derive the deposited acidity (Figure 2.3(a)) the figure is dominated by rainfall. Consequently, it is the mountainous areas to the west and north of Britain that receive the

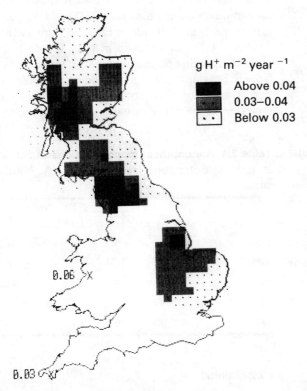

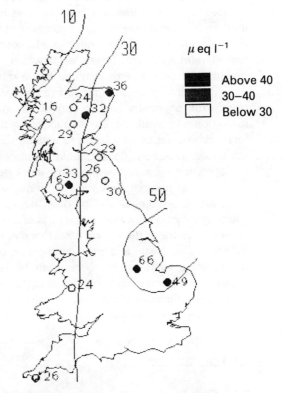

2.3 (a) Wet deposited acidity 1981–85

(b) Rainfall weighted annual average hydrogen ion concentration (μ eq/l) 1981–85. (Maps taken from UK RGAR, 1987).

largest annual inputs of deposited acidity. The Acid Rain Review Group has noted that there are strong similarities in patterns of concentration of acidity, nitrate and non-marine sulphate over the UK and so maps of deposited sulphate and nitrate in rain are rather similar in qualitative terms to those for acidity.

The above conclusions are, however, based almost entirely on rain chemistry measurements made at low elevation sites. Recent research evidence suggests that the true chemical deposition in mountain areas may exceed the estimates discussed here because (i) there is more rainfall at higher elevations, and (ii) the chemical concentrations in rain are sometimes larger at high elevation. The results from very limited experiments to date suggest that the true wet deposition may be a factor of two larger than at low elevations. However this figure is still very uncertain. At present the input of chemical pollutants in wet deposition is not known sufficiently well to allow firm conclusions to be drawn about the threats to terrestrial systems at high elevations.

2.6 OCCULT DEPOSITION

High elevation sites in Britain are frequently enveloped in low cloud. The water drops in such cloud are very inefficiently collected in rain gauges, but when wind driven, cloud drops can be trapped very effectively on the foliage of vegetation. Research measurements at a number of sites in England and Scotland have shown that, on occasions, the chemical contents of waterdrops in cloud can be up to ten times more concentrated than typical rainfall values. There is, however, no routine monitoring network comparable to the UK rain chemistry network, from which annual averages and variations of cloudwater chemistry can be derived. Even if such information was available, the amount of cloudwater captured by vegetation in relation to weather conditions is not known precisely. Consequently inputs of pollutants to vegetation by occult deposition cannot be estimated accurately at present. Tentative estimates suggest that the amount of sulphur and nitrogen deposited by this pathway may be between 10 and 80% of the deposition in rain. Because of the known occurrence of high acidity events in cloudwater and the hidden nature of this input to terrestrial systems, it is important to improve our knowledge of occult deposition input to the main vegetation types characteristic of environments where these occurrences are common.

2.7 TIME TRENDS

2.7.1 Gases

In urban areas, there have been substantial decreases in concentrations of SO_2 over the last 30 years, coinciding

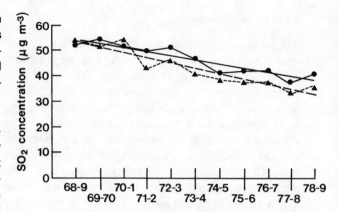

2.4 Trends in annual mean concentrations of SO_2 at country sites of the Warren Spring Survey over the period 1976–79. The dashed line and regression are fitted to arithmetic values, while the solid lines are fitted to means corrected for missing values 1 μg SO_2 m^{-3} = 2.66 ppb SO_2. (The graph is reproduced from Roberts and Lane, 1981).

with decreases in emissions. The situation for rural areas is less clear because of the limited number of monitoring sites. Figure 2.4 indicates that there has been a decline in annual mean concentrations, but the data may not be representative of all rural sites. There are insufficient data to make any statements concerning trends for NO_x or ozone in the UK, although there have been reports elsewhere in Europe that concentrations of both these substances have increased. Table 2.4 shows changes in annual mean concentrations of SO_2 and NO_2 at Bottesford in the East Midlands of England from 1981 to 1985. At this site, concentrations of NO_2 appear to have increased over this period, whereas SO_2 has remained relatively constant, but it is not known whether this situation is representative of other areas where the density of emission sources is different.

Table 2.4 Annual mean concentrations of SO_2 and NO_2 in ppb at Bottesford from 1981–85 (A. Martin, pers. comm.)

	SO_2	NO_2
1981	9.7	11.2
1982	11.3	8.0
1983	9.8	11.3
1984	10.0	16.1
1985	10.8	18.3

2.7.2 Rainfall

Data from Rothamsted Experimental Station indicate that mean concentrations of nitrate in rainfall doubled between the 1850s and 1960, and similar increases in ammonium concentration probably occurred. A recent analysis of data from the European Air Chemistry Network (Rodhe and Rood, 1986) has shown a further doubling in nitrate concentrations between the late 1950s and early 1970s at most stations, with a less pronounced increase in ammonium. It appears that the contribution of nitrogen oxides to the total acidity of rainfall is assuming greater importance in the UK. The ratio of nitrate to sulphate concentration in rain has increased in Scotland but available data show no evidence of an increase in England (UK RGAR, 1987). The Review Group on Acid Rain has also reported a decrease in average rainfall acidity and in deposition of acidity over much of Northern Britain between the two periods 1978–80 and 1981–85. However, consistent long term trends are masked by large year-to-year variability (UK RGAR, 1987).

2.8 FREQUENCY DISTRIBUTION OF POLLUTANTS

2.8.1 Sulphur dioxide and nitrogen oxides

The analysis of short term fluctuations in concentrations from several monitoring sites suggests that the distribution of concentrations of these gases may be approximated by a log normal distribution. Because the form of this distribution is reasonably constant at all sites, it is possible to estimate the frequency of occurrence of large concentrations at a site knowing the measured long-term mean concentration. Table 2.5 makes use of this knowledge to estimate the percentage of time during which concentrations exceed certain thresholds for sites where the annual mean concentrations of SO_2 and NO_2 have

certain values. For a typical mean in central England of 10 ppb, concentrations of NO_2 would be likely to exceed 30 ppb for only 2% of the year. It is important to recognise that, although such episodes are very infrequent, their duration may be very important for effects on vegetation. It is not however possible to estimate mean duration from this type of analysis.

2.8.2 Ozone

Ozone concentrations do not follow the log normal distribution appropriate for other pollutant gases. The values quoted earlier show that much variation from year to year exists in the duration of and frequency of episodes. There are very few sites where there have been sufficiently long periods of measurement to draw any conclusions on the statistical probability of ozone episodes exceeding certain concentrations. These data have recently been reviewed and a separate report by the Photochemical Oxidant Review Group has been published (UK PORG, 1987). At present there are no data in the UK for ozone concentrations at high elevation sites.

2.9 COMPARISONS WITH POLLUTION CLIMATES OF OTHER REGIONS

Table 2.6 summarises some general comparisons of rural pollutant concentrations in the UK, Germany and Eastern USA. The values in the table are taken from a number of sources and should be regarded only as an indication of ranges of concentrations found at each location.

Table 2.5 Expected frequency of large concentrations of SO_2 and NO_2 for a range of annual average concentrations found in UK

Annual arithmetic mean (ppb)	% time during which concentrations exceed				
	20	30	50	100	200 ppb
Sulphur dioxide					
<1.5	<0.01	—	—	—	—
5.0	0.7	0.1	—	—	—
10.0	7.0	2.0	0.25	—	—
15.0	17.0	6.0	1.2	0.05	—
25.0	41.0	21.0	17.0	0.70	
Nitrogen dioxide					
<1.5	—	—	—	—	—
5.0	—	—	—	—	—
10.0	2.5	0.25	—	—	—
15.0	9.0	1.3	0.05	—	—
40.0		62.0	13.0	0.07	—
70.0		97.0	70.0	13.0	0.01

Table 2.6 A comparison of rural pollutant concentrations in UK, Central and Southern Germany and Eastern USA

Concentrations	UK Rural	Remote Rural	Central Germany	Southern Germany*	Eastern USA
Annual mean SO$_2$ in ppb	2–15	<2	5–17	<4	<6
Annual mean NO$_2$ in ppb	2–15	<2	6–12	<4	<6
Annual dry deposition	2–4 g S m^{-2} 1–2 g N m^{-2}	0.4 g S m^{-2} 0.2 g N m^{-2}	2–4 g S m^{-2} 1 g N m^{-2}	1 g S m^{-2} 0.5 g N m^{-2}	0.5–1 g S m^{-2} 0.3–0.5 g N m^{-2}
Annual wet deposition	0.8 g S m^{-2} 0.4 g N m^{-2}	2 g S m^{-2} 1 g N m^{-2}	1–2 g S m^{-2} 0.5–1 g N m^{-2}	1 g S m^{-2} 0.5 g N m^{-2}	0.5–1 g S m^{-2} 0.3–0.5 g N m^{-2}
Hours per year O$_3$ >70 ppb	60–150	5–20	150–300	>250	~550
Rainfall pH	4.1–4.7	4.0	4.0–4.6		4.1–4.3

* (at high altitude sites in Southern Germany, wet deposition of sulphate and nitrate may be three times higher than that at lower altitude sites and concentrations of O$_3$ tend to exceed 70 ppb during more than 350 hours a year. Similar situations may apply at high altitude sites elsewhere.)

2.9.1 Central Europe

The gaseous and wet deposition environment of central and northern Germany is broadly comparable with much of the rural parts of central and eastern England. In contrast, the pollution climate of southern Germany (Bavaria and Baden-Wurtemberg) is distinctive. Annual mean concentrations of SO$_2$ and NO$_2$ are less than 4 ppb and annual wet deposition of sulphate and nitrate is 1.2 g S m^{-2} and 0.5 g N m^{-2}. These amounts of wet deposition are comparable to the wetter parts of Britain. Ozone concentrations in southern Germany are high, exceeding 75 ppb for about 250 hours per year. Comparison with Table 2.6 shows that this is a substantially different ozone environment than is found in Britain. At high elevation sites in Germany, mean ozone concentrations are larger than at low levels by 25–30% and lack a diurnal variation so that the vegetation is exposed for longer periods to high concentrations. In addition, the inputs of sulphur and nitrogen from wet deposition at high elevations may be a factor of two larger than values quoted earlier and the contribution from cloudwater is also likely to be large, but these features of sulphur and nitrogen deposition probably also apply in the uplands of the UK. Consequently, the pollution climate of southern Germany has significantly more frequent ozone episodes, but is in other respects probably similar to that of some parts of the UK.

2.9.2 Eastern North America

Annual mean concentrations of SO$_2$ and NO$_2$ in eastern North America rarely exceed 6 ppb in rural areas. In the north east United States concentrations are larger in winter than in summer when they are scarcely measurable.

This may be because the SO$_2$ and NO$_2$ is oxidised before reaching remote sites in the north east in summer. Ozone concentrations are larger than in the UK, exceeding 70 ppb typically for 10–50 days per year, each event lasting for several hours. The average pH of rainfall in eastern North America is comparable with that over much of Britain and measurements of the chemistry of occult deposition are also comparable. Consequently, compared with the UK, eastern North America appears to have lower gaseous concentrations of SO$_2$ and NO$_2$, more frequent ozone episodes and comparable wet deposition.

2.10 CONCLUSIONS

1. As a result of increased population and industrial and agricultural activity, a general increase in the concentrations of SO$_2$, NO$_x$, ozone, hydrocarbons and other pollutants such as ammonia has occurred during most of the twentieth century throughout developed countries of the world. The UK is no exception to this.

2. As a consequence of the various Clean Air Acts since the 1950s and changes in fuels used, concentrations in the UK of particulate pollutants such as soot have been substantially decreased. However oxidation of SO$_2$ and NO$_2$ can create very fine particles in the atmosphere, producing haze and reducing visibility.

3. Over the past 15 years, there have been substantial decreases in concentrations of SO$_2$ in urban areas coinciding with similar decreases in emissions. Insufficient data exist to demonstrate trends in NO$_x$

and ozone concentrations in UK, although there have been reports elsewhere in Europe of increases in concentrations of these gases.

4. Pollutants rarely occur singly, but are usually found in mixtures of fluctuating concentrations. Although the annual mean concentration of a pollutant may be quite low, short periods of much higher concentration (often referred to as episodes) may occur during the year. The composition of the pollutant mixture is affected by weather and geography and certain areas may be characterised by a particular pollutant mixture or 'climate'. For example remote rural areas of the north and west are characterised by very low concentrations of SO_2 and NO_x, infrequent episodes of ozone and large acid inputs in rain and occult precipitation. In contrast, the south east of England is characterised by moderate concentrations of SO_2 and NO_x and relatively frequent episodes of photochemical ozone in summer.

5.1. Annual mean values, based on results from the UK monitoring network, show that SO_2 concentrations in rural areas range from less than 5 ppb in remote rural areas of Scotland, West Wales and Cornwall to 10–15 ppb in other rural areas of the UK.

5.2. Insufficient data exist to adequately construct maps of NO_2 concentration but available monitoring data suggest that annual mean concentrations of NO_2 are similar to those of SO_2.

5.3. In addition to SO_2 and NO_x in rural areas, photochemically generated ozone may be present. Ozone concentrations exceeding 60 ppb are likely for about 30–300 hours a year.

5.4. The pollutant mixture present in urban areas is often even more varied in both composition and concentration than in rural areas. Typical concentrations range from 17–25 ppb SO_2 and 80–270 ppb NO_x. The large concentrations of the latter are due to vehicular emissions. Ozone concentrations in urban areas tend to be slightly lower than in rural areas.

6. Concentrations of pollutants vary diurnally and seasonally. In rural areas in wintertime, concentrations of SO_2 and NO_2 are as much as 50% higher than the annual mean, whereas episodes of photochemical ozone are mainly a summer phenomenon.

7. Gases and particles are transferred directly from the atmosphere onto plants and soils by the process of dry deposition. This process depends on the movement of pollutants in the atmosphere and their absorption by leaf and soil surfaces. The amount of dry deposition is often assumed proportional to the concentration in the air.

8. At present there are insufficient longterm records of rain chemistry to determine the annual mean concentration of acidity expressed as hydrogen ion concentration (H^+) in rain for much of England and Wales. In the north of Britain, where there has been an adequate measurement network for more than ten years, acidity tends to be twice as great in the east (pH 4.2) as in the west (pH 4.5); concentrations of sulphate and nitrate also follow this trend.

9. Precipitation is three to four times greater in the west than the east and so the amount of acid (and sulphate and nitrate) deposited in a year in northern Britain is greater in the west, particularly in mountainous areas. At high elevations, limited data suggest that wet deposition may be a factor of two larger than at nearby low elevations.

10. There is evidence of increasing nitrate and ammonium concentrations in rain in recent years but no clear trend exists in acid deposition in rain in the UK as a whole. However in Scotland, which has been more extensively monitored, the amount of acid deposited annually in rain has decreased over the past 10 years by about 50%.

11. Wet deposition is highly episodic over large parts of the UK. As much as 30% of acidity deposited in a year occurs on less than 5% of wet days.

12. High elevation sites are frequently enveloped in low cloud and mists. Although cloud water droplets are inefficiently collected in rain gauges, they can be effectively trapped by plant foliage. As yet, input of pollutants to plants by this process of occult deposition cannot be accurately estimated, but current knowledge suggests that measurements that ignore occult deposition may be underestimating sulphur and nitrogen deposition by 10 to 50%.

13. From a general comparison of various pollution measurements, it appears that the pollution climate of central and eastern England is broadly comparable with that of much of central and north Germany. South Germany, however, is not comparable with any area in the UK in respect to ozone but is not unlike some areas of eastern North America. It should be noted that other aspects of climate also differ between these regions, for example the climate of central Europe is of continental type with low winds, large amounts of sunshine and extremes of temperature. Britain, on the other hand, has a maritime climate, mild and windy, with relatively little sunshine. It would be useful to attempt a more detailed comparison of pollution climates, using results from the new UK monitoring network.

EFFECTS ON SOILS

3.1 EFFECTS ON SOIL CHEMISTRY

In contrast to the amount of research performed to assess the impact of acid deposition upon vegetation and natural waters, relatively little attention has been focussed upon its interactions with soils. This is surprising, bearing in mind that soil chemistry, mineralogy and microbiology affect plant growth, and together with hydrological pathways through or over soil, ultimately regulate the chemistry of many freshwater streams and lakes. The neglect stems largely from a once widely-held belief that soils are so well buffered against chemical change that significant modification as a result of pollutant loadings is improbable even on a time scale of a few decades. This concept is now open to question, however.

3.1.1 The nature of soil acidity

Soil acidity,* like water acidity, is expressed in terms of pH.* When the acidity of a *soil* is measured and the result is expressed as a pH value, in practice the concentration of hydrogen (H^+) ions in the soil solution is determined. Both the organic matter and the clay minerals in soils have large surface areas with negatively charged sites. These negative charges are balanced by positive charges on adsorbed cations, including H^+. Generally, the greater the clay or organic matter contents of a soil, the greater its capacity to adsorb cations. The H^+ ions which pass into the water around soil particles are only a small fraction of the total H^+ present on the cation adsorption sites. If the soluble salt concentration of the water is increased, eg. through the addition of a neutral salt such as sodium chloride ($Na^+ Cl^-$), more H^+ ions tend to be displaced into solution by cation exchange, and the water pH falls, ie.:

$$\boxed{Soil}^{-+}H + Na^+ \text{ (solution)} \rightarrow \boxed{Soil}^{-+}Na + H^+ \text{ (solution)}$$

The alkalinity or acidity of a soil depends largely on the relative amounts of different positively charged cations balancing the negative charge on the soil particles. Certain cations (calcium (Ca^{2+}), magnesium (Mg^{2+}), potassium (K^+), sodium (Na^+)) are often called base cations, because when present in excess, they are associated with a low H^+ concentration in soil solution and sufficient hydroxyl anions (OH^-) to make the solution alkaline. When the concentration of adsorbed base cations in the soil increases, the pH rises. When the concentration of acidic cations (H^+, aluminium (Al^{3+})) increases, the pH falls.

3.1.2 Buffering of soil pH

The large pool of exchangeable cations (H^+, Ca^{2+}, Mg^{2+}, K^+, Na^+, $Al(OH)^{2+}$, $Al(OH)_2^+$, etc.) in many soils makes them resistant to rapid pH change. When water drains through a soil, some cations from exchange sites are

---

* For definition of soil acidity and pH see glossary.

leached (ie. washed out). If however the soil contains readily weatherable minerals, the leached cations may be replenished as a result of geochemical weathering reactions, so that the quantities of individual cations stored on soil exchange sites may remain virtually constant. Small additional cation inputs come from precipitation, leaching from vegetation and decomposing litter. The processes which govern the abundance of any particular cation on the exchange pool are represented in Figure 3.1.

As a consequence of H^+ input in deposition, base cations may be leached from the upper horizons (layers) of the soil profile. The smaller the fraction of the cation exchange sites occupied by a particular cation, the less readily that cation will be leached. If its abundance is sufficiently small, no leaching, or even net adsorption, may occur. Calcium usually constitutes a high percentage of total exchangeable bases in fertile soils as it is readily released on weathering and strongly adsorbed onto exchange sites. Adsorption of Ca^{2+} from rainwater inputs is not uncommon in highly weathered acid upland soils, (Cresser et al., 1986). According to Reuss (1983), soil solution cations are dominated by Ca^{2+} when base saturation of exchange sites exceeds 20%, or even when it is as low as 10% in some soils. Below this percentage, aluminium becomes the dominant cation in soil solution and the change is quite abrupt.

3.1.3 The control of pH in agricultural soils

Agricultural soils tend naturally to become more acidic with time, partly as a consequence of leaching of base cations (Ca^{2+}, Mg^{2+}, K^+ and Na^+) by rain and irrigation and partly as a result of the removal of these elements with the crop at harvest. When such soils are limed, inputs of base cations in the liming material displace the H^+ ions starting to accumulate on cation exchange sites. The H^+ ions are neutralised by the anionic component (O^{2-}, OH^- or CO_3^{2-}) of the liming material. The degree of base saturation of the exchange sites and hence the soil pH are thus restored and acid drainage waters are unlikely.

If lime is added to acid organic upland soils, for example to improve the quality of upland pastures, the effect of the lime is confined to a layer very close to the soil surface unless the lime is mixed into the soil by cultivation. If water infiltrates the soil below this depth, the drainage water reaching streams may still remain very acidic after liming. In high rainfall areas where surface runoff is high, liming may very effectively raise the drainage water pH, because this water equilibrates with the neutralised surface soil. For this reason, removal of lime subsidies to farmers in such areas may have far-reaching consequences because it increases the probability of surface water acidification. For example since 1976 there has been a seven fold reduction in the amount of lime ap-

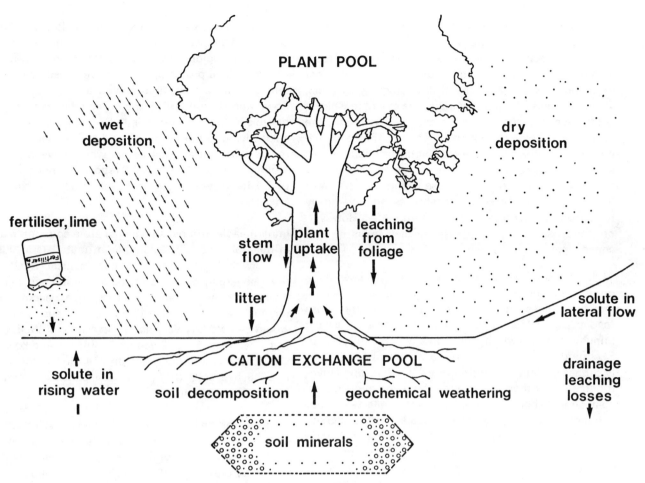

PLANT POOL

wet deposition

dry deposition

fertiliser, lime

stem flow

plant uptake

leaching from foliage

litter

solute in lateral flow

CATION EXCHANGE POOL

solute in rising water

soil decomposition

geochemical weathering

drainage leaching losses

soil minerals

3.1 Processes regulating the distribution of cations in the cation exchange pool.

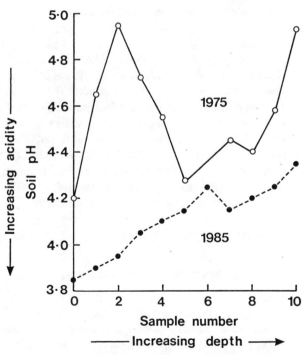

3.2 **Soil pH at various depths in Hallen Wood (near Bristol) in 1975 and 1985. The site is 3 km downwind from the Avonmouth Smelter. Sample number 10 corresponds to 21–31 cm depth (based on the results of Martin and Coughtrey, 1986).**

plied to a Cumbrian catchment and certain fields have received no lime since the liming subsidy ceased. (Crawshaw, 1986). A recent assessment of the state of the environment in the European Community reported that the application of calcium as a fertiliser had decreased by 15–20% in the United Kingdom. (CEC, 1987)

3.1.4 Evidence for soil acidification

Many experiments with lysimeters (columns of undisturbed soils) and simulated rain have demonstrated the acidification of surface soils as a consequence of rainfall acidity (eg. Wood and Bormann, 1977; Killham and Firestone, 1982). Indeed, this has also been done using genuine polluted precipitation reacting with soil columns at various distances from a point pollution source (Killham and Wainwright, 1984). The pH of a surface soil from an unpolluted area placed 0.5 km downwind from a coking works fell from 4.9 to 3.9 over 30 months. The results of Martin and Coughtrey (1987) showed (Figure 3.2) acidification to depth even in a soil with a fairly high clay content at a site 3 km downwind from a smelter near Bristol.

Wood and Bormann (1977) showed that if the base cations leached as a consequence of deposition acidity could be replaced by geochemical weathering, the base status of the soil did not deteriorate and the soil pH did not fall. But in soils where replacement is not adequate, additional leaching caused by acidifying pollutant loadings must lead to surface soil acidification. Replacement of leached cations by geochemical weathering is a much slower process than ion exchange. The extent to which it is effective depends on climate and on how readily the remaining soil mineral(s) will weather. Thus soil acidification is more probable in a high precipitation area with soils where the most easily weathered minerals have already been depleted. Base cations can be taken up from depth in the soil by plant roots, and eventually returned to the surface in litter or throughfall. However, on deep peat this ameliorative mechanism is of little consequence.

At the present time very little direct work has been done on the effect of gaseous pollutants on soil acidification, largely because aqueous acid additions are far more readily simulated. Recent work by Ineson, as yet unpublished, in which soil cores were subjected to SO_2-enriched atmospheres in growth chambers, strongly suggests relatively rapid surface soil acidification (over months rather than years). Work by Skiba and Cresser, also unpublished, indicated that litter collected under conifers growing in polluted areas leads to enhanced soil and water acidification during its subsequent decomposition. These results suggest that gaseous pollutant effects may be far more important than hitherto recognized.

3.1.5 Natural soil acidification

Any changes in soil pH attributable to acid deposition must be assessed against a background of natural soil acidification. The pH of acid-leached (podzol) surface soils derived from granite at a moorland site at Glendye in the Grampian Region of north-east Scotland, falls in the range 3.4 to 3.7 and is more than a whole pH unit lower than that of incoming precipitation (Reid, 1979). At Peatfold, Glenbuchat, where the land use is similar but the parent material is more base-element rich (quartz-biotite-norite) and where geochemical weathering is still substantial in the upper mineral soil horizon, soil pH is only significantly below precipitation mean pH on the upper slopes. Values for four podzol surface horizons were 4.2, 4.3, 4.6 and 4.1. On middle slopes more fertile soils (Cambisols) were dominant, and here the surface horizon pH values were in the range 4.8 to 4.9, coincidentally quite close to the pH of the rain (Creasey, 1984).

Once weathering advances to the point at which hill peat accumulates, horizon acidity may worsen considerably. At sites where rain chemistry and climate are similar, the pH values of hill peat are in the range 3.5–4.0 and measurements suggest that underlying material exerts little influence, the dominant factors being climate and precipitation chemistry.

Soils of granite catchments around Galloway in south-east Scotland, where precipitation is higher than in Grampian Region and acidification of fresh waters is known to be a problem, do not have substantially different pH values from those noted above. According to Bown and Heslop (1979), the organic horizons of peaty podzols in two soils series in this region have pH (water) values lying in the range 3.7 to 4.4. Both series tend to merge with unclassified peats, which have pH values around 3.6 to 3.9. Cuttle (1983) reported a mean pH value of 3.5 for eleven peats from upland sites in southern Scotland.

Impermeable iron pans (placons) are a common feature in mineral soils with acidic parent materials in upland areas with high rainfall. As geochemical weathering must be largely confined to soil above the pan, soil acidification may be rapid once the pan becomes continuous and lateral water drainage over such iron pans would be naturally very acid. The acidity of Welsh soils has recently been reviewed by Thompson and Loveland (1985), who recorded a mean pH of 4.2 ($\pm$0.4) for sixteen acid-leached soils (ferric and iron pan stagnopodzols) under rough grazing.

Evidence for the development of sufficient soil acidity for iron pan formation in upland soils in the absence of acidifying pollutants of anthropogenic origins was presented by Crampton (1961) as a result of examination of soils protected under archeological structures in S. Wales. The acidity of soils would thus naturally move towards pH values at least as low as 4.0.

It is also well known that widespread peat formation often occurred prior to heavy pollution, but a question mark still remains over how much the pH of hill peats is lowered as a result of pollution effects. The pH values of surface mineral horizons from four podzols in the Southern Island of New Zealand, in areas with high precipitation (1800–2500 mm) but relatively little pollution compared with the UK were 3.8, 3.7, 3.5 and 4.5 (Lee et al., 1985), suggesting that pH shifts in Britain caused by moderate amounts of pollutants may generally be modest. However, pollutant inputs may substantially reduce the time scale over which the ultimate degree of soil acidification is finally attained.

3.1.6 The importance of sulphate adsorption

Another factor must be taken into account when considering acid deposition effects upon soils and soil/water interactions, namely sulphate adsorption on anion exchange sites. The displacement by sulphate (SO_4^{2-}) anions of hydroxyl ions (OH^-) from these sites is effectively a neutralisation process (van Breemen et al., 1983b), ie.:

$$\text{soil} \begin{array}{l} -OH \\ -OH \end{array} + SO_4^{2-} + 2H^+ \rightleftharpoons \text{soil} = SO_4 + 2H_2O$$

This reaction occurs to a significant degree in highly weathered and leached soils which are rich in hydrated oxides of iron and aluminium. In a buffered soil system, removal of H^+ implies a corresponding adsorption of base cations on exchange sites to maintain the soil solution pH. Thus sulphate adsorption leads to base cation retention and conversely, when soils become saturated with sulphate, this leads to base cation leaching, ie. soil acidification.

Soils from granite catchments at Glendye are not quite sulphate-saturated (Cresser et al., 1986). In stagnopodzols in much of north-west Wales, sulphate saturation *has* occurred and any sulphate deposited on these soils leaches through the profile, mobilising in this case mainly aluminium in streams because the availability of base cations is severely limited in these very acid upland soils (M. Hornung, pers. comm.). It seems probable that sulphate inputs from acid deposition, superimposed upon already substantial maritime-derived sulphate inputs, may be sufficient to throw a balanced ecosystem off balance at some sites.

Where sulphate is being accumulated by adsorption on to hydrated oxides of iron and aluminium in the lower layers of acid leached soils, changes in hydrological pathways during storm events will occur. These may lead to increased lateral flow of water through surface organic horizons and result in increasing sulphate concentration in river water as discharge rises (Johnson and Henderson, 1979). In upland peaty soils, interpretation of sulphate behaviour is further complicated by reduction/adsorption of sulphate-S into wet peat (Brown, 1985a and b; Brown and MacQueen, 1985). Such soil effects are very important when considering the apparent relationship between H^+ and SO_4^{2-} in river water, since during storms, both may tend to rise coincidentally rather than because of a direct relationship.

3.1.7 Throughfall and stemflow effects

The chemical composition of precipitation is altered by passage through vegetation. Some of the precipitation deposited on plants is intercepted by the canopy, the rest reaches the soil surface as throughfall and stemflow. As a result of leaching of secreted substances from the foliage and wash-off of gases or particles accumulated on the vegetation, throughfall and stemflow tend to gain soluble salts although sometimes absorption of selected species also occurs.

Scherbatskoy and Klein (1983) found that leachates from beech and spruce were generally less acid than applied mists and throughfall collected beneath spruce and maple canopies was less acid than rain and was enriched with Ca^{2+} and K^+. Other workers (Eaton et al., 1973; Hoffman et al., 1980) have also found a reduction in acidity of precipitation collected beneath foliage. However,

throughfall collected beneath hemlock (*Tsuga canadensis*) in the Adirondack mountains of USA (Johannes et al., 1981) and beneath pine, spruce and birch in Birkenes, Norway (Horntvedt et al., 1980) showed an increase in acidity and ion content, particularly SO_4^{2-}. This was ascribed to 'wash-off' of deposited pollutants and to increased leaching from tree crowns, and could be indicative of the widespread occurrence of such acidification in areas of high acidic deposition. Similar effects have been found in Devilla forest in central Scotland, where pH of precipitation was lowered from pH 4.2 to 3.7 after passage through a Scots pine canopy and concentrations of Ca^{2+}, Mg^{2+} and sulphate-S increased (Nicholson et al., 1980). This work has been extended to include a range of species and two other sites, Crathes (Deeside) and Gisburn (north Pennines). Conifers, including the deciduous larch, increased the acidity of throughfall and stemflow all year round whereas hardwood species tended to partially neutralise rainfall acidity when in leaf.

Trees may influence both the rate of soil acidification and the distribution of H^+ through the soil profile. There can be little doubt that trees can trap an additional load of acidifying pollutant. Part of this may be washed to the forest floor. Some of the acid input may be partially neutralised by cation exchange at leaf surfaces. However if base cations leached from foliage are balanced by corresponding root uptake of base cations from soil, the H^+ flux that is apparently neutralized in throughfall is, in effect, transferred to the rooting zone. Even in the absence of pollutants, trees may acidify soils because they take up base cations. Interpretation is further complicated because tree planting changes the water flux through the soil.

The effect of trees upon drainage water pH may be attributed to three main mechanisms:

i)   their effect upon soil pH,

ii) their effect upon neutral salts trapped,

iii) their effect upon water flux.

Once the soil pH is reduced via long-term pollutant loadings, any trapping by trees of additional salts, eg. of maritime origin, will lower the pH of soil solution, and hence of drainage water, even further.

3.1.8 Possible effects of ammonia

In regions where there are high densities of agricultural animals, ammonia released from urine and faeces can be substantial. Over the past few years, work in The Netherlands on effects of ammonia in the atmosphere has attracted considerable attention (van Breeman et al., 1982, 1983a). Ammonia reacts with sulphur dioxide to produce ammonium sulphate, probably in part this reaction takes place on vegetation surfaces. Ammonium sulphate then reaches the soil in rain and as throughfall, where some of it is oxidised to nitric and sulphuric acids:

$$(NH_4)_2SO_4 + 4O_2 \rightarrow 2HNO_3 + H_2SO_4 + 2H_2O$$

At some locations ammonia may therefore be contributing significantly to soil acidification. Ammonium sulphate will ionise in the soil solution giving ammonium (NH_4^+) ions and sulphate (SO_4^{2-}) ions. If plants take up NH_4^+, rather than nitrate (NO_3^-), this is itself an acidifying process. If the NH_4^+ is converted to NO_3^- (the process known as nitrification) and the NO_3^- is taken up by plants, the net effect is still acidifying, since twice as many H^+ ions are produced by nitrification as are used in NO_3^- uptake. Given appropriate environmental conditions, NO_3^- may also be lost from the soil via denitrification. This process has a neutralising effect on the soil, since hydrogen ions are consumed as the nitrate-nitrogen is converted to gaseous form:

$$2\,NO_3^- + 5H_2 + 2H^+ \rightarrow N_2 + 6\,H_2O$$

At high levels of nitrogen pollution, biological nitrogen uptake is unlikely to use all the available nitrogen and soil acidification becomes more probable. Little information is available however on nitrogen behaviour at high nitrogen concentrations in soils which are highly susceptible to acidification.

3.1.9 Acid soils and acid water

Whether or not soil acidification leads to freshwater acidification depends largely upon the pathway the drainage water follows through or over the soil. When the water infiltrates below the near-surface acidified soil layers to zones of higher soil pH and active mineral weathering, acidification of the drainage water is improbable. If overland flow or near-surface flow through acidified surface horizons occur, soil pH reduction can and does lead to water acidification. Such hydrological conditions may only occur for periods of a few hours during storm events in upland areas with modest (ca. 1000 mm) rainfall. They will be much more common in higher rainfall areas, and in areas with thin or impermeable soils and steep slopes. Organic peat soils at such sites will retain lime near the surface and therefore liming would be expected to be most effective for reducing water acidification under these conditions.

3.1.10 Effects on mobility of metals in soils

It is a commonly held view that the deposition of heavy metals (eg. lead, copper, zinc) on to vegetation and soils results in the accumulation of those metals in the surface horizons of the soil and that mobilization and subsequent movement through the soil profile is minimal. Leaching and losses through plant uptake and cropping are also commonly assumed to be minimal (eg. Webber, 1981; Bowen, 1977).

The transport of heavy metals in soils occurs primarily in three ways:

(a) in dissolved and suspended forms. Dissolved compounds in the soil solution move by diffusion and by mass flow with the soil solution. Movement of clay, organic matter and other constituents results in migration of the metals associated with those particles:

(b) by processes of biological enrichment in which metals taken up by plant roots are depleted in the rooting zone and enrich the surface soil horizons during litter decomposition:

(c) by organisms such as earthworms, other macro-organisms and micro-organisms which cause physical mixing and by absorption of metals into these organisms, causing biological redistribution of metals.

Experimental work and predictions from a knowledge of soil chemistry indicate that high cation exchange capacity, high base saturation, high organic matter content and high pH are conducive to the immobilisation of most heavy metals in most soil types. The primary effect of acidifying pollutant deposition is on soil pH but it also affects any other soil properties and soil processes linked to soil pH. This has the effect of changing the equilibrium, partition and speciation of heavy metals in the different soil phases. In general the solubility and hence mobility and potential plant availability, of most heavy metals increases with decreasing pH (eg. Harter, 1983; McKenzie, 1980). This occurs in a well defined sequence (see Figure 3.3). Mobility depends upon soil type, especially in relation to soil texture, soil parent material, porosity and to the existing state of the soil in terms of extent of acidification and/or podzolisation.

Most work on this topic to date has involved laboratory studies and there is very little published literature showing changes in soil pH and heavy metal distribution with time in undisturbed soil profiles. Very few studies have followed relevant soil changes over more than short periods of time. Martin and Coughtrey (1987) have carried out a study over a 10 year period at a site near Bristol heavily contaminated by both acid deposition and heavy metal fallout from industrial sources. Substantial changes in soil pH and metal distribution were recorded in a heavy clay soil, and the movement of heavy metals appeared to be related to pH and the adsorption/desorption characteristics of the metals. There is need for more research of this type, especially in areas where heavy metals are present in large concentrations either for natural reasons or because of pollution.

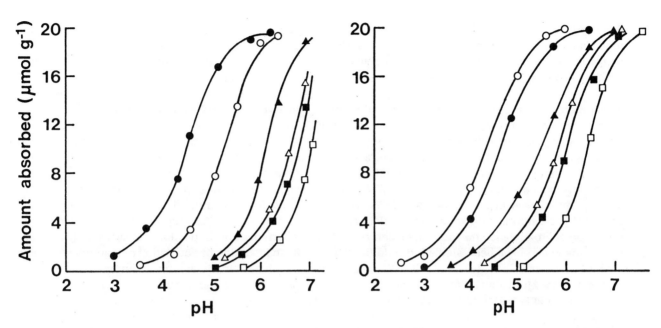

3.3 Effect of pH upon the adsorption of trace metals by hematite (left) and geothite (right). ○ Cu; ● Pb; ▲ Zn; △ Co; ■ Ni; □ Mn (based on McKenzie, 1980).

3.2 EFFECTS ON SOIL BIOLOGY

3.2.1 Role of soil organisms

Soil organisms are important in the maintenance of soil fertility, being responsible for many important reactions which take place within the soil. Of particular importance and central to much of the research into the impact of acid deposition on soil biota, is their ability to convert nutrients held in soil organic matter into inorganic forms, making them available for plant uptake, and their role in the regulation of organic matter accumulation. For example, the breakdown of organic nitrogen is the principle by which non-leguminous trees and vegetation can obtain this important nutrient. The soil population also performs many other functions, such as the mineralisation of organically bound elements, maintenance of soil structure, degradation of pesticides and organic residues and a host of reactions essential for the growth of higher plants.

The suggestion that inputs of acidifying pollutants to the soil may impair biological activity has therefore received considerable research attention in recent years. The threat of acid deposition to the soil biota of managed agricultural systems is considered to be minimal, since management practices are designed to counteract acidification and often override many of the functions of the soil biota. It is the unmanaged natural and particularly forest soils which are considered to be at greatest risk (Department of the Environment, 1976).

3.2.2 Suggested impacts of acidity on soil biota

There have been many studies into the relationships between soil pH and the abundance and activity of soil micro-organisms and fauna, the majority because of interest in natural soil acidification. In general, the more acid a soil the lower is the diversity and activity of the soil biota, because certain groups of organisms are intolerant of acid conditions. Extremely acid soils are often characterised by an accumulation of organic matter, due to a decrease in litter decomposition rates. This is particularly important for forest soils where decomposition of litter on the forest floor is a major source of nutrients for the trees. If the decomposition rate is reduced by incoming acidity then nutrient release will be inhibited and it has been proposed that deficiencies of nitrogen may occur (Tamm, 1976).

Most fine roots of forest trees are intimately associated with fungi in a symbiotic relationship in which the tree supplies the fungus with carbohydrates and the fungus assists the tree in uptake of nutrients. These symbioses are referred to as mycorrhizae, and it has been suggested that acidifying pollutants may damage this delicate relationship between fungus and host (Hutterman, 1982). If the soil pH is reduced as a consequence of medium to long term exposure to acidifying pollutants, mobilisation of heavy metals may also influence mycorrhizal activity.

3.2.3 Available evidence on the effects of acidifying pollutants

Wet deposition of sulphate and nitrate

As long ago as the beginning of this century scientists were investigating the effects of 'acid rain' on soil biological processes in agricultural soils. Crowther and Ruston (1911) collected rainfall from various sites around Leeds in Yorkshire and applied it to soil samples. They noted pronounced effects of rainfall acidity on the nitrogen mineralisation rates of the soils, and concluded that acid rain was reducing the biological activity and fertility of soils in industrial areas.

A resurgence of research effort occurred in the 1970's when Scandinavian soil biologists began a series of laboratory and field experiments in which they acidified forest soils and litters using simulated 'acid rain' solutions, containing sulphate as the acidifying anion (Abrahamsen et al., 1977; Tamm et al., 1977). Subsequently, there have been numerous studies designed specifically to determine the effects of wet deposition of acidity on soil biota and litter decomposition rates. Soil organisms which have been studied include fungi, bacteria, enchytraeids, springtails and mites. A comprehensive review by Morrison (1984) discussed the results of those experiments performed in forest soils. In general terms, it seems that soil flora and fauna are little affected by simulated acid rain treatments except at pH levels well below normal mean rainfall values. Work on the impact of simulated 'acid rain' on decomposition of forest litters in the UK has demonstrated that acidic coniferous litters have a flora and fauna well adapted to acidic conditions (Ineson, 1983), and are little affected by acid rain treatments. Deciduous litters tend to be well buffered and again are little affected unless the base reserve is limited. Soil solution in most cases rapidly attains a pH close to that of the soil, regardless of rainfall pH, as a consequence of cation exchange reactions. Any effect of wet deposition on decomposition is therefore likely to occur only as a result of long term changes in soil pH. Hallbäcken and Tamm (1986) have recently presented strong circumstantial evidence suggesting that such changes have occurred in Swedish forest soils as a consequence of acid deposition.

Although experimental manipulations of non-forest soils have demonstrated that nitrogen mineralisation, nitrogen fixation, nitrification and denitrification can be influenced by short-term simulated 'acid rain', the treatments have often been far in excess of those experienced in rainfall (eg. Alexander, 1980; Brown, 1985c; Firestone et al., 1984). For unmanaged soils in the UK it has been demonstrated that excess inputs of sulphur and nitrate from anthropogenic sources can have effects on both vegetation and associated soils, with subtle effects being observed in the biochemistry of the soils (Press et al., 1985).

The limited amount of work which has been performed to establish the effects of acidifying pollutants on mycorrhizal development has suggested that roots exposed to acid treatments are associated with different mycorrhizal fungal species from roots in unexposed plants. However little is known of the consequent effects on tree nutrition (Dighton et al., 1986). The mechanisms causing such species changes are not yet known, but alterations in

carbohydrate supply or in the amount of toxic aluminium in the soil may be important. Firestone et al. (1984) have demonstrated the potential toxicity of available aluminium to fungi in soils and Ulrich et al. (1980) have proposed that the toxicity of aluminium to roots is a central feature of the forest die-back syndrome.

Although much experimental work has been performed using sulphate as the anion associated with the acidity, nitrate largely has been ignored. Additions of nitrate to soils usually either promote, or have little effect on, soil biological activity and the nutritional benefits of such additions often outweigh detrimental effects. However, when soils are supplied with excess nitrate this can result in an inhibition of nodulation of leguminous species and an increase in the amount of nitrogen lost to the atmosphere through denitrification.

Inputs of wet and dry deposited ammonium to soils can have a marked acidifying affect (see Section 9.1.8), since much of the ammonium is converted to nitrate by bacteria in the soil, with the concomitant production of hydrogen ions. Thus, soil acidification is often caused by the application of ammonium fertilisers to soils. It is being increasingly realised that atmospheric ammonium inputs can have the same effect on natural ecosystems (van Breemen et al., 1984). The acidic pulses associated with nitrification (Ulrich et al., 1980) can result in aluminium solubilisation, with the possible consequences outlined above for both soil micro-organisms and mycorrhizal fungi.

Dry deposition of oxides of sulphur and nitrogen

Technical difficulties associated both with the measurement of deposition rates and the maintenance of controlled low-concentrations of pollutant gases have seriously hindered our appreciation of the role of dry deposition in the acidification of soils. However, recent research in the UK and elsewhere in Europe has highlighted the comparative insignificance of acidification due to wet deposition in some pollution climates, when compared with the acidifying effects of the dry pollutants.

Analysis of those factors giving rise to acidification at the 130-year-old Rothamsted Grass Experiment support the conclusion that wet deposited acidity is a negligible source at that site in central England, although total deposition from the atmosphere was responsible for at least 30% of the acidification observed. Atmospheric inputs to the 'Wilderness' woodland plot within the same experiment were even more extreme (Johnston et al., 1986), and several research groups have recently reported the major importance of dry deposition of sulphur dioxide to the acidification of areas in Central Europe (van Breemen et al., 1984; Paces, 1985). Since the effects of dry deposited air pollutants on soil biological processes may be considerably different from those of the wet deposited forms, it is important in future to differentiate between these inputs. For example, because of our lack of knowledge on the dry deposition inputs of acidity to forests, it is difficult to assess the extent to which the marked acidifications often observed in forest soils are a result of pollutant inputs.

Sulphur dioxide gas is an extremely toxic, anti-microbial agent and the absence of certain lichens and species of pathogenic fungi has been repeatedly correlated with ambient SO_2 concentrations. It has been demonstrated that SO_2 can selectively damage certain soil micro-organisms at high concentrations in-vitro (Grant et al., 1979) and may reduce forest soil respiration at environmentally realistic concentrations (Ineson and Gray, 1980). Recent research (Ineson, unpublished results) suggests that certain species of soil fungi may be specifically damaged by SO_2 concentrations as low as 20 ppb and these effects are associated with soil acidification and enhanced cation leaching. In contrast, oxides of nitrogen stimulate soil microbiological activity at low concentrations and thus in mixtures the effects of SO_2 and NO_x appear to counteract each other, in a non-interactive manner (Ineson, 1983). More information is needed on the impact of these pollutant gases under field conditions, coupled with gaseous measurements at the soil surface within woodland, forest and natural vegetation canopies, before the full impact to the soil biota can be assessed.

The short-term effects discussed above always need to be considered against the background of any longer term soil acidification effects which may also occur.

3.3 CONCLUSIONS

1. Agricultural soils have a natural tendency to become acid and this is generally counteracted by applications of lime. Liming may also prevent acidification of drainage waters in upland pastures. Consequently, the role of liming practices must be carefully considered when formulating land use policies and management programmes.

2. It has only recently been recognised that unmanaged naturally acidic soils, such as the podzols of granitic catchments and upland peat, may be vulnerable to further acidification. The extent to which the acidity of upland peats has increased as a result of pollution is not clear but the potential exists for significant long term changes.

3. Certain geologically acid-sensitive soils in the UK are not fully saturated with sulphate, but others (podzols of north west Wales) have already become sulphate-saturated and further deposition of sulphate leads to increases in acidity and higher concentrations of aluminium in drainage waters. In some sites, the additional sulphate input from acid deposition superimposed upon already substantial maritime-derived sulphate inputs may significantly alter the chemistry of terrestrial and fresh water ecosystems.

4. In general, the solubility of heavy metals in soils increases with increase in acidity. In the context of acid deposition, the implications of their solubility for soil organisms, plant growth and freshwater quality in the UK have received little attention.

5. Large inputs of nitrogen from the atmosphere (in the form of NO_2, NO, NO_3^- and NH_4^+) may have a substantial impact on sensitive soils. Ammonia released to the atmosphere from animal urine and faeces may contribute significantly to soil acidification.

6. The planting of trees may increase the acidity of soils and drainage waters in the absence of pollutants because of:

   i)   trapping of neutral salts from the atmosphere, especially in maritime climates.

   ii) uptake of large amounts of nutrients.

   iii) production of acidic litter horizons.

   Such changes may be offset partly by changes in water flux through the soil.

7. Trees also appear to trap pollutants from the atmosphere more efficiently than shorter vegetation. Unless absorbed by foliage, these pollutants reach the forest soil as throughfall and stemflow. Coniferous species tend to increase the acidity of the rainfall whereas hardwood species (in leaf) tend to partially neutralise rainfall acidity.

8. Soil organisms (both micro-organisms and soil fauna) are important in the maintenance of soil fertility especially by converting nutrients into forms suitable for plant uptake and by controlling soil organic-matter content. In general terms, the more acid the soil the less diverse and less active are the soil organisms.

9. Long term changes in soil pH may reduce the rate of litter decomposition and subsequent release of nutrients.

10. Increased soil acidification may also damage the mycorrhizal relationship between certain fungi and the fine roots of forest trees, either directly or by the mobilisation of toxic heavy metals.

11. In managed agricultural soils, farm practices are designed to provide nutrients as fertiliser and to counteract acidity by liming. The activity of soil organisms is thus of less importance than in natural, unmanaged lowland and upland forest soils which are consequently considered to be most at risk.

THE BIOCHEMICAL AND PHYSIOLOGICAL 4 EFFECTS OF AIR POLLUTANTS IN PLANTS

4.1 INTRODUCTION

Exposure of plants to air pollutants may result in altered growth and development, leading to changes in yield and quality of agricultural crops and forest crops and changes in survival, competition and diversity of species in natural ecosystems. To fully understand these changes, it is necessary to examine the ways in which pollutants affect the normal biochemical and physiological processes in the plant. A pathway of events from pollutant exposure to observed responses and their consequences, is given in Figure 4.1. Air pollutants are

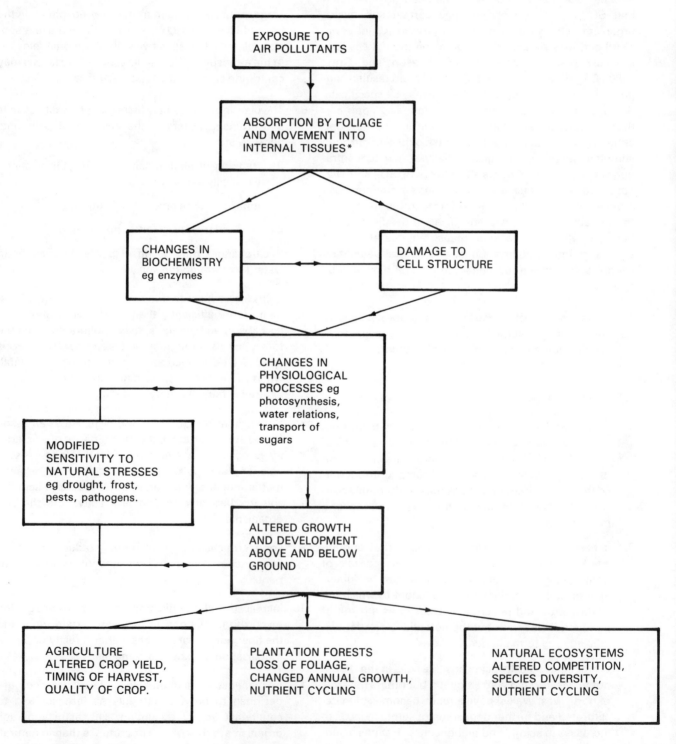

4.1   Stages in plant response to air pollutants.
     *See Plate 2.

absorbed by foliage, primarily through stomatal pores in the leaf surface and enter the leaf tissues where changes in biochemical reactions and/or damage to cell structure may occur. These alterations lead to changes in physiological processes in the plant such as photosynthesis, water relations and translocation of assimilated products and ultimately modify growth and development. Sensitivity to natural stresses such as cold, drought, pests and pathogens may be enhanced by these changes (see Chapter 10), adding to the overall modification of the plant.

The structure of land plants makes them potentially vulnerable to toxic substances in the atmosphere. Leaves are constructed in a way that allows almost unimpeded gaseous exchange with the air surrounding them, at least when stomatal pores are open (see section 4.3). Once inside the leaf, gases come into contact with the walls of cells which are thought to be continuously moist. After solution in this aqueous layer, which bounds the living part of the cell, the molecules can react in various ways or can diffuse into the interior of the cell where they may interact with the functional components.

The diagram below (Figure 4.2) shows the essential structure of a mesophyll cell of a leaf. The primary function of such a cell is photosynthesis, ie. the light-driven reduction of carbon dioxide (CO_2) to produce carbohydrates. The chloroplasts are the sites of photosynthesis and they are located in positions where they can absorb light and receive CO_2 which has first entered into solution in the water contained in the cell wall. Respiration (the oxidation of carbohydrates to CO_2 and H_2O) involves

a series of enzyme-catalysed reactions, many of which are located in the mitochondria.

The boundary to the living part of the cell is a membrane known as the plasma membrane or plasmalemma. Several important cellular activities are located in this membrane, especially those governing the ionic composition of the cell. For example protons (hydrogen ions H^+) can be pumped across the plasmalemma from the cell interior into the wall space. This primary 'proton pump' acts as a basis for ion transport, for example cations such as K^+ can enter the cell in exchange for H^+.

The plasmalemma is the part of the cell with which pollutants first make contact, and very reactive molecules such as ozone may cause considerable damage at this point (see section 4.2.3). Other pollutants such as SO_2 and NO_2 may, in the aqueous layer outside the plasmalemma, form some ionic species that are toxic and others that are familiar components of the cellular environment. In general little is known of the relative concentrations of toxic and non-toxic solution products at this crucial location because it is not yet possible to make measurements on the microscopic scale required.

In this chapter some of the known and postulated responses to air pollutants at the biochemical level are discussed and some of the important consequences for physiological processes are then considered.

4.2 SOME BIOCHEMICAL EFFECTS OF AIR POLLUTANTS

4.2.1 Sulphur dioxide

Sulphur is an important nutrient in plants which is normally absorbed by roots as sulphate and then transported to leaves where it is reduced before being assimilated. Enzymes for the reduction of sulphate are therefore found in leaves. When SO_2 enters the leaves from the atmosphere it first forms a variety of compounds such as sulphite and bisulphite which are not normally present at high concentrations. Although we do not yet understand the precise way in which SO_2 damages plants at the cellular level, we nevertheless have some detailed knowledge of the fate of the solution products of SO_2, and of metabolic disturbances that may be caused.

After it has entered the leaf (usually via the stomatal pores), SO_2 must dissolve in water contained in the cell walls before it reaches the plasma membranes which surround the living part of each cell. As it enters solution it is hydrated and sulphite (SO_3^{2-}) and bisulphite (HSO_3^-) ions are formed. Although it is impossible to measure these ions in the water layer within the cell wall, some sensible deductions can be made from a know-

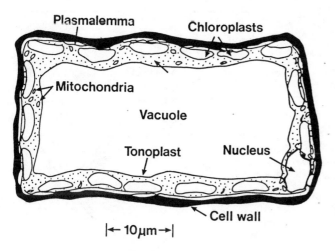

4.2   **Schematic representation of a mature cell from the leaf of a higher plant suggesting some of the complexity resulting from the presence of many membrane-surrounded subcellular bodies. (From PLANT CELL PHYSIOLOGY by P.S. Nobel. Copyright © 1970 W.J. Freeman and Company. Reprinted with the permission of W.H. Freeman and Company.)**

ledge of physical chemistry. The diagram below (Figure 4.3) shows how the percentage occurrence of the ionic species from sulphurous acid is dependent on pH.

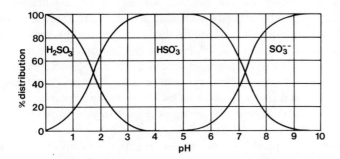

4.3   Distribution diagram of SO_2 solution products. (Reproduced from Puckett et al. 1973). H_2SO_3 is present as dissolved and unreacted SO_2 (Cape, 1984).

It is obvious that the localised proton-pumping activities of the plasmalemma (see section 4.1) will shift the ionic balance. In some cells (eg. stomatal guard cells) the proton movements can be on a very large scale, and considerable differences in pH in the extracellular environment occur at different times of day. Puckett et al. (1973) noted that all the forms of dissolved SO_2 become better oxidising agents as the pH of the medium is lowered. Thus the sensitivity of a cell to SO_2 may depend on the physiological and metabolic state of the cell, which varies considerably at different times of day and in different environments.

The various ionic species (and any dissolved SO_2 which has not yet reacted with water) can then cross the plasma membrane and enter the cytoplasm. At the pH values normally prevailing in the cytoplasm, more bisulphite than sulphite will be present. The proportion of sulphite increases as pH increases. When intracellular compartments have different pH values from the cytoplasm as a whole, the balance between sulphite and bisulphite will therefore change.

Sulphite and bisulphite are both much more toxic than sulphate (Thomas, 1961), and their detoxification can involve oxidation to sulphate. An alternative method of detoxification is reduction to sulphide. These mechanisms are summarised in Figure 4.4.

Much of the SO_2 absorbed by plant tissues is likely to be oxidised to sulphate, which can be achieved in two ways:

(i)   Through a free-radical chain mechanism

(ii) Enzymically, mediated by sulphite oxidase

The aerobic oxidation of sulphite by the first of these mechanisms can generate free radicals which have the potential to destroy many cellular compounds. In chloro-

plasts in the light, free radicals are produced in the thylakoid membranes as an unavoidable consequence of electron transport. These free radicals can begin the chain oxidation of sulphite to sulphate (Asada and Kiso, 1973; Asada, 1980). During this process increased amounts of free radicals are generated, eg. O_2^-, OH and SO_3^-. Further details of the chain reactions are given by Peiser and Yang (1985).

The extent to which free radicals may damage cells *in vivo* is not known with any certainty. *In vitro*, chlorophyll, carotenoids and lipids can be destroyed during the free radical oxidation of sulphite. This may explain why leaf chlorosis is one of the main visible symptoms of damage by SO_2.

The enzyme sulphite oxidase appears to be located in the mitochondria. It may play an important part in detoxification mechanisms for SO_2. Miller and Xerikos (1979) found that SO_2-resistant cultivars of soybean metabolised sulphite more rapidly than did sensitive cultivars. Kondo et al., (1980) studied several species and found that tolerance to SO_2 was correlated with the activity of sulphite oxidase.

An alternative to the oxidation of sulphite is its reduction to H_2S, and the ability to achieve this may also be related to resistance to SO_2 (Sekiya et al., 1982). The conversion of SO_2 to H_2S is apparently light-dependent.

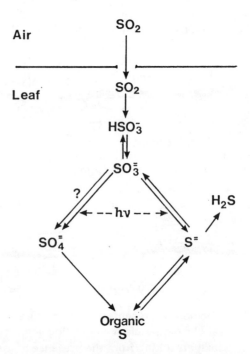

4.4   Pathways for SO_2 metabolism and potential detoxification. The question mark indicates that a nonphotochemical process that oxidises sulphite to sulphate is not certainly known to exist. (Reproduced from Tingey and Olszyk, 1985).

If the solution products of SO_2 are removed from the tissues quickly enough to avoid their accumulation (without the formation of free radicals) then direct damage at the cellular level may be avoided. However, the nutritional balance of the plant may be altered and this may have subtle consequences which are dealt with elsewhere in this report.

Some subcellular effects of SO_2

Sulphite or bisulphite ions can attack disulphide compounds in the following manner:

$$RSSR + HSO_3^- \rightarrow RS^- + RSSO_3^- + H^+$$

This reaction with disulphide bonds could occur with structural and soluble proteins. In the case of enzymes, inactivation would probably occur (Alscher, 1984).

Bisulphite can also be added to compounds such as aldehydes and ketones to produce hydroxysulphonates:

$$R.CHO + HSO_3^- \rightarrow R.CH.OH.SO_3^-$$

The full metabolic impact of reactions of this kind is not known, but there are considerable possibilities of damage to enzymes, etc. and of the production of highly toxic compounds. For example, hydroxysulphonates are chemical analogues of glycollate and they can interfere with its oxidation, an essential step in photorespiration.

Damage to membranes has often been observed during exposure of plants to SO_2. One of the first reports was by Wellburn et al., (1972) who found that swelling of thylakoids in chloroplasts occurred after only a short time in SO_2-polluted air. This effect on chloroplasts has been observed subsequently by many workers. It could be the result of a reaction between SO_2 and proteins and/or fatty acids in the membranes. Disruption of thylakoid membranes is likely to reduce the efficiency of light harvesting in chloroplasts.

Inhibition of photosynthesis is one of the most frequently reported effects of SO_2 in plants and this may be because chloroplasts are cellular locations that are specially sensitive to SO_2. The pH of the chloroplast stroma in the light is generally high (greater than 8.0) so that sulphite ions are likely to make the major contribution to the observed effects. The schematic figure below (Figure 4.5) shows some of the important photosynthetic events thought to occur in chloroplasts. The metabolism of sulphur (and also of nitrogen) is an integral part of photosynthesis which is not, as popularly conceived, solely concerned with carbon metabolism.

Transport of electrons across the thylakoid membranes causes the stroma to become more alkaline and the lumen more acidic. The alkalinisation of the stroma is important for the activity of enzymes of the Calvin cycle, and so any acidification caused by SO_2 is likely to interfere with CO_2 fixation. The gradient of pH across the

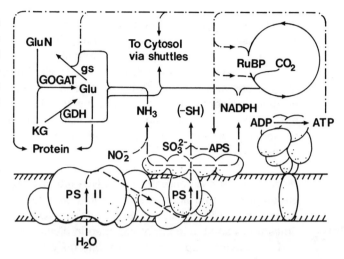

4.5   Scheme to illustrate the various destinations for electrons from the photosynthetic membrane (dashed lines), some of the uses of the reduced products, and the involvement of ATP in various processes that depend on photosynthesis (alternate dots and dashes). As discussed in the text, gaseous pollutants are thought simultaneously to affect several of the processes outlined in this scheme. (Reproduced from Wellburn, 1982).

membranes is also important for the formation of adenosine 5' triphosphate (ATP) (ie. photophosphorylation). Fumigation with SO_2 has been shown to reduce the ATP content of leaves (Wellburn, 1985a). Cerovic et al. (1983) examined the effects of SO_2 on rates of ATP formation in envelope-free chloroplasts from peas. The rates of photophosphorylation fell with increasing amounts of SO_2.

There is evidence that the key enzymes of photosynthetic CO_2-fixation are adversely affected by sulphite (Libera et al., 1975). The activity of ribulose 1,5-bis-phosphate carboxylase may be directly affected, but it is perhaps more likely that inhibition is caused because sulphite binds to the enzyme in the same manner as bicarbonate (Ziegler, 1972). Some new data from Parry et al. (1983) suggests that sulphite has a variable effect on the affinity of this enzyme for CO_2.

A problem in making further advances in biochemical studies is lack of information on internal concentrations of toxic anions. Wellburn (1985b) has recently made the first attempt to analyse the anions in chloroplasts taken from leaves that had been fumigated with SO_2 and NO_2. The results of such studies will play an important part in enabling further advances to be made in understanding the effects of air pollutants at the cellular level.

4.2.2 Nitrogen oxides

Nitrogen dioxide reacts with water to form nitrous and nitric acids. Nitrous acid is a weak acid which will be present as a mixture of nitrite (NO_2^-) ions, protons (H^+) and undissociated molecules (assuming the pH of the extracellular water to be between 5 and 6). Most of the nitric acid, on the other hand, will ionise to yield nitrate (NO_3^-) ions and protons. Only nitrate and protons are normally present in large quantities inside cells and so nitrite ions and undissociated nitrous acid must be regarded as unfamiliar, and potentially toxic, chemical forms.

Most research has concentrated on NO_2 rather than NO, although the latter is often a major component of NO_x. Anderson and Mansfield (1979) found that NO was five times more soluble in xylem sap than in distilled water, and since xylem sap is continuous with the extracellular water in the leaf mesophyll, it seems likely that uptake of NO into plants may be greater than would be predicted from its water solubility. Preliminary determinations by Law and Mansfield (1982) confirmed that this was the case. The fate of NO after solution in water is uncertain. It has been considered to be non-reactive with water (Bonner, 1970), but isotopic exchange between ^{15}NO and solutions of $N^{18}O_3^-$ and $N^{18}O_2^-$ has been observed (Bonner and Jordan, 1973; Jordan and Bonner, 1973). It is, therefore, possible that NO, like NO_2, can produce nitrate and nitrite ions in solution. More needs to be known about the behaviour of NO after it has entered the leaf, because one recent investigation has suggested that NO is much more toxic than NO_2 (Saxe, 1986). This is very difficult to explain on the basis of existing knowledge.

Nitrate and nitrite ions are normal intermediates in the pathway leading to the production of ammonia, prior to amino acid synthesis in plants, as depicted in figure 4.6 below (see reviews by Beevers and Hageman, 1980 and Guerrero et al., 1981).

Nitrate and nitrite are the substrates for two reductase enzymes normally present in leaves, namely nitrate and nitrite reductases. The usual source of substrate for nitrate reductase is nitrate transported into the leaves from the roots and the reduction of this nitrate produces nitrite which then acts as the substrate for nitrite reductase.

Nitrites are known to be toxic to plant cells and they do not accumulate in leaves under normal conditions. Precise regulation of the reduction pathway to ammonia is required to prevent their accumulation and the activity of nitrate reductase is thought to provide the necessary rate control. This enzyme appears to be located outside the chloroplasts (Wallsgrove et al., 1979) whereas nitrite reductase is within the chloroplasts. Presumably the potentially toxic nitrite ions are kept apart from sensitive sites during their relocation within the cells. It is likely that the appearance of nitrite ions in extracellular water, after the uptake of NO or NO_2 by leaves, represents an abnormal situation with which the cell is not able to cope easily. The passage of nitrite ions (and possibly undissociated nitrous acid) across the plasma membrane does not occur to any marked degree during normal metabolic activities.

Figure 4.7 shows the relationship between nitrate and nitrite reduction and the synthesis of amino acids in chloroplasts.

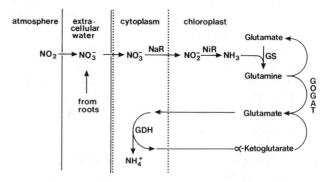

4.7 **The relationship between nitrate and nitrite reduction and the synthesis of amino acids in chloroplasts.**

Amundson and Maclean (1982) suggested a link between the location of nitrate reduction and the susceptibility of different plant species to NO_x. They pointed out that in C_4 plants both nitrate and nitrite reductases are present in mesophyll but neither are present in bundle sheath cells. They suggested that accumulation of nitrite in the bundle sheath could account for the damage reported after exposure of maize to NO_2 overnight. They also suggested that some woody plants might be specially sensitive to NO_x because they use only the roots to reduce nitrate to ammonia.

	Enzyme	Probable location
NO_3^-		
↓	Nitrate reductase (NaR)	Cytoplasm
NO_2^-		
↓	Nitrite reductase (NiR)	Chloroplasts
NH_3 (NH_4^+)		

4.6 **Reduction pathway of nitrate to ammonia, prior to amino acid synthesis in plants.**

Nitrate and ammonium ions are normally absorbed by the roots of higher plants. Ammonium ions are normally assimilated in roots and do not enter the xylem stream in appreciable concentrations. Nitrate may be reduced either in the root, in the root and shoot, or in the shoot, depending on the species. Consequently, primary assimilation of ammonia is not a normal function of plant shoots and nitrate assimilation may not occur in a species in which nitrate reductase activity is confined to the root. Plant shoots may, therefore, not have the ability to readily detoxify gaseous nitrogen-containing gases.

Several researchers have found that the activities of nitrate and nitrite reductase are affected by exposure to NO_x. Levels of nitrite reductase are usually enhanced (eg. Wellburn et al., 1976; Wellburn et al., 1980), but the effects on nitrate reductase are less clear. Amundson and Maclean (1982) suggested that the direct supply of nitrite ions can reduce the demand for the reduction of nitrate, so the activity of nitrate reductase declines. This may mean, however, that the normal rate control of the pathway is lost. The incorporation of ammonium into amino acids is regulated by other enzymes, as shown in figure 4.7. The normal route is via glutamine synthetase and glutamate synthase (Miflin and Lea, 1976) but another pathway via glutamate dehydrogenase is available. The reasons for these alternative pathways in higher plants are not clear, but the activity of glutamate dehydrogenase can be increased by exposure to NO_x (Wellburn et al., 1976; Wellburn et al., 1980). This may be the result of enhanced deamination to remove extra amino acid.

Much of the work quoted above has been performed with relatively high concentrations of NO_x, but Wellburn et al. (1981) found that a 20-week exposure of several grasses to 68 ppb NO_2 increased the activity of nitrite reductase.

Most of the published biochemical studies have considered that the pathways described above, starting with nitrate reduction, are responsible for the detoxification of NO_x by plants. There are, however, other metabolic processes that may be important, eg. production of polyamines and gaseous emissions of N_2, NO and NH_3 from leaves. These other possibilities (largely speculative at present) have been discussed by Rowland et al. (1987).

4.2.3 Ozone

Ozone differs from SO_2 and NO_x insofar as its entry into a plant does not supply an essential nutrient. The full metabolic consequences of the input of sulphur and nitrogen need to be examined when the toxic effects of SO_2 and NO_x are being assessed. In the case of ozone, on the other hand, it is the reactivity of the molecule itself rather than the contribution of elements towards metabolism that is important.

Once ozone has entered a leaf there is thought to be very little resistance to its diffusion through the moist cell walls. However, when it is in solution, ozone immediately begins to form derivatives with varying levels of reactivity, for example hydroxyl radicals, monatomic oxygen, hydrogen peroxide and superoxide radicals (O_2^-). These derivatives may be responsible for most of the harmful effects of ozone, for example damage to membrane proteins and to unsaturated regions of the fatty acids within membranes. There are natural systems in cells for scavenging free radicals so that their damaging effects are restricted, but free radicals on or near the outer surface of the plasma membrane may cause damage before the scavenging systems can operate.

Most studies (biochemical, microscopical, electrophysiological) have indicated that a major early effect of ozone is on the plasma membranes. Once this damage has taken place, secondary effects such as leakage of potassium ions occur. Other cellular membranes such as those of mitochondria and chloroplasts are damaged in the same general way but to a lesser degree, presumably because the free radical scavenging systems give them protection which is not available to the plasma membrane. Nevertheless, there is some damage to these organelles in moderate to high exposures to ozone. This may affect the ability of the cell to achieve repairs to the plasma membrane and other sites of injury. Repair mechanisms must invariably consume energy.

Recently Mehlhorn and Wellburn (1987) have obtained an important clue to the mechanism by which ozone injures plant tissue. They found that pea seedlings were only sensitive to visible injury by ozone when they were emitting ethylene. Ethylene is a gaseous plant growth regulator which is formed naturally in tissues, especially at times of physiological stress and during particular stages of development, eg. fruit ripening. Mehlhorn and Wellburn suggest that the high toxicity of ozone to plant tissues may be the result of it reacting with ethylene to produce water-soluble, highly reactive free radicals which damage cellular components.

In general, it can be predicted that damage to membranes will affect the ability of cells to retain solutes, to maintain osmotic pressure and to perform normal transport functions which are dependent on primary processes located in membranes. Further information may be found in the papers by Mudd et al. (1984) and Ballantyne (1984).

4.2.4 Mixtures of pollutants

When plants are exposed simultaneously to more than one pollutant the responses are complex. Knowledge of effects at the biochemical level is so sparse that it is not possible to offer a complete explanation of the range of responses that has been observed in experiments. It is unlikely that the range of responses is only the result of inter-related biochemical processes, because physiological phenomena can also play an important part. For example, SO_2 and ozone can both cause substantial changes in stomatal behaviour and these gases will therefore not only influence their own uptake into leaves but also the uptake of any other pollutant species present.

In spite of these complications some indications of the causes of synergistic effects of SO_2 and NO_2 exist. Determinations of the activity of nitrite reductase over a period of several days have suggested that SO_2 may affect the ability of plants to metabolise the potentially toxic ions resulting from the uptake of NO_2 (Figure 4.8).

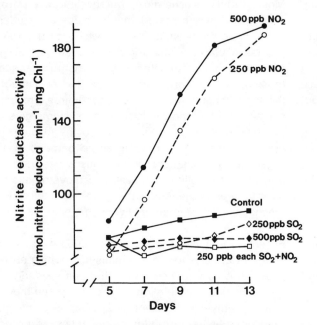

4.8   Levels of nitrite reductase activity in extracts of ryegrass (*Lolium perenne* L.) laminae which have been exposed to clean air or various combinations of SO_2-polluted and/or NO_2-polluted air for 5–15 days. (Reproduced from Wellburn, (1982)).

Fumigation with NO_2 alone induces a significant increase in nitrite reductase activity, but in the presence of SO_2 this increase does not occur. This suggests that SO_2 interferes with an essential detoxification mechanism for removing nitrite ions. The situation is not, however, simple. Studies of pH gradients across isolated thylakoid membranes suggest that relatively high levels of nitrite or sulphite are required to disrupt photosynthetic electron flow, but mixtures of nitrite and sulphite are highly disruptive at concentrations as low as 0.1 mM. It is not, however, known how these concentrations relate to those in polluted atmospheres. The reasons for such synergism are also not known, and further studies at the

subcellular level are required to explore them. This toxicity of a combination of nitrite and sulphite to membranes may be why mixtures of SO_2 and NO_2 often cause visible symptoms of injury that resemble those produced by ozone (Reinert *et al.*, 1975).

4.2.5 CONCLUSIONS

1.   Sulphur and nitrogen are both essential plant nutrients and their normal route of entry in high quantity is not from the atmosphere into the leaf, but from the soil into the root. When they do enter through the leaf, normal metabolic control points may be bypassed.

2.   The metabolism of sulphur and nitrogen is an integral part of photosynthesis. However the conversion of SO_2 and NO_2 to forms utilisable by plants requires considerable expenditure of energy.

3.   When SO_2 enters the leaf, compounds such as sulphite and bisulphite are formed and these can inhibit key enzyme activity. Exposure to SO_2 may also result in damage to membranes, and this affects photosynthesis and energy production. Nitrogen dioxide reacts in the leaf to form nitrates and nitrites. Nitrates are essential for protein production but nitrites are toxic to plant cells and their accumulation is normally prevented by cellular controls of enzymes and substrates. Uptake of NO_2 from large concentrations may disrupt these controls. Until recently, NO was not thought to react with plants to any great extent, but new evidence suggests that NO can also form toxic nitrites in cells.

4.   As ammonia and oxides of nitrogen are increasingly to be found alongside one another in parts of the UK, their effects in combination need to be studied.

5.   Ozone is a very reactive molecule and once it has entered the leaf, it readily attacks cells. Plasma membranes are important points of attack but symptoms thereafter at the cellular level are non-specific. Direct and indirect effects often cannot be separated, but there is new evidence that ethylene produced in stressed plants may be involved in the responses of plants to ozone. Ethylene and ozone can react to produce very reactive free radicals.

6.   Insufficient knowledge exists of precise mechanisms behind phytoxicity and of ways in which species differ in their sensivitiy to pollutants.

7.   More biochemical research is needed to improve our understanding of the effects of mixtures of pollutants. For example some unexpectedly large effects of SO_2/NO_2 mixtures may occur because SO_2 interferes with the normal mechanism for removing nitrite.

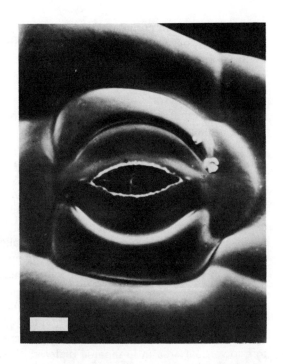

4.3 THE EFFECT OF AIR POLLUTANTS ON PHYSIOLOGICAL PROCESSES

Physiological processes within the plant centre around the production and distribution of carbohydrates for plant growth and development. Carbohydrates are produced by a process known as photosynthesis, during which CO_2 from the atmosphere is fixed in green tissues utilising energy from the sun. The products are then translocated to various parts of the plant and utilised for growth. The processes of translocation and growth require carbohydrates as a source of energy and the release of CO_2 in dark respiration often provides a useful measure of this activity.

The exchange of CO_2 and oxygen between plant cells and the atmosphere occurs through pores on the leaf surface known as stomata (see Plate 2). As leaf tissues contain a high proportion of water, the simultaneous loss of water vapour to the atmosphere by transpiration is therefore inevitable. The structure of a typical stomatal pore is shown in Figure 4.9. Opening or closing of the central pore occurs when a change in turgor pressure of the guard cells or surrounding cells causes the guard cells to move apart or to close together along their length. Any increase in size of the stomatal pore is likely to increase stomatal conductance (decrease stomatal resistance) and the rate of water loss or transpiration from the leaf. Conversely a reduction in the pore size usually reduces stomatal conductance and decreases the rate of transpiration.

The mechanism behind air pollutant effects can only be understood if these key physiological processes and their effects on plant growth and development are considered in detail (see Figure 4.10).

4.9   Scanning electron micrograph of a stomatal pore on the leaf surface of dayflower (*Commelina communis*). a) Grown in clean air. The pore is surrounded by two 'guard cells'. b) Exposed to sulphur dioxide. In this picture strain lines are seen on the surface of the two 'subsidiary cells' on either side of the guard cells. Such physical change can occur when subsidiary cells are damaged by pollutants, and the stomatal pore may then be forced to open ie. the guard cells lose full control of the aperture. Bar = 10 μm. (Provided by K. Oates, Lancaster University).

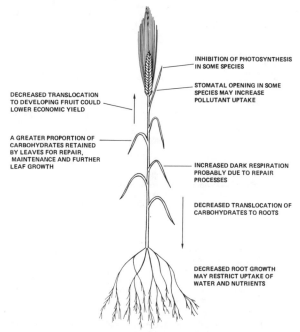

INHIBITION OF PHOTOSYNTHESIS IN SOME SPECIES

STOMATAL OPENING IN SOME SPECIES MAY INCREASE POLLUTANT UPTAKE

DECREASED TRANSLOCATION TO DEVELOPING FRUIT COULD LOWER ECONOMIC YIELD

A GREATER PROPORTION OF CARBOHYDRATES RETAINED BY LEAVES FOR REPAIR, MAINTENANCE AND FURTHER LEAF GROWTH

INCREASED DARK RESPIRATION PROBABLY DUE TO REPAIR PROCESSES

DECREASED TRANSLOCATION OF CARBOHYDRATES TO ROOTS

DECREASED ROOT GROWTH MAY RESTRICT UPTAKE OF WATER AND NUTRIENTS

4.10 Possible effects of air pollutants on physiological processes.

4.3.1 Photosynthesis

Sulphur dioxide

Published data record a wide range of plant sensitivity to short-term (<8 hours) fumigations with SO_2 (Figure 4.11). In the majority of species significant inhibition of photosynthesis was first detected at 200–400 ppb. Recovery was found to commence immediately, and when the level of inhibition had not exceeded 20%, recovery was complete within two hours (Bennett and Hill 1973; Darrall 1986). Following greater levels of inhibition recovery was complete after 24 hours (Bennett and Hill, 1973). In general, inhibition has been found to be more severe in individuals with higher rates of photosynthesis, either in particular cultivars or under certain conditions of light and temperature. The role of humidity as a modifier has not been found to be consistent.

Photosynthetic responses to recurrent short-term fumigations were found to be dependent upon the frequency of such episodes as well as the concentration. In rice, the rate of recovery declined after hourly fumigations leaving an increasing residual level of inhibition (Matsuoka,

1978). However, no cumulative effect was detected following daily or weekly exposures (McLaughlin *et al.*, 1979; Takemoto and Noble, 1982).

Data from long-term fumigation with SO_2 are scarce despite the fact that such work would be more representative of ambient conditions in the UK than short term episodes. There are few dose-response data available and currently the lowest concentration reported to inhibit photosynthesis is 60 ppb over 28 days in silver birch (Freer-Smith, 1985). Comparison with the sensitivity to short term (<8 hour) fumigations does not give a clear picture; lower threshold concentrations and increased levels of inhibitions have been reported (Hällgren and Gezelius, 1982; Keller, 1978; Saxe, 1983) but also no change in response and a loss of initial inhibitory response (Taylor *et al.*, 1986). Effects were found to be completely reversible after a five-day fumigation (Hällgren and Gezelius, 1982). However, after 4–5 weeks, effects were only partly reversible and this was attributed to a lower leaf area in fumigated material (Saxe, 1983). An integrated measure of photosynthesis, net assimilation rate, can be obtained from the analysis of plant weight changes during fumigation. The lowest concentration at which effects have been reported is 75 ppb over 166 days in lucerne. Other data report effects at between 100 and 250 ppb over 21 to 49 days. More detailed information on photosynthetic responses is available in review articles eg. Black, 1982; Hällgren, 1984; Darrall, 1987.

Ozone

Few authors have tested a sufficient range of concentrations to draw conclusions about threshold concentrations and dose-response relationships. In short-term fumigations inhibition has been reported at 100 ppb for one hour in alfalfa and other authors have found reductions at 200–500 ppb (see Darrall, 1987).

In long-term fumigations (>1 day) inhibition of photosynthesis was seen at lower concentrations, for example at 35–54 ppb over a three week period in a number of agricultural crops (Reich and Amundson, 1985). In coniferous and hardwood trees inhibition was only seen at higher rates of ozone. The lowest reported inhibitory dose was 50 ppb in a 126 day exposure (Barnes, 1972). Effects were seen in other species at concentrations of 150 ppb or above (Carlson, 1979). Measurements of net assimilation rate also confirmed effects on carbohydrate production at 270 and 250 ppb (Oshima *et al.*, 1979; Walmsley *et al.*, 1980; Jensen, 1981).

Sulphur dioxide and ozone

In comparison with the effects of each gas singly, fumigations with a mixture of SO_2 and ozone were found

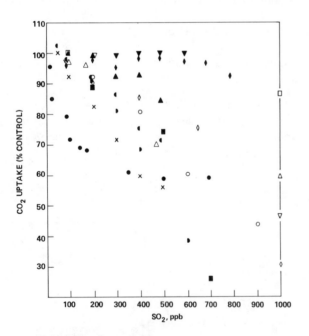

□ *Phaseolus vulgaris*, pinto bean (NOYES, 1980)
△ *Oryza sativa*, rice (MATSUOKA)
▽ *Hordeum vulgare*, barley and *Medicago sativa*, alfalfa (BENNETT AND HILL, 1973)
◇ *Diplacus aurantiacus* (WINNER AND MOONEY, 1980)
○ *Helianthus annuus*, sunflower (OSHIMA et al., 1973)
● *Vicia faba* cv Dylan, field bean (BLACK AND UNSWORTH, 1979)
■ *Glycine max*, soya bean (CARLSON, 1983)
◀ *Vicia faba* cv Threefold white, field bean (DARRALL 1986)
▸ *Vicia faba* cv Blaze, field bean (DARRALL 1986)
▲ *Hordeum vulgare* cv Sonja, winter barley (DARRALL 1986)
▼ *Triticum aestivum* cv Virtue, winter wheat (DARRALL 1986)
✦ *Brassica rapa* cv Rafal, oil-seed rape (DARRALL 1986)
✕ *Lolium perenne* cv S23, ryegrass (DARRALL 1986)

4.11 Effects of short term (1–8 hours) fumigation with SO_2 (<1000 ppb) on net photosynthesis, summary of published data.

to have a greater effect upon net photosynthesis, except where either gas alone substantially reduced the rate of photosynthesis (Carlson, 1979; Chevone and Yang, 1985; Black et al., 1982). Inhibitory effects increased with the duration of the fumigation period up to 8 hours, but not during a longer term exposure (1–7 days) Black et al., 1982; Carlson, 1979). Recovery following exposure to ozone and SO₂ occurred within 24 hours where the level of inhibition had been small. At higher concentrations the effect was not readily reversible (Black et al., 1982).

Nitrogen oxides alone and in combination with sulphur dioxide

The process of photosynthesis is much less sensitive to the presence of NO$_x$ than other pollutants, for inhibition has only been detected at 500–700 ppb in short-term fumigations (<8 hours) and 250 ppb over a 20 hour period (Hill and Bennett, 1970; Capron and Mansfield, 1976).

As a result of exposure to combinations of SO₂ and NO₂, inhibition of net photosynthesis was observed at lower concentrations than when plants were fumigated with these gases singly. Effects were seen at 200–250 ppb NO₂ and SO₂ (White et al., 1974; Carlson, 1983).

4.3.2 Stomatal responses to air pollutants

Sulphur dioxide

There are more than 30 published papers dealing with this topic, reporting observations on a range of agricultural species and trees and a number of comprehensive reviews have been published (Black, 1982; Mansfield and Freer-Smith, 1984; Darrall, 1987). A comparison of varieties sensitive and tolerant to SO₂ showed that in some cases the more sensitive varieties had higher intrinsic stomatal conductances and a greater increase in transpiration and stomatal conductance in the presence of SO₂ (Winner and Mooney, 1980a, b and c; Pande, 1985). At low concentrations (<200 ppb) an opening response in field bean was found to be a result of damage to epidermal cells adjoining the stomata (Figure 4.8) rather than a direct effect on the stomatal guard cells.

At intermediate concentrations (200–700 ppb) the different responses could not be attributed to environmental factors such as humidity or light intensity.

Ozone

At ozone concentrations below 200 ppb, no clear picture of stomatal responses could be seen (Darrall, 1987). Both increases and decreases as well as no change in stomatal conductance or transpiration have been reported. Above 200 ppb, reductions in transpiration and stomatal conductance occurred in the majority of species exposed to ozone, and in the remainder, no response was detected. Varietal and species differences were found to be similar to those reported for SO₂.

Ozone and sulphur dioxide

No clear picture of stomatal response to mixtures of ozone and SO₂ can be seen from the published data. Of the thirteen species for which data have been published, five show stomatal closure and three stomatal opening. The different results could not be attributed to ozone or SO₂ concentration, length of exposure, humidity, temperature or light intensity.

Sulphur dioxide and nitrogen oxides

There are few reports of stomatal responses to NO₂ alone or in combination with SO₂. An increase in stomatal conductance at 100 ppb NO₂ has been reported in one woody plant (Naturi and Totsuka, 1984), but in general there is no response except at concentrations above 1000 ppb when decreased conductances occur. On fumigation with the mixture of gases, reductions in stomatal conductance and a decrease in transpiration were reported in some species which were greater than additive (Carlson, 1983).

Changes in stomatal opening, measured either as the rate of transpiration or as stomatal conductance, have been frequently reported in response to various air pollutants and a summary of the data is shown in Table 4.1.

Table 4.1 Summary of Stomatal Responses to Air Pollutants

Response / Pollutant	Increased stomatal conductance. Increase in transpiration or no change	Increase or decrease in stomatal conductance. Increase or decrease in transpiration or no change	Decrease in stomatal conductance or decrease in transpiration
SO₂ (ppb)	<100	100–950	>1865
ozone₃ (ppb)		≤ 200	> 200
NO₂ (ppb)	<100	≤1000	≥2000
NO (ppb)		≤1000	>1000

4.3.3 Changes in assimilate distribution

Changes in the partitioning of manufactured carbohydrates between shoot, root and developing fruits have been reported in response to air pollutants (see 5.5.2, 6.4.2). Where effects have been detected, a decrease in carbohydrates to the roots has generally been found. This is likely to lead to an imbalance between the roots which exploit available water supplies in the soil and the shoots which utilise the water in transpiration. A deficit in water available to the plant can be anticipated although this may not be evident except in conditions of limited supply from the soil, eg. drought. Decreased allocation of carbohydrates to developing fruits has also been reported and this is likely to have a disproportionate effect on the economic yield of crops when compared with an overall reduction in plant weight.

In silver birch, the effects of exposure to 40 ppb SO_2 for 9 weeks were detected as changes in the root:shoot ratio (Freer-Smith, 1985). There are numerous other reports of effects between 50 and 500 ppb SO_2 based on changes in root to shoot ratio or changes in carbohydrate movement. Effects have been reported at concentrations below those at which inhibition of photosynthesis has been detected (Noyes, 1980) and decrease in export of carbohydrates from source leaves has been found to be more pronounced in sensitive than tolerant plant material (McLaughlin and McConathy, 1983; Taylor et al., 1986).

Similar results have been found upon fumigation with ozone; a decreased root to shoot ratio has been reported at 50 ppb in a 40 hour fumigation over 5 weeks (Tingey et al., 1971) as well as at higher concentrations. However at 150 ppb ozone, an increased allocation to the roots occurred in a fumigation of 24 hours over 6 days (Blum et al., 1983). Recent work indicates that such responses are dependent upon plant water availability, because a drought-induced stimulation of root growth was suppressed by ozone, whereas in irrigated material, a reduction in shoot weight was detected at mean concentrations of less than 100 ppb (NCLAN report, Kress et al., 1986). There are no reports of significant changes in carbohydrate resource allocation in response to fumigations with nitrogen oxides at 40-400 ppb NO_2.

The changes in carbohydrate allocation in response to fumigation with mixtures of SO_2 and ozone and/or NO_2 do not present a clear picture. There are some reports of greater than additive effects upon fumigation with SO_2 and ozone or NO_2 and other reports of additive or less than additive effects (Freer-Smith, 1985; Darrall, 1987). Clearly, as these pollutants generally occur as mixtures this area of research is important.

4.3.4 Respiration

Respiratory losses normally represent a small proportion of assimilated carbohydrates. However, if changes persist for a considerable period after exposure to an air pollutant then they would represent a significant influence on the carbon balance of the plant.

In general, respiration has been found to increase in response to fumigation with air pollutants in the absence of visible injury.

There are some reports of both increased levels and no change in dark respiration in shoots fumigated with sulphur dioxide (20-400 ppb) (Darrall, 1987). The magnitude of a reported increase was found to be independent of concentration between 35 and 175 ppb and persisted for 24 hours following the cessation of the fumigation episode (Black and Unsworth, 1979).

Stimulation of dark respiration in shoots by ozone has been reported both in the presence and absence of visible injury (Pell and Brennan, 1973) but not at concentrations below 150 ppb. In a single study on root respiration, ozone (150 ppb) decreased respiration levels but in combination with SO_2 (150 ppb) or with SO_2 alone there was no change.

No effect of nitrogen oxides on respiration has been reported in the range 40-400 ppb.

4.3.5 Conclusions

1. Pollutant gases enter plants mainly through the stomata and to a lesser extent through the cuticular surfaces of leaves and may directly affect stomatal movements which are essential for both gas exchange and water conservation in plants.

2. Short exposure (8 hours) to small concentrations (20-80 ppb) of SO_2 cause stomatal opening in some species but similar concentrations of other pollutants generally have no effect.

3. Exposure to large concentrations of most pollutant gases (200 ppb SO_2; 2000 ppb NO_2; 1000 ppb NO; 200 ppb ozone) tend to cause stomatal closure.

4. Exposure to more than one pollutant causes variable responses, frequently different to those caused by exposure to single pollutants.

5. Stomata also respond directly to other environmental stresses such as drought, and it is becoming increasingly evident that the interrelationships between these responses and pollutant exposure are complex, but extremely important in our understanding of observed effects.

6. Short term exposures of many plants to SO_2 concentrations ranging from 200-400 ppb produce signi-

ficant reductions in net photosynthesis. In sensitive plants, reductions have been detected after exposure to only 35 ppb.

7. Oxides of nitrogen inhibit photosynthesis only at high concentrations (500 ppb) but SO_2 and NO_2 together cause inhibition at lower concentrations than when SO_2 is present singly.

8. Short term exposure to ozone causes inhibition of photosynthesis at concentrations above about 100 ppb.

9. In the absence of visible injury, recovery of photosynthesis is completed within 24 hours of exposure to SO_2, but effects of exposure to ozone or ozone + SO_2 are not so readily reversed.

10. There is increasing evidence that photosynthetic response to pollutants can be greatly modified by environmental factors such as light intensity and fluctuations in relative humidity or temperature and by genetic factors responsible for variation between species.

11. The distribution of assimilates in the phloem has been found recently to be more sensitive than photosynthesis when plants are exposed to SO_2 (40 ppb over 9 weeks or higher concentrations over shorter periods) and ozone (50 ppb over 40 hours during 5 weeks). Interference with assimilate distribution can result in reduced export to the roots, leading to a decrease in the root:shoot ratio, with serious implications where water and nutrient supplies are limited. Similarly, reduced export of assimilates to developing fruits is likely to have a disproportionate effect towards decreasing fruit and seed yield.

12. Fumigation with SO_2, or ozone increases the rate of dark respiration, results for oxides of nitrogen are not consistent. After the cessation of fumigation, recovery to pre-fumigation levels occurs over a number of days, which is in contrast to photosynthesis where recovery commences immediately.

EFFECTS ON GRASSLANDS

5.1 INTRODUCTION

Grasslands are reviewed separately from other crops in view of their considerable importance in British agriculture. Intensively managed grasslands and grasses in rough grazing occupy about 57% of the UK land area, a larger percentage than of most other European countries. Grasses have special characteristics which result in their reacting in a particularly complex manner to air pollutants. Unlike arable crops, most grass species are perennial and may be subjected to atmospheric pollution for many years. This is especially relevant in the case of permanent pastures which contain native species and have been established in some cases for many hundreds of years. Such pastures receive minimal management, in contrast to short term leys which are sown with specially bred cultivars, often including clovers, and which may last for only 2–3 years. Grasslands are also used for amenity purposes, such as parks and sports fields, which are usually located in urban areas where the highest concentrations of SO_2 and NO_2 tend to occur. Most grasslands contain a mixture of species and thus their response to air pollutants cannot readily be understood on the basis of experiments with monocultures. There is no evidence that UK grasslands are directly damaged by acid rain but there has been considerable research effort on effects of gaseous pollutants on grasses.

5.2 FIELD OBSERVATIONS

The earliest reports from the field of the effects of ambient air pollution on grassland species were by Cohen and Ruston (1925) who noted the absence of clovers from lawns in industrial areas, as well as species of fescue (*Festuca*). They pointed out that in order to maintain a lawn in the industrial centre of Leeds, it was necessary to reseed annually. A later study by Bleasdale (1952) showed a marked decline in productivity of the important pasture species perennial ryegrass, (*Lolium perenne*), exposed in standard cultures at different sites along two transects between the Cheshire countryside and central Manchester. However, the best evidence from the field for serious effects occurring on agricultural grasslands was reported for a hill-farming region of East Lancashire by Bell and Mudd (1976). This region had experienced high concentrations of SO_2 for a long time, with winter means of about 45 ppb up to the mid-1970s. During and after the Second World War, attempts were made to improve the productivity of the local farms by ploughing up the permanent pastures and reseeding with high yielding bred grass cultivars, including perennial ryegrass. In many cases the results were disappointing, with a fall-off in productivity. This was generally ascribed to air pollution, reflecting the somewhat similar experience of the Forestry Commission when attempting to establish conifer plantations in polluted parts of the southern Pennines around the same time (see Chapter 7). Indeed, both chlorosis and characteristic acute SO_2-injury were observed on the introduced grass cultivars on various occasions.

More recently, further field trials were carried out from 1976–81 by Colvill et al. (1985) at sites in north-west England with a range of pollution levels, using ryegrass populations differentially sensitive to SO_2, in order to minimise the confounding effects of climatic differences between sites. In initial trials, SO_2-sensitive plants were reduced in yield at high SO_2 sites, particularly after a winter with a mean of 53 ppb, while tolerant plants showed a smaller effect. Concentrations of SO_2 declined during later trials (at about 30 ppb) and yield losses became more difficult to detect. In these later trials, sensitive plants were not affected more than tolerant plants, suggesting that the lower yields at urban sites were probably caused partly, at least, by other factors such as the presence of other pollutants with SO_2 and increased drought.

It is well known that SO_2 can contribute to the nutrition of sulphur deficient plants (Cowling et al., 1973). Over the last 40 years there has been a progressive rise in the application of inorganic nitrogen fertilisers to grasslands in the United Kingdom. At the same time there has been a reduction in sulphur inputs via fertilisers, largely as a result of substitution of ammonium sulphate by compounds with a higher nitrogen content per unit weight. However, both nitrogen and sulphur are essential for plant growth and a sulphur-deficiency is likely to occur when the ratio of nitrogen:sulphur falls below 16:1 (Murphy, 1978). There is now evidence that both dry-deposited and wet-deposited sulphur may be acting as nutrients in managed agricultural grasses in the United Kingdom. Most of the country receives at least 15 kg ha^{-1} annual total sulphur deposition from the atmosphere and there are no signs of sulphur-deficiency in crops. However, in the Republic of Ireland, where annual sulphur deposition is less than 15 kg ha^{-1}, many productive grasslands have shown positive responses to the addition of sulphur fertilisers (Murphy, 1979). Furthermore, there are indications that some areas of the United Kingdom with low sulphur deposition, such as northern Scotland and west Wales, are marginally sulphur-deficient (Bell, 1984). It should be noted, however, that these apparent benefits of air pollution can readily be replaced by addition of sulphur to nitrogen fertilizers, with an estimated minimum increase of 10% in production costs (Bache and Scott, 1979). An interesting development in this respect is the current promotion of sulphur-fertilisers in northern Scotland.

5.3 EVOLUTION OF SULPHUR DIOXIDE TOLERANCE IN THE FIELD

Particularly important evidence for adverse effects of ambient SO_2 on grasslands arises from the demonstration that grass species can evolve tolerance to SO_2 in polluted areas. Grass swards are characterised by intense competition both between species and also between individuals of the same species. Thus any change in environmental conditions which has a more adverse effect on some plants than others is liable to cause a shift in the genetic composition of the sward in favour of more tolerant individuals. Evolution of tolerance to heavy metal pollution in grass species growing on severely contaminated sites has been recognised for many years, but it is only relatively recently that a similar phenomenon has been demonstrated with respect to air pollution. The first indication of this resulted from observations that native ryegrass plants growing in polluted hill-farming regions of east Lancashire (see Section 5.2) were apparently unaffected by air pollution incidents which injured bred cultivars of the same species (Bell and Mudd, 1976). Subsequently controlled fumigation experiments demonstrated that the native Lancashire populations were indeed considerably more tolerant to SO_2 than either bred cultivars or individuals from clean sites (Bell and Mudd, 1976; Horsman et al., 1979). Furthermore, it was shown that a similar phenomenon occurred in a range of grass species at other polluted sites (Horsman et al., 1979; Ayazloo and Bell, 1981). It has recently been demonstrated that tolerance can evolve extremely rapidly, having been shown for three species over 3–5 years in Philips Park, Manchester where annual mean SO_2 concentrations were 35–60 ppb (Wilson and Bell, 1985). However, these concentrations subsequently fell to 20–30 ppb and the populations of all three species lost their tolerance. This is probably a reflection of tolerant plants invariably showing poorer growth in clean air than sensitive individuals (Bell, 1985), which raises the important point that favourable genetic characteristics may be lost as the result of selective pressure by air pollution on a grass sward.

5.4 FILTRATION EXPERIMENTS

The observations of poor growth of bred cultivars in polluted areas of the southern Pennines (see Section 5.3) led to the first filtration experiments performed in Britain. These were carried out in the early 1950s, with ryegrass grown in a pair of chambers in Manchester, ventilated with ambient air or water-scrubbed air, respectively (Bleasdale 1952, 1973). Yields were reduced by up to 57% in ambient air over periods up to 6 months when the mean SO_2 was 50–60 ppb. More recently, similar experiments have been performed in Sheffield during the 1970s, with grass and clover species grown in chambers ventilated with charcoal-filtered or ambient air (Crittenden and Read, 1978, 1979; Awang, 1979). In this case reductions in yield of ryegrass, Italian ryegrass (L. multiflorum) and cocksfoot (Dactylis glomerata) of up to 42% were found after exposure to ambient air containing mean SO_2 concentrations of 10–30 ppb. The growth of

white clover (Trifolium repens) proved to be even more susceptible to the effects of ambient air pollution than the grass species investigated (Awang, 1979).

The chambers used in filtration experiments at Manchester and Sheffield were all of the closed greenhouse type, which substantially modify ambient climatic conditions and which are likely to alter plant sensitivity to pollutants. Open-top chambers have proved more satisfactory in emulating conditions of temperature and humidity, and, to some extent, light levels, present in the field. Such chambers were developed to assess effects of ambient urban air pollution between 1977 and 1980 on ryegrass in St. Helens, Lancashire (Roberts et al. 1983; Colvill et al. 1983). In three experiments no overall effects on growth were found of filtering air containing about 30 ppb SO_2, although yield losses occurred in the early spring growth period, possibly as a result of carry-over effects of winter mean concentrations of >45 ppb SO_2. These results are clearly at variance with those from Sheffield, but may be explained by different microclimates in the two types of chambers, a lower filtering efficiency at St. Helens, and differences in the quantities of other pollutants present. This latter point makes the interpretation of earlier filtration experiments very difficult as SO_2 was the only gaseous pollutant monitored regularly, while it is now apparent that both NO_2 and ozone are likely to contribute to growth reductions in the field (see Sections 5.5.2; 5.5.3). Furthermore, although activated charcoal removes SO_2, NO_2 and ozone, NO is not absorbed and may influence growth in the control chambers in urban areas.

The effects on ryegrass of ambient air containing mean SO_2 concentrations similar to those in Sheffield were examined in the early 1980s with closed chambers at three London sites (Usher, 1984) and a semi-rural location at Leatherhead, Surrey (Lane, 1983). The results present an extremely confused picture, with both growth reductions and stimulations occurring in ambient compared with charcoal-filtered air. The most consistent effect at the London sites was an increase in leaf senescence. The two experiments at Leatherhead are particularly difficult to understand. One hundred and forty seven days exposure to a mean of 11 ppb ambient SO_2 and about 17 ppb NO_2 over the winter 1980–81 produced almost 50% stimulation in shoot dry weight, whereas a similar experiment over the ensuing winter with 13 ppb SO_2 and 29 ppb NO_2 for 180 days showed no significant effect. Our present knowledge of dose-response relationships and the way in which these interact with other stresses may provide an explanation of these apparently conflicting observations, (see Section 6.4.2 and Chapters 9 and 10).

There is only one published report of filtration experiments designed to determine the impact of ozone at a rural site in Britain on grassland species. Ashmore (1984) grew ryegrass and clover as monocultures in a 50:50

33

Table 5.1 Growth of perennial ryegrass (*Lolium perenne*) and white clover (*Trifolium repens*) alone or together (from Ashmore, 1984)

Species	Monoculture Above-ground dry weight (g) in		Mixture Above-ground dry weight (g) in	
	Filtered air	Unfiltered air	Filtered air	Unfiltered air
Lolium perenne	5.9	7.2	10.0	13.3***
Trifolium repens	5.9	5.0	4.9	2.7***
Total	11.8	12.2	14.9	16.0

Significance levels are indicated as:– ***, P > 0.001.

mixture in open-top chambers at Ascot, Berkshire for 6 weeks in summertime. Filtration of ambient air for 6 weeks did not significantly affect growth of the monoculture or the total yield of the mixture. However, the composition of the mixture was altered by ambient air containing a mean daily (hourly) maximum concentration of only 42 ppb ozone. The yield of the more ozone-tolerant ryegrass was significantly greater in the mixture at the expense of the more sensitive clover (Table 5.1). This has important implications for the quality of grasslands in that ambient rural air has the demonstrated potential to reduce the abundance of the nitrogen-fixing clovers which contribute to overall yield and fodder value. The greater sensitivity of clover than grass species to ambient Sheffield air, reported by Awang (1979), adds further weight to this argument. The relative insensitivity of grasses to ozone was further demonstrated by Ashmore (1984). He found that, out of seventeen British crop species studied in rural filtration experiments over a number of years, none of the five grass species responded to ambient pollution, in contrast to significant reductions of growth in seven out of the remaining twelve species (see Section 6.4.3).

The conflicting results of filtration experiments performed at relatively low ambient SO_2 concentrations point towards the need for considerably more research in this field in order to understand current effects on grasslands in urban, urban/fringe, and rural locations. In particular the role of different mixes of ambient pollutants and their interaction with climatic factors must be elucidated. However, it is noteworthy that relatively small effects have been produced in recent filtration experiments carried out during wintertime in contrast to the summertime experiments when ozone is present at phytotoxic levels on occasions.

5.5 CONTROLLED EXPOSURE EXPERIMENTS

5.5.1 Exposure to sulphur dioxide alone

Several British research groups have examined the effects of long-term fumigation of grass species, particu-larly ryegrass, with low to moderate concentrations of SO_2. Fumigation techniques have differed between groups, as have other factors between consecutive experiments, such as season and duration of exposure and concentration of SO_2. Consequently results have been very variable and relationships until recently, at least, have proved extremely difficult to determine with confidence. The first attempt to obtain a dose-response relationship was published by Bell (1982), using data for ryegrass, which was the only species at that time that had been fumigated with a wide range of SO_2 levels. No correlation could be found between growth reduction for duration of exposure, and SO_2 concentration. The data were examined by Mansfield and Freer-Smith (1981) who, in an attempt to achieve improved homogeneity of types of experiment, removed all fumigations lasting less than 40 or more than 160 days. This resulted in a significant positive relationship, although with a considerable scatter of data points. The establishment of a dose-response relationship by inclusion of experiments of 40–160 days duration only, was later justified by Bell (1985). He noted the extreme sensitivity to SO_2 of very young grass seedlings and the apparently seasonally-induced changes in the magnitude and direction of growth responses to SO_2 when exposures in outdoor chambers were continued for more than 6 months (Whitmore and Freer-Smith, 1982). When data points from filtration experiments in which plants were subjected to ambient air of known SO_2 concentration are included, it is clear that many of these indicate a much greater sensitivity than would be expected on the basis of the fumigations. The possible reasons for this will be discussed in Section 5.5.2. A further attempt has been made to establish a dose-response relationship for ryegrass by Roberts (1984) and McQueen (1985) who incorporated all available results from fumigation experiments, but omitted a number of data points where air changes in the chambers were less than one per minute. This gave a linear regression which could explain 60% of the scatter, with a threshold of about 20 ppb SO_2 (Figure 5.1). Exclusion of experiments with slow air flow was justified on the grounds that these did not realistically represent field conditions due to increased boundary layer resistance to

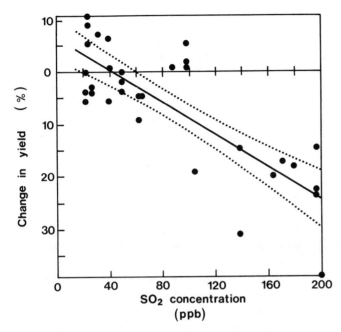

5.1 Linear regression of SO_2 concentration and percentage yield reduction of perennial ryegrass (*Lolium perenne*) exposed for more than 20 days at <200 ppb in chambers with more than 1 air change per minute; 33 data points were included. The regression equation was: percentage yield loss = 7.33 − 0.21 SO_2 (ppb) (p<0.001). The dotted lines show the 95% confidence limits of the regression. (Reproduced from Roberts, 1984).

SO_2 uptake. However, it seems difficult to explain on this basis the findings of Bell *et al.* (1979) that 16 ppb SO_2 for 173 days over winter with slow air flow reduced the growth of ryegrass by 68%, this being the lowest concentration so far reported to have adversely affected a grass species. A possible interaction with climatic factors (see Chapter 10) cannot be excluded.

Clearly a relationship does exist between yield loss and exposure to SO_2 or ambient air but interactions with environmental conditions, both ambient and imposed by the chambers themselves, leave a high degree of uncertainty. Overwinter exposure to SO_2 in outdoor chambers has tended to produce larger detrimental effects than exposure to similar concentrations under experimental conditions conducive to high growth rates. Thus Whitmore and Mansfield (1983) (Figure 5.2) found that between October and May, slow-growing smooth-stalked meadow grass (*Poa pratensis*) exposed to SO_2, suffered a 45% reduction in total plant weight, but during rapid summer growth this disappeared and a slight stimulation occurred by the end of the summer. Similar effects were found for ryegrass by Colvill *et al.* (1983), with yield reductions being greater in winter than summer. Such marked seasonal effects are clearly of considerable importance when considering the impact of ambient air

pollution on perennial grass species, but nothing is known about their cumulative effect over a number of years.

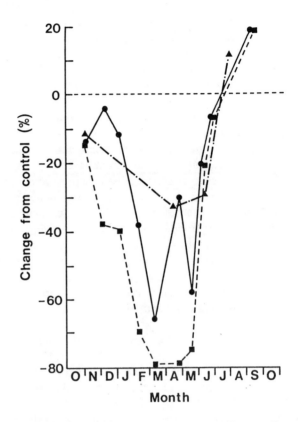

5.2 Seasonal differences in the effects of SO_2 (and SO_2 + NO_2) on the growth of grasses. ▲ ——— *Lolium perenne*, 50 ppb SO_2; ● ——— *Poa pratensis* 68 ppb SO_2; ■ _ _ _ _ _ *Poa pratensis* 68 ppb SO_2 + 68 ppb NO_2. Data for *Lolium perenne* (shoot weight only) taken from Colvill *et al.* (1983). Data for *Poa pratensis* (shoot-root weight) taken from Whitmore and Mansfield (1983). (Reproduced from Roberts, 1984).

Plant age, density and cultivar also influence the magnitude of the response of grass species to SO_2. Bell *et al.* (1979) found that a greater effect of SO_2 on ryegrass occurred in early stages of exposure, while Whitmore and Mansfield (1983) found that newly emerged seedlings of smooth-stalked meadow grass, cocksfoot and timothy grass (*Phleum pratense*) were more sensitive than 42-day old plants. Hence, if meaningful dose-response relationships are to be achieved, fumigation must start at planting or emergence. Many chamber experiments use spaced plants rather than swards and although the former resemble newly sown grassland, swards are more relevant to permanent pastures. Whitmore and Mansfield (1983) exposed single seedlings and small swards to 66 ppb SO_2 from October–June and found no effect on the former, but a reduction of 27% in the shoot dry weight of the latter. This suggests that the use of spaced plants may be underestimating the impact of SO_2 on a sward in the field, although the situation is complicated by the evolution of SO_2-tolerance under the intense competition occurring in a sward (see Section 5.3). Whitmore and Mansfield (1983) also demonstrated considerable differences in sensitivity to SO_2 of different cultivars of three grass species, highlighting a further difficulty in making generalisations about the impact of ambient SO_2 on grasslands.

It is now apparent that if future attempts to establish dose-response relationships are to succeed, a more standardised approach to controlled exposure experiments is necessary. Realistic concentrations of SO_2 should be used over several consecutive seasons, while chamber systems should be designed so that climatic conditions within them resemble the ambient as closely as possible. Furthermore, standard soil mixtures, sowing densities, and management practices should be employed. At the same time, complementary investigations are necessary to determine the modifying impact on pollutant response of the range of climatic and edaphic factors found in the field (see Chapters 9 and 10).

In view of the fact that annual mean ambient SO_2 concentrations in rural areas are currently 5–15 ppb, pasture grasslands are unlikely to be affected directly if SO_2 is the sole pollutant. However, amenity grasslands in urban areas with mean SO_2 concentrations of 15–25 ppb SO_2, with levels as high as 100 ppb for <1% of the time, are quite likely to suffer adverse effects without taking into account the presence of other pollutants.

5.5.2 Exposure to sulphur dioxide and nitrogen oxides

It has already been noted (see Section 5.4) that yield reductions resulting from exposure to ambient air containing a known mean concentration of SO_2 are frequently greater than those resulting from a controlled fumigation with the same concentration. Mansfield and Freer-Smith (1981) suggested that this might be explained by the presence of fluctuating concentrations of pollutants and/or the combined impact of other pollutants with SO_2. There is now limited evidence that the effects of fluctuating concentrations may not be important (Lane and Bell, 1984; Bell, 1985), but it has become increasingly apparent that interactions with other pollutants play a key role in affecting growth in the field. It is known from Chapter 2 that SO_2 is invariably accompanied by oxides of nitrogen, in concentrations that may be considerable in urban areas owing to the contribution from vehicular emissions, while ozone may also be present at phytotoxic levels from time to time in both urban and rural areas in summertime.

Although NO and NO_2 differ in rate of uptake by plants, at the cellular level their mechanism of action may be similar (Mansfield and Freer-Smith, 1981), and most fumigation experiments utilise NO_2 rather than a mixture of NO and NO_2. Many studies of the effects of NO_x on plants have used very high concentrations. Lower concentrations of NO_x on its own do not appear to damage plants and may even stimulate growth. However, ambient air commonly contains both SO_2 and NO_2 at concentrations ranging from 5–15 ppb of each in rural areas to 15–30 ppb SO_2 and 40–70 ppb NO_2 in urban areas, and plant pollution research has moved to the consideration of the effects of pollutant mixtures rather than individual pollutants.

The effects of long term exposure to SO_2 and NO_2 on four common grasses (cocksfoot, timothy, smooth stalked meadow grass and Italian ryegrass) were investigated by Ashenden and Mansfield (1978, 1979, 1980). The grass seedlings were exposed to weekly mean gas concentrations of 68 ppb for 20 weeks over the winter period in glasshouses. By the end of the exposure, growth of all four grasses was severely inhibited by the mixture of SO_2 plus NO_2, Italian ryegrass weighing 52% less than the controls and Timothy 86% less. The effects of the mixture were additive in smooth-stalked meadow grass but synergistic in the other three species, and had the toxicity of the mixture of $SO_2 + NO_2$ been taken as the sum of their individual effects, it would have been drastically underestimated for three out of the four species examined, and, in the case of Italian ryegrass, the pollutants would have appeared innocuous. From monthly measurements of growth, growth inhibition generally increased with length of exposure.

In further experiments carried out on smooth-stalked meadow grass (Whitmore and Mansfield, 1983), seedlings were exposed to 62 ppb SO_2 and 62 ppb NO_2 and their mixture from October until June in glasshouses. Total dry weight of plants was reduced by 45% by single pollutants and by 74% by the SO_2 and NO_2 mixture. Interactive effects of SO_2 and NO_2 were found in late winter, but not during later growth (Figure 5.2). Growth inhibitions were not only associated with slow winter growth, but also with early stages of plant development: plants fumigated over winter from emergence were more severely affected than those fumigated from the age of 42 days (see Section 5.5.1).

The problems of establishing dose/response relationships with SO_2 have been described. Clearly the presence of pollutants other than SO_2 plays an important role in the response of plants to ambient air. Mixtures of SO_2 and NO_2 appear to be far more toxic to growth than SO_2 alone and attempts to establish dose/response relationships between SO_2 and NO_2 mixtures and plant yield must be a research priority. To date, a key study has been the investigation by Whitmore (1985) into the relationship between $SO_2 + NO_2$ dose and yield of smooth-stalked meadow-grass using three exposure concentrations, (40, 70, 100 ppb) in environmentally controlled wind tunnels, for periods of 20, 34 and 38 days. Effects ranged from small non-significant stimulation at 40 ppb for 20 days to a 77% reduction at 100 ppb for 38 days. Some evidence of equivalent doses of SO_2/NO_2 mixtures (composed of different concentrations and time exposures) causing reductions of similar magnitude suggested that effects of the mixture could be related to dose (concentration $\times$ exposure time) within the experimental limits. A plot of dose against % change in dry weight yield showed that exposure to only 40 ppb SO_2 and NO_2 for 34–38 days severely inhibited dry-weight gain (Figure 5.3) and that transition from little effect to severe inhibition was very sharp. So rapid a change over a small dose increment implies that a slight variation in concentration or exposure time could result in a large variation in response, not only in magnitude but also in direction.

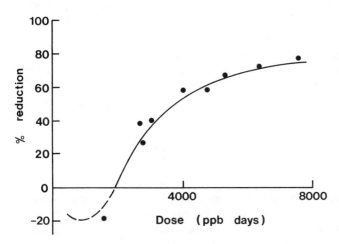

5.3 **Relationship between dose (concentration of SO₂ plus concentration of NO₂ times the duration) of SO₂/NO₂ mixture and response of *Poa pratensis* in terms of percentage inhibition in dry weight relative to dry weight of controls. (Reproduced from Whitmore, 1985).**

As in the case of SO_2, the effect of $SO_2 + NO_2$ appears to depend greatly on the vigour and growth of the plant. In the experiments of Whitmore and Mansfield (1983), during the winter period the detrimental effect of the mixture was greater than additive and occurred sooner than those of the individual pollutants. These results suggest that experiments should be carried out over a wide range of temperatures, representing those occurring in the field, particularly in view of the recently demonstrated interaction between SO_2 and cold stress on ryegrass (see Chapter 10.3).

A serious obstacle to quantifying the impact of ambient $SO_2 + NO_2$ mixtures on grass species is that most experiments have been performed at concentrations in ex-

cess of those currently found in rural areas. An attempt to expose grasses to long-term realistic pollutant regimes was reported by Lane and Bell (1984). In one experiment, ryegrass and timothy were exposed in outdoor chambers for 6 months, starting in January, to means of 32 ppb SO_2 and 21 ppb NO_2, singly and in combination, with pollutant concentrations fluctuating independently at hourly intervals to simulate ambient levels recorded at a site in central London. In the case of ryegrass, growth reduction occurred during the winter in both treatments containing SO_2, but with subsequent faster growth, these effects disappeared and ultimately none of the pollutant regimes differed from the control. A somewhat different pattern was seen for timothy with no effect of the pollutants initially, but some small stimulations in growth on occasion during the spring and summer.

A second experiment, which also included cocksfoot, using similar concentrations for seven months and starting in November, was complicated by low temperature damage occurring in some treatments, but again effects were generally small at the final harvest. The results of Lane and Bell (1984) are somewhat difficult to reconcile with earlier fumigation work and with the results of filtration experiments, but again highlight the complexity of the effects of mixtures of pollutants under uncontrolled climatic conditions.

The emphasis in this section has been on the effects of pollutants on the growth of the shoots of grassland species, these representing the economically important part of the crop. Indeed, in many experiments root growth has not been measured, because of the difficulties in separating the roots from the soil. However, there are many examples of root growth being more severely affected than shoot growth in controlled exposure experiments, primarily due to a change in the allocation of assimilates. For example, shoot/root ratios of smooth-stalked meadow grass exposed to SO_2, NO_2, and $SO_2 + NO_2$ were high during winter but declined as shoot dry weight was affected (Whitmore and Mansfield, 1983). Such an effect may explain the apparent small response of the grass species in the experiments of Bell and Lane (1984), where in most cases only the dry weight of the shoot was measured. Experiments where root growth is reduced but minimal effects are observed on the shoots may, at first sight, suggest that no effects of economic consequence are taking place. However, an increase in shoot/root ratio will predispose plants to drought injury and will reduce the potential for regrowth after grazing, mowing, and trampling, these latter factors being of particular significance in the case of grasslands.

5.5.3 Exposure to ozone

Relatively few experiments have been performed in which grass species have been fumigated with ozone. Ashmore (1984), in reviewing the ozone-sensitivity of thirty-eight British crop species, listed only one grass (timothy) as 'very sensitive', a category in which, however, he placed both white and red clovers. The significance of such differential sensitivity between different grassland species for sward composition under pollution stress has already been described in Section 5.4. This has been confirmed by controlled exposure to ozone of clover/grass mixtures, eg. Montes *et al.* (1982) found a marked increase in the proportion of tall fescue (*Festuca arundinacea*) in a mixture with white clover after exposure to 80 ppb ozone for 7 hours per day after 4 months; the same treatment had no effect on tall fescue but reduced the dry weight of white clover when these were growing alone. Bennett and Runeckles (1977a) similarly showed a shift in favour of the grass species in a mixture of Italian ryegrass and crimson clover (*Trifolium incarnatum*) after 6 weeks fumigation with 90 ppb ozone for 8 hours daily. The extreme sensitivity of crimson clover was further demonstrated by Bennett and Runeckles (1977b) who showed that only 30 ppb for 8 hours per day for 6 weeks reduced its root/shoot ratio but had no significant effect on Italian ryegrass, in single species swards. Ashmore (1984) classed ryegrass, the most important pasture grass in the United Kingdom, as 'slightly sensitive' to ozone. The only published work on the effects of an ozone fumigation on the growth of this species showed a 17% reduction in total dry weight after treatment with 90 ppb for 4 hours per day 5 days per week over 5 weeks (Horsman *et al.*, 1980); this is a concentration well above that experienced over such a time-scale in the United Kingdom. Despite many grass species being relatively insensitive to ozone, a recent series of fumigation experiments showed that 50 ppb over 3 weeks reduced the total dry weight of common bent (*Agrostis capillaris*), as well as white clover, by 40–50% (Ashmore and Tickle, 1988). This is a mean concentration which has been reached occasionally over similar periods during summertime in south-east England and raises the very real possibility of marked growth reductions in the field. Furthermore, it adds weight to the argument that pollutants other than SO_2 have contributed to the large depressions in growth observed on grass species in some urban filtration experiments (Section 5.4). In order to understand fully the significance of ozone episodes superimposed upon the continuous presence of SO_2 and NO_2, it is necessary to carry out controlled exposure experiments with the three pollutants in different combinations. Unfortunately there are no published reports of such experiments on grasslands species where growth parameters have been measured, although work in The Netherlands has demonstrated marked increases in the degree of leaf injury produced on clovers when ozone is added to an SO_2/NO_2 mixture.

5.6 CONCLUSIONS

1. There is no evidence that UK grasslands are directly damaged by acid rain in the strict sense.

2. Effects of urban air pollution on grassland species were reported as early as 1925.

3. There are indications that some areas with low sulphur deposition in the UK (eg. northern Scotland and west Wales) are marginally sulphur-deficient. In other areas, deposited sulphur may be acting as a nutrient in managed agricultural grasslands.

4. The evolution of tolerance in grasses to SO_2 in polluted areas is widespread in respect to species and location. It has occurred at a range of sites at annual mean SO_2 concentrations of 37–56 ppb over as short a period as 4 years. At one site, as SO_2 annual mean concentrations have declined to 20–30 ppb, this tolerance has disappeared.

5. Early winter-time filtration experiments in urban areas showed reductions in growth caused by ambient air. More recent experiments (early 1980s) in urban/urban fringe areas produced somewhat conflicting results, with both positive and negative effects, which are difficult to interpret but may involve interactions with other environmental stresses; in general, the mean SO_2 concentrations in these experiments were well below those used in most fumigation experiments.

6. An experiment carried out in summertime in a rural area of south east England, where episodes of photochemical ozone occur, has shown that ambient air can reduce the proportion of clover to grass in a sward. Such a presumed causal link to ozone has implications for the forage quality of grassland in these areas.

7. Controlled exposure experiments with grasses in the 1970s showed that concentrations of SO_2 exceeding 30 ppb may adversely affect growth without visible damage. Annual mean ambient SO_2 concentrations in rural areas are currently 5–15 ppb, and so pasture grasslands are unlikely to be affected directly if SO_2 is the sole pollutant. However, amenity grasslands in urban areas with mean SO_2 concentrations of 15–25 ppb and with higher concentrations for short periods, could suffer adverse effects without taking into account the presence of other pollutants.

8. Although relationships between yield loss and exposure to SO_2 or ambient air have been demonstrated, interactions with environmental conditions leave a high degree of uncertainty in estimating losses in the field.

9. Evidence from a limited number of species indicates that exposure over winter to concentrations of 40 ppb SO_2 + 40 ppb NO_2 can produce substantial reductions in growth, but continuation into summer

is generally accompanied by a progressive lessening of this effect.

10. Effects of the pollutant mixture, in general, are far greater than the effect of SO_2 alone and can be additive for some species and synergistic for others.

11. Few experiments with $SO_2 + NO_2$ mixtures have been carried out at concentrations currently found in rural areas. Limited studies at about 20 ppb SO_2/NO_2 on grasses have not shown consistent yield reductions.

12. Root growth is frequently more severely affected by exposure to pollutants (SO_2, NO_2 and $SO_2 + NO_2$) than shoot growth. An increase in the shoot/root ratio may predispose plants to drought injury and reduce potential for regrowth after grazing, mowing or trampling.

13. The few controlled experiments in which grassland species have been exposed to ozone have shown that UK grasses tend to be relatively insensitive to ozone whereas clovers are fairly sensitive.

EFFECTS ON ARABLE AND HORTICULTURAL CROPS

6.1 INTRODUCTION

The term arable is used to refer to 'ploughed' areas and arable crops include cereals, potatoes, sugar beet, oilseed rape, fodder crops and field-scale vegetables such as peas and beans. Horticulture, is the cultivation of fruit, flowers and ornamental trees and shrubs in addition to intensively grown vegetables (market gardening). There have been far fewer studies of the long-term effects of air pollutants in the UK on arable or horticultural crops than on grassland species. In particular, there has been little work on flowers, fruits and ornamental trees. This has arisen because the early work which showed growth reductions in the absence of visible injury was done with agricultural and amenity grass swards. In addition, grasslands cover 12 million hectares of the UK compared with just under 4 million hectares for cereals and about 0.2 million hectares for sugar beet, potatoes and fodder crops. Nevertheless, the value per unit area of even the most productive permanent pasture is well below that of other field crops. Consequently, as it has become easier to use large exposure chambers and open-air fumigation systems, so a number of studies of the effects of air pollutants have been carried out on cereals and other crops.

Horticultural crops have a high value per hectare compared with cereals yet the effects of air pollutants on these crops have received little attention in the UK. Two thirds of the 0.25 million hectares (excluding potatoes) used for horticultural crops lies in ten counties (Bedfordshire, Cambridgeshire, Greater London, Kent, Norfolk, Suffolk, Lincolnshire, Humberside, Merseyside, Worcester and Hereford). This reflects the fact that market gardening has always been concentrated in the vicinity of cities. Seven percent of land use in counties to the north of London is used for horticultural crops. In these areas the mean annual SO_2 and NO_2 concentrations range from 5–20 ppb and frequent episodes of ozone (>60 ppb) may occur in summer. More attention has been given recently to horticultural crops, following observations that some cultivars of peas and beans are among the most ozone-sensitive crops in the UK. Changes in crop quality are particularly important for horticultural crops but little work has addressed this important issue.

The limited data on the effects of air pollutants on arable and horticultural crops in the UK come from transect studies, air filtration studies and controlled exposures in chambers or open-air fumigation systems.

6.2 TRANSECT STUDIES

Field evidence for the effects of ambient air pollution on these crops is based very largely on experiments in which standard cultures of plants have been exposed at different points on transects located along gradients of pollution from city centres and into the surrounding countryside. Surprisingly few of these simple but effective experiments have been performed, but these span a long period from the early years of this century up to the present day. The difficulties which arise in interpretation stem from the fact that there are climatic as well as pollutant gradients in the vicinity of urban areas.

The first published report of such work with arable crops was by Cohen and Ruston (1925) who grew radish (*Raphanus sativus*), lettuce (*Lactuca sativa*), cabbage (*Brassica oleracea*), wallflower (*Cheiranthus cheiri*) and cereals at five locations along a 7 km transect from the centre of Leeds, immediately prior to the First World War. All species showed a progressive fall in yield as the most polluted site was approached, where the relative weight ranged between 3 and 46% of that at the cleanest site on the edge of the city. The total deposition of sulphur compounds showed a 3-fold range along the transect but massive deposition of particulates in the inner-city will also have contributed towards the observed effects. A similar study by Bleasdale (1952) in Manchester in the early 1950s showed a progressive fall in the growth of forget-me-not (*Myosotis vulgaris*) and wallflower along a 16 km transect into the city centre. Furthermore, survival overwinter was markedly reduced at the more polluted sites in both the Leeds and the Manchester studies, foreshadowing the recent experimental evidence for frost/SO_2 interactions (see Chapter 10). A similar result was observed for spring cabbage in a comparison between a Manchester city centre and a rural location.

Both these studies were performed when concentrations of SO_2 and smoke were considerably higher than at the present day. Of more relevance to current problems, is the transect study by Imperial College, operated between 1983 and 1986 inclusive, using up to eighteen sites along a 40 km transect from Central London to Ascot. Several crops were grown in standard soils at these sites and the results for four cultivars of pea (*Pisum sativum*), were reported by Ashmore and Dalpra (1985). The pea cultivars showed a statistically highly significant trend of reduction in dry weight of seed, stem and leaves, and increased ozone injury with proximity to the centre of the conurbation (Figure 6.1). This was attributed, tentatively, to the enhanced effect of ozone in the presence of increasing concentrations of $SO_2 + NO_2$ with decreasing distance from London.

The regional distribution of ozone has been mapped for the UK using the degree of visible injury on the indicator plant BEL-W3 tobacco placed at a range of sites

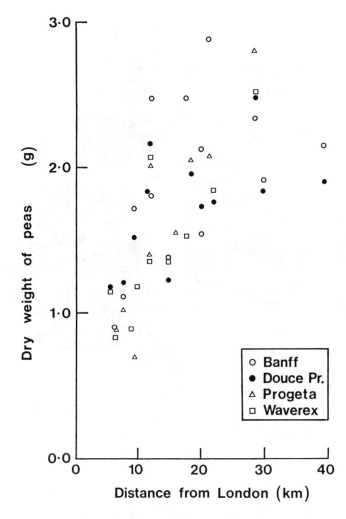

6.1 Seed dry weight per plant of peas grown at various distances from London. (Reproduced from Ashmore and Dalpra, 1985).

(Ashmore *et al.*, 1987). Symptoms such as brown or white flecks appear after exposure to concentrations above 40 ppb ozone which is just above the natural background. In 1977 and 1978 the survey showed that ozone levels were above the natural background over large areas of the UK and the degree of injury was related to the hours of sunshine and the wind direction from urban areas (Figure 6.2). It has been proposed that ozone concentrations will be elevated most frequently in average summers in the south of England and particularly in the agricultural areas around London, but this has not yet been supported by monitoring data.

The regional and temporal distribution of ozone in the UK has been reviewed in detail by the Photochemical Oxidant Review Group (UK PORG, 1987).

6.3 FILTRATION EXPERIMENTS

Early pollutant exclusion experiments were carried out in urban areas by supplying air to half of a greenhouse after the pollutants had been removed by a water scrubber or by charcoal filters. Studies comparing growth in filtered and unfiltered air, carried out prior to 1977 in Manchester (Bleasdale, 1952) and Sheffield (Awang, 1979) indicated that air filtration improved the growth of buckwheat (*Fagopyrum esculentum*) and barley (*Hordeum vulgare*), respectively.

Filtration studies using improved air flow and closed and open-top chamber systems which reduce climatic modification by the chambers have been carried out more recently around Merseyside and London. Filtration studies carried out overwinter have shown small responses, which ranged from both positive and negative effects, on growth of a small number of arable crops following the removal of SO_2 and NO_2. The variability in results may reflect important interactions between SO_2, NO_2 and other environmental stresses.

Winter filtration experiments were carried out on winter barley by Lane (1983) at Leatherhead, Surrey, an urban fringe area, between November and May 1980–81 and 1981–82. Growth was 13% higher in unfiltered air in 1980–81 and 12% lower in 1981–82. The unfiltered air contained ~12 ppb SO_2 and 17–29 ppb NO_2. Similar filtration experiments were carried out in the winter of 1980–81 at three sites in London where the mean SO_2 and NO_2 levels ranged from 12–21 and 15–19 ppb respectively (Usher 1984). Filtration produced both positive and negative effects on stem weight of cabbage (*Brassica oleracea*) but consistent reductions in stem and root weight of forget-me-not (*Myosotis alpestris*).

In recent exclusion experiments carried out on winter barley at Glasgow from 1982–85 by the Institute of Terrestrial Ecology (Fowler *et al* 1988), annual mean concentrations of pollutants were also low (6 ppb SO_2; 16 ppb NO_2; 17 ppb NO; 17 ppb ozone) and air filtration did not significantly affect yield of spring barley in 1983 or 1984, although some yield differences between winter barley crops grown in polluted and unpolluted air occurred. These differences were not consistent probably due to major climatic differences in 1984 and 1985 which could have led to additional stresses on crop yield. Thus although earlier experiments have shown a beneficial effect of filtration, more recent results are conflicting.

From 1976–80, exclusion experiments were carried out on spring barley in an agricultural area, Marston Vale in Bedfordshire, which is subjected to air pollution (mainly SO_2 and fluorine) from several brickworks (Buckenham *et al.*, 1982). In unfiltered ambient air (mean SO_2 concentration 19 ppb), reductions in grain, ear and straw yields

6.2 Geographical distribution of leaf-injury to Bel W3 indicator plants during May–September 1977 and June–August 1978 together with the distribution of sunshine over the same period. The blank areas in each map represent the areas with the lowest injury/sunshine hours, while the dotted areas, horizontal hatching, vertical hatching and then black areas represent increasing levels of both parameters. (Reproduced from UK PORG, 1987).

Table 6.1 Effects of filtering ambient air pollutants, in closed and open-top chambers in the Bedfordshire Brickfields on the yield of Barley (1976–80) (Buckenham et al. 1982, and M. Parry, pers. comm.)

Year	Site	Chamber Replication Closed (C)	Chamber Replication Open-top (OTC)	Cultivar	Pollutant Effect* Grain C	OTC	Pollutant Effect* Straw C	OTC	SO_2 in Unfiltered chambers (ppb)	SO_2 in Filtered chamber (ppb) C	OTC	Foliar F in Unfiltered chamber (ppb) C	OTC	Foliar F in Filtered chamber (ppb) C	OTC	Ambient** ozone (hours >60 ppb)
1976	Woburn	1	2	Abacus	−30	−48	−33	−60	23	11	12	8	32	6	11	251
1977	Woburn	1	2	Maris Otter	−28	+18	−24	−23	20	8	15	54	58	6	60	98
1978	Thrupp End	1	2†	Porthos	−10	−24	−7.5	−35	19	3	7	39	53	9	33	80
1979	„ „	—	4†	Magnum	—	−37	—	−27	18	—	6	—	34	—	18	64
1980	„ „	—	4†	Magnum	—	−7.5	—	−16	20	—	7	—	27	—	18	11

Note: * Percentage difference between unfiltered and filtered chambers.
 ** Data taken from UK, PORG (1987) for Stevenage.
 † Modified Open-top chambers with collar and lip.

Foliar F figures relate to leaf content of F.
SO_2 concentrations in the unfiltered chambers are the same for both closed and open-top chambers.

occurred compared with plants grown in chambers where filtering reduced the SO_2 concentration to 50–70% of ambient (Table 6.1). However, there was also a mean concentration of 0.1 ppb fluorine present, probably mostly as the gas hydrogen fluoride and this may have affected yield. Ozone concentrations were measured intermittently but detailed values are not available. The Photochemical Oxidant Review Group (UK PORG, 1987) summarised the concentrations from 1971–85, and it is probable that the US National Air Quality Standard (120 ppb for 1 hour) was exceeded in 1976 and 1977 and probably also in 1979. Thus a role of ozone in the reduction in yield of barley at Marston Vale cannot be discounted, particularly as the greatest effect was seen in the summer of 1976 when the highest UK ozone concentrations were recorded.

These studies were all carried out in, or close to, urban areas or industrial sources with the objective of assessing the effect of removing the mixture of pollutants of which SO_2 was considered to be the main phytotoxic component. Establishing significant effects of filtering urban air overwinter became progressively more difficult as urban SO_2 levels declined steadily after 1970. In contrast, in the last two decades there has been an increased concern that reactions of hydrocarbon and nitrogen oxides in summer may produce potentially phytotoxic levels of photochemical oxidants.

The results of ozone monitoring in the UK between 1971 and 1985 have recently been summarised by the Photochemical Oxidant Review Group (UK PORG, 1987). There is considerable variation from site-to-site and year-to-

year which is largely of meteorological origin. Typically the USA National Ambient Quality Standard (120 ppb for 1 hour) is exceeded in most years in the south of England. Hourly mean ozone concentrations in rural or suburban locations typically exceed 60 ppb for 100–200 hours in the summer (2.2–4.6% of the time).

Information on ozone effects on crops and its relevance to the UK has been collated by Roberts et al. (1984). The first field experiment using charcoal-filtered (CF) and non-filtered (NF) air to assess the effect of oxidants was initiated in California with Citrus species. In plastic-covered closed chambers, lemon and orange yields were reduced by as much as 50% in the NF air, largely due to premature leaf and fruit drop. Similar studies revealed smaller but significant yield effects of oxidants in California on grapes, cotton and other species (EPA, 1984). Concentrations of oxidants in California are much higher than in the UK, 100 ppb is exceeded on at least 15 days per month in the summer and hourly peaks reach 400–600 ppb. However, the hourly peak concentrations of 100–250 ppb which occur in the eastern United States are more similar. Studies near Washington DC by Heggestad et al. (1980) between 1972 and 1979 showed that yield reductions of snap beans, sweet corn, potatoes and tomatoes attributed to ambient oxidants were 4%, 9%, 10% and 17% respectively (Table 6.2). There was also considerable variation between cultivars with the oxidant effect on four snap bean cultivars, ranging from a 12% yield reduction to a 4% yield increase. High oxidant concentrations varied from year to year with only one hour above 100 ppb in 1972 compared with 40 hours in 1975.

Table 6.2 Effects of photochemical oxidants on growth and yield of 5 crop species grown at Beltsville, Maryland, and the Dalmarva Peninsula (from Heggestad 1980)

Species	Varieties tested each year No.	Years[a]	Yields as compared to chambers with carbon filtered air	
			Non-filtered chambers %	No chambers %
Potatoes	3.1	1973–77	90	112[b]
Soybean	4	1973–75	80	101[b]
Sweet corn	4	1972–76	91	93
Snap beans	3.3	1972–76	96	96
Tomatoes	1	1979	83	65
Average			88.0	93.4

[a] Four replications each year except for tomatoes (3 replications).
[b] Higher values than in non-filtered chambers may indicate chamber effects.

It is difficult to make direct comparisons between eastern North America and the UK as differences in cultivar sensitivity and seasonal variations in temperature, relative humidity and soil moisture availability may greatly influence the response. In addition, the distribution of ozone episodes is different in the UK due to the more variable climate. In the UK, most evidence for the effects of ambient ozone on plants has been accumulated at Silwood Park, Ascot, where from 1977–85 ozone concentrations have exceeded 60 ppb (one hour mean) on 5–20% of summer days (ie. 9–18 days) (UK PORG 1987) and annual mean concentrations of SO_2 and NO_2 were 10 and 7 ppb respectively (Ashmore 1984). The number of days with one hour above 100 ppb varied from nil in 1980 to 6 days in 1977.

During incidents of high ozone concentrations (>100 ppb) at Ascot, visible plant injury was observed in the field on a number of species including vine (*Vitis vinifera*), bean (*Phaseolus vulgaris*), tomato (*Lycopersicon esculentum*), sweetcorn (*Zea mays*), petunia (*Petunia hybrida*), lucerne (*Medicago sativa*) and spinach (*Spinacia oleracea*). The Processor and Growers Research Organisation at Peterborough has received reports from growers of leaf injury on peas resembling that caused by ozone on various occasions over the last 10 years following periods of hot, dry weather, (A. Biddle, pers. comm.). Air filtration experiments at Ascot have shown that these symptoms were reduced on peas or clovers grown in charcoal-filtered air on three occasions when ozone exceeded 100 ppb between 1978 and 1983.

Information on yield reductions from these filtration experiments have also been collected at Ascot. Sensitive cultivars of some horticultural crops showed growth reductions in periods with relatively high ozone concentrations. These included peas, lucerne, clover, french bean, barley, spinach and radish. Arable crops where growth reductions did not occur included broccoli, wheat, rye and oats.

The effect of filtration on the yield of radish in experiments lasting one month was related to the ambient levels of ozone during the experiment. Significant reductions in yield of 10% or more were found in experiments during which the mean daily maximum ozone concentration reached 40 ppb and there were 3 or more days with concentrations above 60 ppb. However, the timing of these days also appeared to be critical. Only if levels above 60 ppb were recorded during the period in which the radish was actually swelling were significant reductions in yield found (UK PORG, 1987).

The appearance of short-term reductions in growth during ozone episodes does not necessarily mean that crop yield will be reduced. Ashmore (1984) gave the results of successive harvests of three barley cultivars growing in filtered and unfiltered air between April and August 1983. The mean daily maximum was 51 ppb ozone and 60 ppb was exceeded on 28% of days. Two of the cultivars showed no significant difference between treatments at any of the harvests. For the third cultivar, up to 27% reductions of both grain and straw dry weight in unfiltered air were found at the June and July harvests, but by the time of the final harvest in August there were no significant differences between the two treatments. This can be interpreted as meaning that the crop grew and developed more slowly in unfiltered air, but that it eventually reached the same final yield. For crops such as winter barley for which harvest date is not critical, this may not imply any economic loss. For other crops, such as certain vegetables where market price is often dictated by harvest date, slower development may be extremely important.

Plate 1. Low cloud causing occult deposition on upland forest.

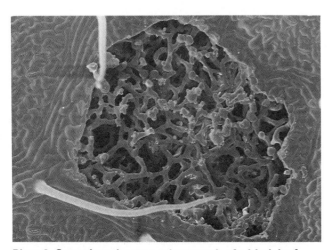

Plate 2. Scanning electron micrograph of a birch leaf (*Betula pubescens*). On the leaf surface, epidermal cells, hairs and stomata can be seen. The hole reveals the internal structure.

Plate 3. Field exposure of winter wheat at University of Nottingham School of Agriculture, to sulphur dioxide released from a system of pipework.

Plate 4. 'Solardome' glasshouses at Lancaster University used for controlled exposures of crops and trees.

Plate 5. Open-top chambers at Forestry Commission Research Station, Alice Holt used for air filtration experiments on trees.

Plate 6. Heavy industry in the UK is often in close proximity to agriculture and natural vegetation.

Plate 7. Polluted area of the southern Pennines showing erosion of peat and mosses.

Plate 8. A podzol profile at Glendye, North-East Scotland showing an organic layer of slowly decomposing material above an iron pan which is relatively impermeable.

Plate 9. Winter desiccation of Yew shoots. Injury was caused in February 1986, but characteristically, the symptoms developed later in March when the weather warmed up.

Plate 10. Forest decline at Fichtelberg, Fichtelgebirge West Germany showing foliar thinning and yellowing.

6.4 CONTROLLED EXPOSURE EXPERIMENTS

6.4.1 Exposure to sulphur dioxide

Most experiments using controlled exposures to SO_2 in chambers have been done with pasture grasses. The difficulties of working with cereals in chambers led to the development of two open-air fumigation systems in the UK. These have been used for a number of years to expose field plots of winter cereals to controlled concentrations of SO_2. Some results remain to be published but limited conclusions can be reached based on the available data.

The first system was set up at Sutton Bonington in Leicestershire when the background seasonal mean SO_2 concentration was 15 ppb (Baker et al., 1986). Winter barley (Hordeum vulgare cv. Igri) was exposed in three 20 m square, fumigated plots to different concentrations of SO_2. In 1983/84 these were 50, 100 and 200 ppb above ambient and in 1984/85 40, 80 and 120 ppb above ambient. The system achieved concentrations close to the required values (Table 6.3). Exposure commenced in late December/early January, 89 days after sowing in 1983 and 67 days after sowing in 1984. Because of interruptions to fumigation caused by equipment failure and low windspeed, the mean concentration over the whole season was considerably lower than the average concentration during periods when gas was released. During winter and early spring, plant growth was depressed at the two highest treatment concentrations but later recovered. Visible leaf damage was caused to the plants in the fumigated plots following treatment with two herbicides, a fungicide and a growth regulator in April 1985 (Baker and Fullwood, 1987) (see Chapter 10) and the data from the highest treatment was therefore excluded from the subsequent dose-response analysis. In spring and summer, the lowest treatment concentrations produced an increase in plant growth above that of the controls but no corresponding increases in grain yield occurred. In both years the grain yield was depressed by SO_2 treat-

ments (Figure 6.3). A linear regression fitted to the data relating percentage yield reduction to SO_2 concentration produced a slope corresponding to a loss of 2.2% yield per 10 ppb above the 15 ppb background for the site.

At Littlehampton, where the annual mean ambient SO_2 concentration was 10 ppb, winter barley (Hordeum vulgare cv. Sonja) was exposed in 1982/83 to different levels of SO_2 in four 27 m diameter fumigated plots (McLeod et al., 1986). The exposure concentrations were taken from a data set for an ambient monitoring site at Bottesford in central England and used either directly or with an additional 30 and 60 ppb SO_2 to produce the exposures in the three plots. The fumigation commenced on 1 November, 51 days after sowing and continued until final harvest on 5 July 1983. There was no evidence of a depression of growth over the winter period. During the spring there was an interaction between SO_2 treatment and the occurrence of the fungal pathogen, brown rust (Puccinia

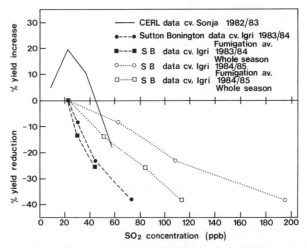

6.3 A comparison of data from Sutton Bonington and CERL for percentage yield reduction in winter barley (Hordeum vulgare) after long term SO_2 exposure (CERL data from McLeod et al., 1986; Sutton Bonington data from Baker et al., 1986).

Table 6.3 SO_2 concentrations used in the open-air fumigations of winter cereals at Sutton Bonington and Littlehampton

Site and season	Period of exposure	SO_2 mean concentration (ppb)			
		Ambient	Treatments		
Sutton Bonington* 1983–84	Average during fumigation only, 18 Jan–8 July	—	63	108	196
	Whole season average, 1 Oct–28 July	15	30	44	73
Sutton Bonington* 1984–85	Average during fumigation only, 24 Dec–10 July	—	51	84	113
	Whole season average, 1 Oct–21 July	16	30	44	55
Littlehampton** 1982–83	Average throughout fumigation period, 1 Nov–5 July	10	23	38	58

* Data from Baker et al. (1986)
** Data from Mcleod et al. (1986)

hordei), which was greatly reduced in all fumigated plots (McLeod, 1987). Subsequently both positive and negative interactions with other pathogens have been recorded (see Chapter 9). At the highest treatment concentration there was a decrease in grain yield, grain size and grain weight at final harvest (Figure 6.3). At the lowest SO_2 treatment concentration all these parameters increased. The increase in grain size was attributed to a delay of leaf senescence, increased leaf area duration and lengthened grain-filling period. The explanation provided was a reduction in the number of leaf-surface micro-organisms involved in the senescence process.

The dose-responses from the two studies are compared in Figure 6.3. Their interpretation is complicated by the use of different cultivars, different ambient SO_2 concentrations at the two sites and the different definitions of experimental exposure. Additionally the background concentrations of NO_x and ozone may also have been different. The increase in yield between 9 and 22 ppb at Littlehampton may not be detectable at Sutton Bonington where there was a higher background of 15 ppb SO_2 and a lowest treatment concentration of 30 ppb. Furthermore the comparison of fumigation average and whole-season average from Sutton Bonington with the exposure period average from Littlehampton is not appropriate. Calculation of the exposure period average for Sutton Bonington, thus excluding the pre- and post-fumigation periods without treatment (109 days in 1984 and 71 days in 1985), produces yield changes for the medium and high treatments of both studies that may be closer to a common response.

The interaction of fungal pathogens and leaf-surface micro-organisms at Littlehampton and chemical treatments producing acute injury at Sutton Bonington suggests that details of crop protection procedures should be clearly described with the final yield results. Both studies reported that they followed the usual farming procedures for their area.

The concentrations of SO_2 used in all treatments, except the lowest at Littlehampton, exceed the range of annual mean SO_2 concentrations observed within the UK. The highest annual mean for 1984/85 measured in the National Survey of Smoke and SO_2 was 27 ppb at an urban location in Doncaster (WSL, 1986). The mean concentrations experienced in agricultural areas are lower. It is therefore essential to determine further dose-response patterns within the ambient range, to evaluate the importance of higher concentrations of short duration and the extent of biotic interactions involving pathogens under field conditions.

6.4.2. Exposure to sulphur dioxide and nitrogen oxides

Studies of the effects of NO_2 alone on arable crops have usually involved concentrations higher than those found in the UK ambient air, often resulting in acute effects. The occurrence of interactions between SO_2 and other pollutants was reviewed by Ormrod (1982). In general NO_2 alone is less phytotoxic to crops than SO_2. In combination with SO_2, NO_2 can cause effects which may be antagonistic, additive, or synergistic. The effects of mixtures of SO_2 and NO_2 on grasses have been extensively studied at Lancaster University (Whitmore, 1985).

Investigations also carried out at Lancaster into the effects of SO_2 and/or NO_2 on the growth of young barley are an important supplement to the field exposures described in the previous section (Pande and Mansfield, 1985a). Seedlings of spring barley (*Hordeum vulgare* cv. Patty) were exposed to 100 ppb SO_2 and 100 ppb NO_2 alone and in combination for 20 days. Despite the high dose, single pollutants produced only a slight effect on growth. A further exposure was performed for 14 days with mixtures of SO_2 and NO_2 ranging in concentration from 40–140 ppb. Growth reductions increased with increasing dose and a good dose/response relationship was obtained (Figure 6.4) with a threshold for damage

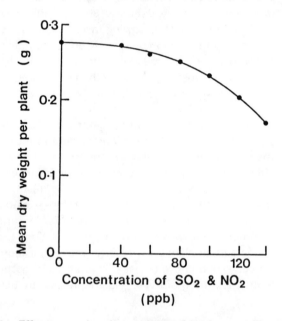

6.4 **Effects on the dry weight of barley seedlings of fumigation for 2 weeks with mixtures of SO_2 and NO_2. The concentrations of both gases were equal on a per unit volume basis (ppb). Fumigation began 3 or 4 days after germination. (Reproduced from Pande and Mansfield, 1985).**

occurring just below 40 ppb. As concentrations of pollutants increased, root growth was affected more severely than shoot growth resulting in an increase in shoot/root ratio. The dose/response curve can be used in a predictive manner for controlled fumigations but cannot be used in field situations because of interaction with climatic and other stresses. Although greater reductions in root than shoot growth have been found previously for grasses (Jones and Mansfield, 1982b), no clear dose/response relationship had been shown before. Mansfield et al., (1986) have suggested that impact of pollutants in the field may be greater in conditions of water shortage due to reduced root growth.

Clearly, the results of short-term exposure can be misleading as shown by fumigation of winter barley with 62 ppb SO_2 + 62 ppb NO_2 throughout the season (Pande and Mansfield, 1985b). Despite reductions in growth during winter months, effects on grain yield were slight suggesting that there may be little adverse effect of SO_2 and NO_2 in polluted rural areas on final yield of winter barley. Similar results were found by Roberts et al. (1983) when winter barley was exposed to fluctuating concentrations of SO_2 and NO_2 for 8 months. A mixture of 45 ppb SO_2 + NO_2 caused some growth reductions but a mixture of <30 ppb SO_2 + NO_2 had no effect, or a slight stimulation (Figure 6.5). Polluted plants tended to be taller than controls at Lancaster, an effect also found by Baker et al. (1986) and could be more susceptible to storm damage. Growth reductions during winter could also affect susceptibility to other stress factors such as pests, pathogens, frost and exposure (see Chapters 9 and 10).

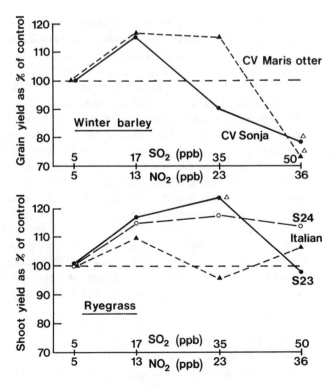

6.5   Effects of SO_2 + NO_2 mixtures on yields of winter barley (_Hordeum vulgare_), ryegrass (_Lolium perenne_ cv. S23 and S24), and Italian ryegrass (_Lolium multiflorum_). (Reproduced from Roberts et al., 1983).

6.4.3 Exposure to ozone

Crop plants have not been experimentally exposed to ozone for long periods in the UK. Ashmore (1984) carried out a series of acute fumigations at 250 ppb for 4 hours to determine the range of sensitivity (based on visible injury) of plant species and crop cultivars (Table 6.4). One important conclusion was the classification of legumes as ozone sensitive. In contrast, the brassicas and beets were relatively resistant. The grasses and cereals were considered to be of intermediate sensitivity. Evaluation of the sensitivity of native species by this method showed that sensitivity decreased in the order: Legumes>Chenopodiaceae>Graminae = Cruciferae> Compositae. Differences between habitats were also observed, in that species of cultivated land or calcareous soils were more sensitive in general than species of acid, nutrient-poor soils.

The threshold for visible injury symptoms after exposure to peak concentrations varies considerably between species. For example, the most sensitive plant (the tobacco cultivar Bel-W3) can be injured by hourly mean concentrations above 40 ppb. However, other relatively sensitive species may only be injured when the concentrations reach 100 ppb for several hours. Sensitivity also depends on environmental conditions. Plants are generally less sensitive during periods of low light or low relative humidity. Drought conditions which induce stomatal closure can also lead to greater resistance. Consequently a specific ozone episode may cause little or no injury at one time or location and extensive injury at another time or in a different location.

In the absence of long-term studies of the effects of continuous fumigation with ozone on growth and development in the UK, conclusions have been derived from extensive work in North America. There is considerable support in the North American literature for effects on growth, stem elongation, leaf area, root weight and flower production as well as fruit and seed set in a range of crops after long-term exposures to >100 ppb ozone (Jacobson, 1982). Current interest lies in quantifying the effect of long-term exposure to between 50 and 100 ppb. Heck et al. (1982) have argued that for a given day, the diurnal cycle for many sites in the USA was quite regular and the changes in ozone concentrations during the period of maximum absorption (9.30 a.m. to 4.30 p.m.) were quite small. Consequently, the daytime 7 hour mean (9.30 a.m. to 4.30 p.m.) was considered most relevant to long-term effects on crop growth. A series of experiments were carried out in open-top chambers, at a range of sites to determine the effect of seasonal daytime 7 hour mean ozone concentrations ranging from 50 to 150 ppb on the yield of crops under the auspices of the National Crop Loss Assessment Network (Heck et al., 1982 and 1983). As with the studies on visible injury, there were considerable differences in sensitivity be-

Table 6.4 Summary of the ozone sensitivity of British crop species (from Ashmore, 1984)

Very sensitive		Moderately sensitive	
White clover (*Trifolium repens*)	*†	Barley (*Hordeum vulgare*)	*
Red clover (*Trifolium pratense*)	*†	Cocksfoot (*Dactylis glomerata*)	††
Pea (*Pisum sativum*)	*†	Tomato (*Lycopersicon esculentum*)	†
Lucerne (*Medicago sativa*)	*†	Oats (*Avena sativa*)	††
Spinach (*Spinacia oleracea*)	*†	Maize (*Zea mays*)	†
Radish (*Raphanus sativus*)	*	Carrot (*Daucus carota*)	
Vine (*Vitis vinifera*)	†	Onion (*Allium cepa*)	
Hop (*Humulus lupulus*)		Parsnip (*Pastinaca sativa*)	
Broccoli (*Brassica oleracea* var. Italica)	††	Broad bean (*Vicia faba*)	
Timothy (*Phleum pratense*)	††	French bean (*Phaseolus vulgaris*)	*†

Slightly sensitive		Resistant	
Wheat (*Triticum aestivum*)	††	Sugar beet (*Beta vulgaris*)	
Rye (*Secale cereale*)	††	Oilseed rape (*Brassica napus*)	
Fescue (*Festuca spp.*)	††	Mangel (*Beta vulgaris*)	
Italian ryegrass (*Lolium multiflorum*)	††	Kale (*Brassica oleracea* var. Acephala)	
Perennial ryegrass (*Lolium perenne*)	††	Brussel sprouts (*Brassica oleracea* var. Gemmifera)	
Potato (*Solanum tuberosum*)		Lettuce (*Lactuca sativa*)	
Beetroot (*Beta vulgaris* var. Esculenta)		Cabbage (*Brassica oleracea* var. Capitata)	
Leek (*Allium porrum*)		Cauliflower (*Brassica oleracea* var. Botrytis)	
Swede (*Brassica rutabaga*)			
Turnip (*Brassica rapa*)			

Note: The sensitivity categories are based on a standard acute ozone exposure.

† indicates that visible leaf injury to this crop has been observed in the field.
* indicates that significant adverse effects of ambient ozone on the growth of this crop has been found.
†† indicates that no significant adverse effects of ambient ozone on the growth of this crop have been found.

tween crops. The concentration required to produce a 10% yield reduction varied from 40 ppb in the case of soybean and cotton to over 70 ppb for wheat and corn (Table 6.5). The Photochemical Oxidant Review Group (UK PORG, 1987) recently assessed the NCLAN results in

Table 6.5 Seasonal ozone concentrations averaged over a seven hour day (0900 to 1600 ST) required to produce a 10% yield reduction (from UK PORG 1987 based on Heck et al. 1982 and 1983)

Crop	Ozone concentration (ppb)
Corn	75–132
Wheat	64–93
Soybean	38–43
Peanut	43–49
Kidney bean	72–86
Cotton	41
Turnip	40–61
Lettuce	53–57
Spinach	41–60

The range of values for each crop are due to a range of different varieties being studied in different seasons. These values were calculated from fitted dose-response models based on 7-hours per day fumigations.

the context of UK ozone concentrations using the data from a rural background site at Bottesford, Leicestershire from 1978–85. The 0900–1600 h ozone concentrations over the summer averaged 32 ppb (range 26–42 ppb) compared with the 'zero-effect level' of 25 ppb (Figure 6.6). The Review Group concluded that the NCLAN dose-response data suggested that 'only in exceptional summers will the yield of even the most sensitive crops be reduced by ozone on its own'. However, the NCLAN exposure pattern had several features which limit its relevance to UK conditions. Firstly, the period of exposure did not coincide with the time of day at which highest concentrations occurred at Bottesford where episodes above 60 ppb often persisted beyond 1600 h. Secondly, the NCLAN procedure added constant amounts to filtered air day after day, which is different from the UK pattern in which periods of relatively low concentration are interspersed with episodes of elevated concentrations. It is apparent that a programme should be set up in the UK to determine the effects of ozone on crop growth by a combination of long term filtration experiments accompanied by controlled exposures simulating the ozone concentrations typical of UK conditions.

6.4.4 Exposure to ozone sulphur dioxide and nitrogen oxides

Few attempts have been made to fumigate with mixtures of SO_2, NO_2 and ozone despite the need to determine the

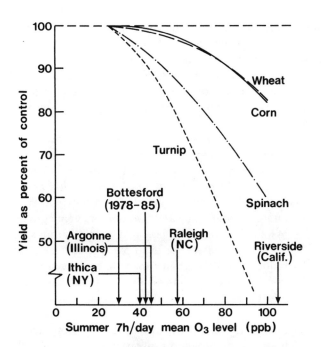

6.6 Data from the US National Crop Loss Assessment Network on the effect on crop yield of daily exposure to ozone (7 h/day). Also shown are mean ozone concentrations in two years at a UK site and at 3 sites in the eastern USA.

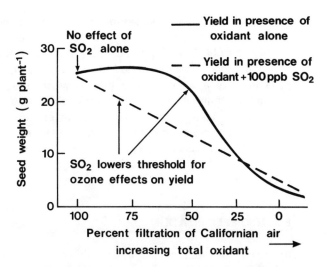

6.7 Effect of ambient ozone in California on the yield of red kidney bean (*Phaseolus vulgaris*) and interactions with added SO_2. (Reproduced from Roberts *et al.*, 1983).

influence of sub-threshold concentrations of SO_2 + NO_2 on the growth responses of crops to ozone. The most recent review was prepared by Lefohn and Ormrod (1984). The effects of 3-combination mixtures have mainly been studied in short-term experiments in relation to visible injury. Although the highest SO_2 concentrations occur in winter, concurrent peaks of SO_2 and ozone do occasionally occur in summer. Studies of concurrent exposure to mixtures have produced variable results ranging from antagonism (Ashmore and Onal, 1984) to synergism (Jacobson, 1982). Ozone episodes in summer are more frequently preceded by SO_2 peaks in the UK. Exposure to SO_2 prior to ozone peaks produced greater injury in cucumber but less injury in bean (Hofstra *et al.*, 1985). A limited number of studies have exposed crops to SO_2 and ozone mixtures and assessed growth responses over the full season. Oshima (1978) examined the interactive effects of SO_2 with ambient, filtered and part-filtered air at Riverside, California. Red kidney bean yields were not affected by SO_2 alone but both seed and total plant weight were reduced by SO_2 in 50% filtered air (Figure 6.7). Snap beans also suffered greater yield losses when SO_2 was added to ambient air compared with charcoal filtered air (Heggestad and Bennett, 1981). In contrast, neither Kress *et al.* (1986) nor Reich and Amundson (1984) found significant interactions between SO_2 and ozone on yield of soybean. It should be noted that the intermittent pattern of SO_2 treatment in these studies does not simulate the continuous, fluctuating exposures which occur in the UK.

Rural areas of UK which are most likely to experience elevated ozone concentrations may also receive moderate concentrations of SO_2 and NO_2. Thus the importance of experiments using controlled exposures to SO_2, NO_2 and ozone cannot be stressed too strongly. No data have yet been published on this important aspect in the UK although a limited number of studies are underway. In North America, Reinert and colleagues found that, in most crops examined, exposure to repeated short-term peaks of SO_2 + NO_2 + ozone caused more subsequent yield loss than the single gases or two-pollutant mixtures (Reinert and Gray, 1981; Reinert and Sanders, 1982).

Wolting (1983, 1984 and 1985) gave brief summaries in the Annual Report of the Research Institute for Plant Protection (Wageningen, Netherlands) of the effects of SO_2 + NO_2 + ozone mixtures on a range of indicator plants and native species. In 1983, 35 ppb NO_2 + 35 ppb SO_2 added to the ozone in unfiltered air in open-top chambers reduced the yield of great plantain (*Plantago major*), an ozone indicator species, after 4 weeks but radish and lettuce were less sensitive. In 1984, yields of both great plantain and radish but not spinach were reduced by 75 ppb NO_2 and 70 ppb SO_2 added to unfiltered air. In 1985, great plantain showed 40% leaf injury and 12% yield loss after a 3 week exposure to 22 ppb NO_2 + 25 ppb SO_2.

Bel-W3 tobacco plants showed leaf injury but no yield reduction. Two legumes showed slight visible symptoms and four native species showed no negative reactions. Ryegrass (*Lolium perenne*) showed a slight discolouration of leaf tips but, even after 6 weeks exposure, dry matter production was not affected (Posthumus and Tonneijck, 1984).

Experiments are in progress at Ascot, near London where SO_2 and NO_2 are being added to filtered or ambient air (J.N.B. Bell, pers. comm.) at concentrations typical of those measured at Kew in London. Results with peas indicate a greater effect of SO_2 when added to ambient air than when added to filtered air, but no such effect was seen with spinach. However, the pea experiment was carried out in summertime when ozone concentrations exceeded 60 ppb on 21 days, whereas the spinach experiment took place in autumn when ozone never exceeded 60 ppb.

6.5 ACID PRECIPITATION

In a review of effects of acid precipitation on crops, Irving (1983) concluded that the growth of the majority of species studied in both field and controlled environment experiments was not affected by simulated acid rain. In fact, when the acidity of ambient rain was compared with acidity causing foliar injury to experimental vegetation grown in controlled conditions, (Jacobson 1984) it was found that most reports of foliar injury occurred at pH values of 3.5 or less, values which are generally more acidic than those occurring in ambient rain (Figure 6.8).

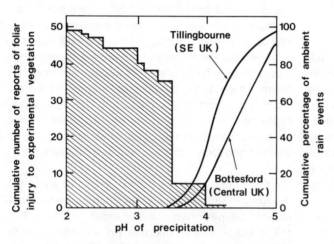

6.8 Effect of acid sprays on visible injury to vegetation (reports up to 1983). Also shown are the distributions of rain acidity at 2 sites in the UK.

As glasshouse grown crops have been found to be more sensitive to acid precipitation than the same species grown in field (Jacobson 1982, Evans et al., 1982), it is fairly clear that field grown vegetation is not in any great danger of foliar injury from current levels of acid precipitation in Eastern USA and, by analogy, in Europe.

However growth and yields of some crops appear to be negatively affected by acidic rain and others positively affected. It has been suggested (Irving 1983) that the net crop response is the result of the interaction between negative effects of acidity and the positive benefits of sulphur and nitrogen fertiliser together with other en-

vironmental conditions. In addition, the ratio of sulphate to nitrate may also determine the magnitude of the response (Irving, 1985). In some of these studies, crops would have been exposed to ambient concentrations of gaseous pollutants, especially ozone and this combination of stresses would clearly complicate interpretations.

Many problems exist in attempting to compare the divergent experimental responses to simulated acid rain. Experimental procedures are frequently inadequately described. Not only is chemical composition and concentration important but the size of droplets in sprays and intensity, frequency and duration of events greatly affect results. Different cultivars also have different susceptibilities. In soybeans, for example, 'Amsoy' seed yield was reduced by 10% when subjected to daily simulated acid rain of pH 4.1 whereas yields of 'Williams' were not affected.

Rainfall is episodic, occurring for 4–8% of total available hours of the growing season in Eastern USA (Niemann, 1984) and acid deposition is even more episodic. In the UK, 30% of total acidity was deposited on 3% of wet days at a number of sites during 1979/80 (Barrett et al., 1983). Comparisons between studies would be improved by knowledge of percentage time with rain, average duration of wet periods, average duration of dry periods between events and total amount of rain received. Rain-free intervals allow plants time to recover from injury. When radish was exposed to acid rain (Jacobson et al., 1985) the capacity to recover (measured as dry weight of hypocotyl) increased with increase in interval between rain exposures. Similar recoveries (measured as decrease in leaf conductance) were recorded for various grasses following exposure to wind (Pitcairn and Grace, 1985), a phenomenon that, like acid rain, damages surface structure.

Acid rain occurs in many areas of Eastern USA where oxidant levels are considerable but very few studies of interactive effects on ozone and acidic rain on vegetation have been reported. One such study (Troiano et al., 1983) on soybean (Glycine max L. Merr. cv. Beeson) concluded that increased acidity of applied acid rain increased the reduction in total dry weight caused by ambient ozone, and acid rain × ozone interactions also affected components of yield. In contrast, Rebbeck and Brennan (1984) found no interaction between ozone and acid mist on the growth of lucerne. However, there is sound theoretical support for the view that rain and ozone may have additive or greater-than-additive effects on plants (Irving, 1986).

6.6 CONCLUSIONS

1. Early studies showed the detrimental affects of urban pollution on crops. More recently (1983–86), it

has been demonstrated that there is a progressive decrease in yield of some crop plants (eg. peas) in summer experiments along a transect from the countryside into central London. This effect was tentatively ascribed to the combined effects of ozone with SO_2 and NO_2.

2. In the middle of the 20th Century, winter-time filtration experiments in urban areas showed that plants grew less in ambient air than in filtered air. Later experiments (1970s), carried out mainly in summertime in urban and rural areas also showed growth reductions in ambient air. However, recent experiments in summer and winter in urban/urban fringe areas have produced somewhat conflicting results with both positive and negative effects of pollution on growth. This may be because pollutant concentrations (especially SO_2) are lower than in the past or because the pollution mixture is different.

3. There is evidence from experiments in filtered and unfiltered chambers at rural sites in south-east England that ambient air reduced the yield of some horticultural species such as peas, beans and spinach in many summers. However, the growth of other arable crops such as wheat, and broccoli has not been affected in these experiments. Effects show some correlation with ambient ozone concentrations.

4. After experiments in chambers in which ozone concentrations exceeded 100 ppb, visible injury to peas and clovers has been observed. Visible symptoms resembling ozone injury have also been observed in the field on species such as spinach and petunia, species in which injury is likely to directly affect economic value.

5. Recent experiments in which cereals were exposed in the field to SO_2 released from pipes have shown that concentrations above 40 ppb reduce growth of winter barley, although some stimulation of yield were recorded at lower concentrations. Components of grain yield such as grain number and grain weight responded differently to fumigation, emphasising the importance of examining crop responses in terms of all components rather than only absolute yield.

6. Concentrations of SO_2 used in these experiments exceeded rural annual mean SO_2 concentrations observed in the UK. It is important to determine dose-response patterns in the ambient range but it is difficult to do so with realistic field exposures.

7. The available evidence from controlled exposures indicates that for the limited number of species (spring and winter barley) investigated, exposure over winter to concentrations of 40 ppb SO_2 + 40 ppb NO_2 produced substantial reductions in growth, but continuation of exposure into summer was generally accompanied by a progressive lessening of this effect. There are few studies of long term exposures below 40 ppb.

8. Over long periods, growth of many crops is reduced by exposure to a mean concentration of 40 ppb ozone or above. A substantial body of evidence exists in North America on which dose-response relationships have been based. Growth of certain sensitive species, including soybean, peanut, spinach and turnip, was reduced above a threshold of about 40 ppb ozone (7 hour/day seasonal mean), although in others, growth was only reduced after exposure to over 70 ppb (7 hour/day seasonal mean). Owing to different patterns of ambient ozone pollution, climatic interactions and the wide range of sensitivity of species concerned, these relationships are unlikely to be directly applicable to the UK.

9. A limited number of studies of controlled exposure of plants to mixtures of SO_2, NO_2 and ozone are in progress in UK. Fumigation studies in The Netherlands have shown visible injury to great plaintain (used as an indicator species in that country) resulting from exposure to 25 ppb SO_2 + 25 ppb NO_2 + 20 ppb ozone for 3 weeks.

10. Few experiments have been carried out in the UK on agricultural and horticultural crops using simulated acid rain or mist of realistic chemical composition. Most North American studies do not show effects on crops after exposure to realistic concentrations over long periods.

11. Arable land in and around urban areas is commonly used for horticultural crops. These crops with high economic value are thus vulnerable to pollution damage and require further research to identify sensitive species.

EFFECTS ON TREES

7.1 EVIDENCE FROM FIELD OBSERVATIONS AND POLLUTANT EXCLUSION EXPERIMENTS

During their long life-span, trees may be subjected repeatedly to environmental stresses, including atmospheric pollution, which may not cause visible injury but may seriously weaken the tree in the long term. The damage resulting from atmospheric pollution may be manifested not only in loss of or damage to foliage but in reduction of wood production and quality or in increased susceptibility of the tree to other stresses such as cold, drought and disease.

Many of Britain's forests are situated in rural areas of the north and west where mean annual concentrations of SO_2 and NO_2 are below 5 ppb. In contrast, some forests (Forest of Dean, New Forest and those in the south Pennines) and amenity plantings close to sources of emission are exposed to appreciably larger concentrations of SO_2 and NO_2. Trees in both rural and urban areas are subject to ozone episodes.

Evergreen trees retain their foliage in the winter when air pollution emissions from domestic heating sources are highest. Consequently initial studies of effects of air pollution on trees in the UK were concentrated on the growth of evergreen species in industrial or urban areas.

7.1.1 Evidence from areas affected by urban development

A survey of the distribution of Scots pine (*Pinus sylvestris*) made by Farrar *et al.* (1977) in the southern Pennines in response to reports of poor performance in forestry trials in the area revealed that the species rarely occurred in an area of land extending north and east from Greater Manchester and Merseyside. The occurrence showed a significant negative correlation with mean winter concentrations of SO_2. Similar results were also obtained from the Ruhr area in West Germany (Knabe, 1970).

The rarity of Scots pine in the Pennines may be partly a result of the policy of the Forestry Commission in species choice for the area since the early 1950s. However a recent survey (Lines, 1984) of species trials planted in the southern Pennines between 1951 and 1977 by the Forestry Commission indicated that Scots pine had grown slowly but with some success. The overall conclusion of the survey was of improved growth since the 1960s, (accompanying falling SO_2 levels), particularly of Sitka spruce (*Picea sitchensis*), the potentially most economic crop in this area. Deep, thorough cultivation techniques used in 1972 on one site produced very satisfactory growth. One reason for this may be the provision of more fertile and easily rootable soils which could have compensated in part for deleterious effects of pollution past and present.

London ambient air has also been shown to reduce tree growth. Garsed and Rutter (1982) grew seedlings of Scots pine, Lodgepole pine (*Pinus contorta*), Norway spruce (*Picea abies*) and Sitka spruce in the same soil at sites in central London and Ascot. All species grew better in London over the first year probably due to more favourable urban temperatures, but after the second year, relative growth rates were significantly lower for Norway and Sitka spruce (25% and 45.6% respectively).

Some hardwoods are also sensitive to urban air. Premature leaf fall was a symptom of chronic pollution damage to Canadian poplar (*Populus canadensis*) sited near the industrial complex of Bratislava (Navara *et al.*, 1978) and attributed mainly to SO_2 pollution. It must be emphasised that, although the pollution concentration along a gradient from a pollution source is frequently expressed in terms of the major pollutant, other pollutants, especially particulates, are almost always present to some degree. Growth reductions, visible injury and death were recorded in Norway spruce in the Erzgebirge region of Czechoslovakia (Materna 1973) and attributed to SO_2, although again other agents may have contributed to phytotoxic effects. Because of the presence of other phytotoxic agents and climatic variation, it is obviously difficult to derive dose-response relationships specific to SO_2 from field studies.

Pollution impact can sometimes be more readily assessed by means other than growth performance. In a mixed oak forest near a coal burning power station in Pennsylvania USA (Rosenberg *et al.*, 1979), species richness and diversity proved more sensitive indicators of pollution than growth assessments of individual species. A decrease in species diversity was also noted by van Haut and Stratmann (1970) in a beech-oak forest in Germany due to emissions from an iron-ore smelter.

7.1.2 Effects on annual rings

It is frequently difficult to distinguish low level pollution response in trees over a period of time, from growth variations due to climate or other environmental variables (Briffa, 1984). However, provided that other sources of environmental variation can be accounted for, analysis of annual rings in trees can be a useful method of measuring pollution impact on growth and has been used extensively in USA. Radial growth increments were calculated from cores in forty-eight red spruce stands throughout the Appalachian Mountains. Mean radial growth was approximately 30–50% slower during the past 10 years compared with a standard 30 year reference period (1932–61) and was not affected by stand age, but causes of the reduced growth and vigour are as yet only speculative (McLaughlin, 1985). Comparisons of white oak (*Quercus alba*) tree ring chronologies among five sites representing an apparent gradient of industrial pollution in the Ohio valley (McClenahen and Dochinger,

1985), suggested that air pollution had reduced growth in nearby forests. Similar methods were used to show a relationship between decreasing growth of pines in New Jersey and stream pH. It has been suggested that acid precipitation may have been limiting growth for the past two decades (Johnson et al., 1981).

Bunce (1979) was able to show more conclusively that emissions from an aluminium smelter, mainly fluorine, had reduced growth measured as annual ring increment in surrounding forests. Scandinavian studies of ring width and wood density data have shown some changes indicative of changes in pollution concentrations (Arovaara et al., 1984; Wigley et al., 1986). In the UK, extensive studies have been made of ring width variation in oak (Briffa et al., 1983; Briffa, 1984) and there is scope for further studies on coniferous species with the aim of examining tree growth in relation to pollution concentrations.

7.1.3 Photochemical oxidants

Photochemical oxidant pollution was first recognised in coastal parts of California in 1940. Severe damage was caused by ozone in areas remote from local sources. In the San Bernardino mountains, 40,000 acres of mixed conifer woodlands have been moderately to severely damaged. In eastern USA, various needle disorders of eastern white pine were attributed to ozone damage in the 1960s and damage has since been caused by high concentrations of ozone to white pine and other species. Considerable variation in the sensitivity of white pine to ozone was found (Dochinger et al., 1970; Costonis, 1970; Costonis and Sinclair, 1969) and made use of in subsequent research. Clones were produced from trees of desired sensitivity in the form of either rooted cuttings or grafts (see Section 7.2.2) providing material of known response for use in research, including biological monitoring of ozone (Berry, 1973).

Symptoms of damage were also observed in other indigenous trees in eastern USA, and open top pollutant exclusion chambers were used to test effects of ambient ozone on growth of eight forest species native to the Blue Ridge Mountains from 1979–81 (Duchelle et al., 1982). Height growth was suppressed in all species by the end of the second growing season mostly without evidence of ozone-induced foliar symptoms.

Open top chamber experiments were performed on native British deciduous trees and ozone-sensitive American white ash (*Fraxinus americana*) at Ascot, near London throughout the summer of 1979 (Ashmore, 1984). In ambient air, compared with charcoal filtered air, there was a significantly increased amount of foliar chlorosis in early September on silver birch (*Betula pendula*), European ash (*F. excelsior*) and two out of five strains of white ash. Beech (*Fagus sylvatica*) was not affected, suggesting that it is relatively tolerant to ozone.

Effect of altitude

The occurrence of higher concentrations of ozone at higher altitude forest sites has been observed in south Germany (Reiter and Kanter, 1982) and western and eastern USA and some values are given in Chapter 2. Tree injury was also found to increase with site elevation at both regions of the USA (Miller et al, 1982; Skelly et al. 1983) and there is a suggestion of greater forest damage at high altitude in south Germany (Ashmore et al., 1985). The possible role of ozone in forest decline is discussed in Chapter 11.

7.2 EVIDENCE FROM CONTROLLED EXPOSURE EXPERIMENTS

Trees are probably the most difficult group of plants to examine for effects of air pollution. Conifers are grown for up to 60 years in the UK before harvesting and often for up to 100 years in Europe and so any feasible experimental exposures to pollutants occupy only a very small part of the life cycle. Thus the dangers of extrapolating from short-term fumigations, often at high pollutant concentrations, to effects of ambient air in the field are evident. Effects of ambient pollution may be cumulative and manifested only in the form of reduced growth some time later. Such latent or invisible injury may be indicated by physiological, biochemical or ecological reactions as well as increased susceptibility, depression of vigour etc. (Keller, 1984).

The size of mature trees makes controlled exposure difficult and costly. Seedlings are frequently used, needing little space. In some species they are highly susceptible to pollutants and allow early detection of effects. However, mature trees may differ considerably in their susceptibility to pollutants.

7.2.1 Variation in response

Considerable variation in growth response to pollutants exists between and within species. The relative susceptibility of different tree species to acute injury from SO_2 has been assessed from field studies around point sources of SO_2 (Last, 1982). Hardwoods tend to be less sensitive than conifers and most conifers grown in Britain (Scots pine, Norway spruce, Sitka spruce and larch) tend to be at the sensitive end of the scale, although lodgepole pine is classed as intermediate. Long term studies at less polluted sites (Garsed and Rutter, 1982; Lines, 1984) showed that Norway and Sitka spruce were more sensitive than Scots and lodgepole pine. The order was reversed when the trees received acute SO_2 fumigation (Garsed and Rutter, 1982), indicating that acute fumigation may be of little use as a screening procedure for selecting tree species for resistance to chronic exposure. Large variation within species also occurs. Differences in % leaf injury of more than 30% have been found between clones of larch (*Larix decidua*) exposed to SO_2 and Scots pine exposed to ozone (Bialobok, 1977) and between clones of aspen (*Populus tremuloides*) exposed to SO_2 + ozone (Karnosky, 1977). Variations in CO_2 uptake in spruce shoots from different clones after exposure to SO_2 were also recorded (Keller, 1984).

Variation within a species can be minimised for experimental studies by using genetically uniform material produced by vegetative propagation (cloning). The parent tree used for cloning may simply be a strong, healthy individual, or a tree that has been selected for a particular pollutant sensitivity. Propagation is either by means of rooted shoot cuttings or by grafting shoots or buds onto established rootstocks. In both cases the resulting plants possess the same genetic characteristics as the parent tree. Cuttings have the advantage of being quick to produce and more uniform than grafts. However certain species, particularly some conifers, do not root easily. It is also more difficult to take cuttings from older trees, which is a disadvantage when clones are required from mature trees. In such circumstances, grafts are preferable. The shoot or bud may be taken from a mature tree and grafted onto an established rootstock thus avoiding juvenile delays in fruiting and sources of variation in the rootstock can be minimised by using clonal rootstocks.

The use of clones limits variability but does not necessarily add to the knowledge of species response. However in most controlled exposure experiments, replication is restricted so that overall species responses cannot in any case be characterised. Variation is also a valuable asset for withstanding effects of pollutants. Progenies of stands of trees growing near point sources of pollution showed less damage than those transplanted from unpolluted sites (Thor and Gall, 1978). Individuals in which resistance has developed in response to pollutant exposure can be used in plant breeding programmes, as can individuals which show (through screening tests) inherent pollution resistance. Resistance to atmospheric pollution has consciously been included in plant breeding programmes for eastern white pine (Thor and Gall, 1978) and must also have been an unconscious part of all breeding programmes carried out in polluted areas (Roberts *et al.*, 1983). The genetic variation in growth responses to mixtures of pollutants is not well understood, and further studies are needed to measure tolerances to combinations of multiple pollutants at low concentrations (see 7.2.7) (Karnosky, 1985; Kress *et al.*, 1982a).

7.2.2 Controlled exposure to sulphur dioxide

Short term (10 weeks) exposures of potted grafts of fir and spruce to 50–200 ppb SO_2 in outdoor chambers resulted in decreased CO_2 uptake (Keller, 1978a). Annual ring width was reduced by 10 weeks of SO_2 exposure, particularly in summer, concentrations of 25 ppb and

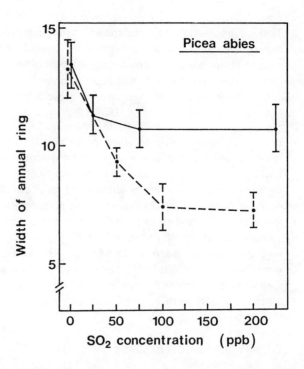

7.1 The effect of a ten week SO_2 fumigation at different concentrations during summer (broken line) or winter (solid line) on the relative width of the subsequent annual ring in two combined spruce clones. Vertical bars denote standard errors. (Reproduced from Keller, 1984).

50 ppb causing 15% and 18–25% reductions respectively (Figure 7.1). Broadleaved trees were also affected. 50 ppb SO_2 produced necrotic spots on beech (*Fagus sylvatica*) and alder (*Alnus incana*) after 7 weeks of exposure in spring (Keller and Bucher, 1976), and, in winter, fumigation at 50 and 100 ppb SO_2 resulted in reduced numbers (by 10% and 70% respectively) of terminal buds developing in the following spring (Keller, 1978b). A similar 'latent injury' occurred when white pine (*Pinus strobus*) seedlings were exposed to 50 ppb SO_2 for 11 weeks (Percy and Riding, 1981). No significant differences in external parameters were recorded but needle ontogeny was slowed down.

Longer term (6 months–2 years) exposure of Scots pine caused small reductions in relative growth rates (Farrar *et al.*, 1977, Garsed and Rutter, 1982) although younger trees were more sensitive. Exposure of young plants (6 –12 months) to ~60 ppb SO_2 for 6 months reduced the dry weight by 20%. Exposure of 3-year old trees to ~60 ppb SO_2 for 12 months depressed root growth only and exposure for 18–24 months produced a 14% reduction in mean relative growth rate (Garsed and Rutter, 1982) (all reductions are relative to growth in charcoal-filtered air).

Ryskova (1978) exposed 2-year old Scots pine seedlings and 3-year old Norway spruce seedlings for 2 years to

87 ppb SO_2 in the first year and 52 ppb in the second year. He observed a 10% weight reduction in growth increment in both species and mild chlorosis at the end of the second year. A number of tree species were exposed in the open field to a mean concentration of 50 ppb SO_2 for 3 years (Bonte, 1977). Yield was reduced by 10–40% in seven fruit trees and height and circumference increase were reduced in five out of seven conifer species. Oak (*Quercus* spp.) and beech were moderately affected but silver fir (*Abies alba*) and Corsican pine (*Pinus nigra*) were resistant. A further 2 year fumigation with only 19 ppb SO_2 reduced height growth in larch only (Bonte *et al*, 1981).

The experiments described, with the exception of the last, have used higher concentrations of SO_2 than those normally experienced in the field and the need for long term exposures of trees at low concentrations is clear. However, in the long term study of conifer growth in clean and polluted air carried out by Garsed and Rutter, (1982), London air containing ~30 ppb SO_2 caused greater growth reductions than would be expected from SO_2 alone. This suggested that the presence of other pollutants and/or other stresses such as temperature and light may have acted additively or even more than additively to limit growth.

7.2.3 Controlled exposure to sulphur dioxide and nitrogen oxides

Oxides of nitrogen invariably accompany SO_2 in polluted air. A number of broadleaved tree species (alder, apple, lime, birch, poplar) commonly grown for amenity purposes in urban areas were exposed to SO_2 and NO_2 singly and in mixtures at concentrations of 62 ppb over 60 weeks, with an intermediate harvest in the summer after 21 weeks (Whitmore and Freer-Smith, 1982). Responses were varied. Significant growth stimulations were produced by NO_2 alone in lime (*Tilia cordata*) and alder (*Alnus incana*) after 21 and 60 weeks respectively, whereas SO_2 generally reduced growth. The gas mixture caused greater-than-additive effects (50–60% growth reduction in some cases) in the first season. In the second season, interactive effects between SO_2 and NO_2 were lost as SO_2 damage became more marked and enhancement due to NO_2 was lost. Greater-than-additive effects also occurred when black poplar (*Populus nigra*) cuttings were exposed in summer to SO_2 and NO_2. Winter exposures to SO_2 or NO_2 delayed leaf growth the following spring.

The sensitivity of Scots pine, lodgepole pine and Sitka spruce to 62 ppb SO_2 and 62 ppb NO_2 was tested (Freer-Smith, 1984) over a period of 138 weeks. Premature needle loss was the main symptom of chronic SO_2 pollution, but beneficial effects of NO_2 were seen in three out of four provenances of lodgepole pine and no effect on growth occurred in the other two species. The pollutant

mixture was more toxic than SO_2 alone to the pine species in the second season but effects of $SO_2 + NO_2$ were roughly additive in Sitka spruce. The toxic effects took at least a year to develop. Since gas concentrations used were higher than those generally found in forests of Western Europe, it is clear that long term experimentation is required to determine whether similar responses occur at more typical concentrations.

Some of the experiments carried out in The Netherlands on poplars have used lower concentrations of SO_2 and NO_2, more similar to ambient concentrations. Exposure of a pollution-sensitive clone (*Populus* × *interamericana* 'Donk') to a mixture of 22 ppb SO_2 and 12 (Night)/30 (day) ppb NO_2 for only 6 weeks (Mooi, 1985), resulted in cumulative leaf fall six times greater than the control. The increased leaf fall obviously reduced the dry weight of the plants and exposure to low concentrations over a long period may result in decline in performance and vigour of the tree.

7.2.4 Controlled exposure to ozone

There have been many studies of plant response to ozone in USA, although fewer with trees than crops. Several eastern forest tree species were exposed to 59 –150 ppb ozone for 28 days (Kress and Skelly, 1982). Exposure to 50 ppb ozone significantly reduced growth of Loblolly pine (*Pinus taeda* L.), American sycamore (*Plantanus occidentalis* L.) and yellow poplar (*Liriodendron tulipifera* L.). Yellow poplar and Virginian pine (*Pinus virginiana* Mill.) were not adversely affected by exposure to 150 ppb ozone.

Long term exposure to ozone can affect leaf ageing in poplar and this has been much researched in The Netherlands where premature poplar defoliation is suspected. Fumigation of two cultivars of *Populus* × *euamericana*, 'Dorskamp' and 'Zealand' with 40 ppb ozone, 12 hours per day for 5 months (Mooi, 1980) induced severe defoliation (60%) and slight reduction in stem dry weight (4–12%) compared with control trees in clean air. A long term concentration of 40 ppb ozone is close to maximum natural concentrations of ozone in unpolluted areas of The Netherlands. Far higher concentrations can occur from time to time, suggesting that ambient concentrations of ozone may be responsible for leaf drop of poplar in The Netherlands.

Ozone may however affect trees in less obvious ways, eg. pollen germination in eastern white pine was significantly reduced by 150 ppb ozone for 4 hours under wet conditions (Benoit *et al.*, 1983), a possibly serious consequence, as ozone episodes of 100–200 ppb lasting several hours may occur often in the eastern USA.

The results of Reich *et al.* (1986), show that short periods of low concentrations of ozone can reduce photosynthesis without visible injury and often without accompanying growth reduction. This raises the suspicion that over a number of years, reduced photosynthesis may lead to reduced vigour which could increase susceptibilities to other stresses.

7.2.5 Controlled exposure to ozone and sulphur dioxide

The effect of concentrations of SO_2, representative of an urban area, with and without ozone, has also been investigated for poplars (Mooi, 1981). Total dry weight was reduced by 5% by exposure to 60 ppb SO_2, 7–13% by exposure to 35 ppb ozone and 27–40% by exposure to SO_2 + ozone indicating a strongly synergistic interaction. Leaf drop was also significantly increased.

Conifers too exhibited more serious damage when exposed to mixtures of SO_2 + ozone than to either gas alone at similar levels. A striking example of this synergism is to be seen in chlorotic dwarf of white pine, symptoms of which are produced by mixtures of SO_2 and ozone (Dochinger and Seliskar, 1970). Of a number of white pine clones tested, all were injured by 25 ppb SO_2 + 50 ppb ozone, whereas none were injured by 50 ppb ozone alone and only one by 25 ppb SO_2 (Houston, 1974).

However, there have been a few reports of antagonistic interactions in the effects of SO_2 + ozone on trees. Exposure of new needles of SO_2-sensitive eastern white pine to 50 ppb SO_2 + 50 ppb ozone for 2 hours resulted in less injury than exposure to 50 ppb SO_2 alone (Costonis, 1973). The ozone, which alone did not cause injury, appeared to reduce the toxicity of SO_2. A similar antagonism was recorded in Scots pine by Nielsen et al. (1977), but at higher gas concentrations. The responses of plants to pollutant mixtures are likely to vary according to such factors as species, age, dosage and ratios of pollutants in mixture, environmental conditions etc. In view of the number of reports of less than and more than additive effects of SO_2 + ozone on crop species and the possible effects of such interactions on the results of field fumigation and filtration experiments, further investigations into antagonistic and synergistic interactions in the effects of SO_2 and ozone on trees are obviously required.

7.2.6 Controlled exposure to sulphur dioxide, nitrogen oxides and ozone

Ozone monitoring data and surveys with a bioindicator species have shown that ozone can occur throughout the UK and Europe in phytotoxic concentrations, although such concentrations are reached infrequently and are usually of short duration. However, because of interactions between air pollutants which alone may affect plants, damaging concentrations of mixtures of gases can be lower than thresholds for single components.

In The Netherlands, ozone concentrations may average 50–100 ppb during some weeks and peak concentrations of 200–250 ppb can be measured (Mooi, 1983, 1985). Fumigation experiments on poplars with SO_2 + NO_2 already described formed part of a series examining effects of SO_2, NO_2 and ozone in various combinations and concentrations based on actual air pollution measurements made in The Netherlands. Addition of low concentrations (~29 ppb) of ozone to 21 ppb NO_2 or 22 ppb SO_2 for 6 weeks caused severe premature defoliation and a reduction in dry matter, doubling the detrimental effects of SO_2 + NO_2. A range of poplar species and clones of poplar were used and although differences in sensitivity were found, all were negatively affected by the combination of gases. However this experiment was not fully factorial.

Conifers have also been exposed to mixtures of pollutants. The differing sensitivities within eastern white pine were revealed in fumigations with low doses of SO_2, NO_2 and ozone (50 and 100 ppb) alone and in combination for 4 hours per day for 35 consecutive days (Yang et al., 1983). Both positive and negative effects were observed and complex pollutant interactions occurred. Seedlings (families) from seed of two self-pollinated trees of loblolly pine (*Pinus taeda*) expressing different sensitivities to ozone were exposed to 50 ppb ozone, 100 ppb NO_2 and/or 140 ppb SO_2 for 6 hours per day for 28 consecutive days (Kress et al., 1982a). Significant growth suppressions occurred with the relatively sensitive family in all but the NO_2 alone treatments, and ozone + SO_2 caused the greatest suppressions. In the relatively insensitive family, only ozone + SO_2 and ozone + SO_2 + NO_2 caused significant suppressions. The latter combination caused a 30% height reduction in the relatively sensitive family compared with 14% in the insensitive family. Little foliar injury occurred and thus in ambient air in the field, growth suppressions may go undetected unless either clean air controls or known sensitive and non-sensitive trees are used for comparisons.

Similar experiments were carried out with seedlings from seed of two trees of American sycamore (*Platanus occidentalis*) (Kress et al., 1982b). Significant growth suppressions were noted for both families when exposed to the pollutant mixtures and both families showed significant recovery in rate of height growth 2 weeks after removal of the pollutant stress.

7.2.7 Effects of ozone and acid mist

Although direct ozone fumigation of trees in the UK has not received high priority, the possible interactive effects of ozone with acid rain and mists at high elevation on forests in Europe has led to considerable research on these mixtures. However conclusions based on experimental results in this field must be viewed with uncertainty. Insufficient information is available from monitoring to provide a basis for realistic simulations of acid mists and experiments to date have only been carried out on young trees.

Evidence of increased leaching from ozone pre-damaged trees has come from West Germany. More ions were leached from predamaged Black Forest Spruce than from healthy nursery stock trees grown in Black Forest soil (Krause et al., 1985). At 100 ppb ozone, increase in acidity of the mist increased efflux of heavy metals, Ca^{2+}, Mg^{2+} and SO_4^{2-} but not Cl^- and NO_3^-. When acid mist at pH 3.5 was applied, increased ozone concentrations resulted in increased proton concentration in the leachate. Skeffington and Roberts (1985) found additive or less-than-additive effects of combined ozone/acid mist on needle chlorosis after exposing 3-year old Scots pine and Norway spruce saplings to four ozone concentrations and acid (pH 3) or distilled water mist for 60 days (Figure 7.2). They also found that exposure to ozone enhanced leaching of ions from needles with or without

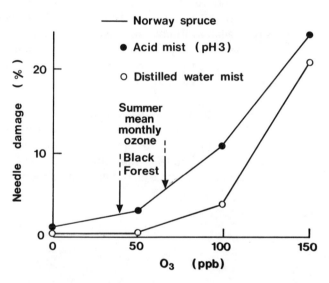

7.2 **Effects of constant exposures to ozone and mist of acid or distilled water over 60 days (July/August 1984) on the percentage of needle damage in Norway spruce. Also shown is the range of summer monthly mean ozone concentrations in the Black Forest, West Germany.**

acid misting but the treatments also increased needle concentrations of most ions. Rehfuess (1986) also found that leaching losses of Mg^{2+} and Ca^{2+} from 3-year old rooted Spruce cuttings were increased by acid (pH 3.0) mist and further increased by acid mist together with 45 ppb ozone (compared with clean air and distilled water treatments). Thus these experiments indicate that ozone concentrations of 45–100 ppb together with acid mist, could cause indirect damage as a result of increased nutrient efflux, without visible symptoms. Values of 50–75 ppb ozone occur in Germany in spring and summer, and thus increased leaching may occur in

the field. The result would be more serious in nutrient deficient ecosystems than in nutrient rich soils.

7.2.8 Effects of acid precipitation

As with arable crops, experiments with simulated acid rain (SAR) on trees are very difficult to compare and simulations often bear little relationship in composition, intensity, frequency, etc., to ambient precipitation. The acidity of distilled water in equilibrium with atmospheric CO_2 (pH 5.6) is normally used as a control although unpolluted rain may be as acid as pH 4.5 in some circumstances (Charlson and Rodhe, 1982). There is some evidence of damaging effects of rainfall of pH 3.5 or below on trees and some evidence exists of stimulatory growth effects, presumably due to extra sulphur and nitrogen available as nutrients.

In four out of seven North American tree species, percentage seedling germination was significantly stimulated by acid rain (pH 4, 3.5 and 3). Similarly, growth of seedlings of Douglas fir (*Pseudotsuga Douglasii*) and cuttings of some clones of Norway spruce was increased by SAR of lower pH (Lee and Weber, 1979; Tveite, 1980).

However, five weeks treatment with acid rain of pH 4.6 significantly reduced seedling elongation and needle differentiation in several conifer species (including red spruce (*Picea rubens*) which is known to be declining in parts of north east USA) compared with rain of pH 5.6 (Percy, 1986).

Pollen germination of sugar maple (*Acer saccharum*), quaking aspen (*Populus tremuloides*), paper-bark birch (*Betula papyrifera*), and eastern white pine (*Pinus strobus*) showed an LD50 (median lethal dose) of pH 3.6–3.95, levels of acidity not uncommon in ambient rain (Cox 1983). In longer term Norwegian experiments, growth increases of Scots pine found in 1976 and 1977 following applications of water of pH 3.2, ceased by 1979 and the most acid plots showed significantly less growth (Abrahamsen, 1984).

Growth of temperate forest trees may be limited by supplies of nitrogen, phosphorus, magnesium and potassium. As the latter two nutrients, particularly magnesium, are affected by leaching, tree growth may be reduced by acid rain in regions receiving large amounts of acid deposition where magnesium and perhaps potassium are deficient. In other areas where nitrogen or sulphur may be deficient, acid deposition may increase forest production.

7.3 CONCLUSIONS

1. Many of Britain's forests are situated in rural areas of the north and west where mean annual concentra-

tions of SO_2 and NO_2 are below 5 ppb. In contrast, some forests in southern and central England and trees growing close to sources of emission are exposed to appreciably larger concentrations of SO_2 and NO_2. Trees in both rural and urban areas are subject to ozone episodes.

2. The effects of pollutants on trees are difficult to determine because:
   i) trees are long-lived and have juvenile and mature forms which may differ in sensitivity;
   ii) effects on trees may be cumulative and will also depend in part upon changes in the weather from season to season and year to year;
   iii) genetic variation in trees is large compared with agricultural crops;
   iv) trees are grown on a wide range of soil types, often low in nutrient availability, in contrast to agricultural crops;
   v) mature trees are more self sufficient in nutrients than crops.

3. There is evidence from field observations and controlled experiments that growth of some tree species (Scots pine, poplar) may be decreased in or near urban areas. These effects may be attributed to SO_2, NO_2 and perhaps periodic episodes of ozone.

4. Controlled exposures of trees to SO_2 have shown reductions in annual ring width, changes in growth rates of shoots and roots, and reduced numbers of buds developing the following spring. Such exposures have usually been at SO_2 concentrations larger than those commonly experienced in Britain.

5. Exposure to SO_2 and NO_2 gives responses that may be more than additive and sometimes take more than one season to develop, emphasising the need for longer term studies. Sensitive clones of poplar, studied in The Netherlands, show large increases in leaf fall after only short exposures to concentrations of SO_2 and NO_2 that are close to ambient.

6. Growth of seedlings of some tree species is significantly reduced after exposures to ozone concentrations in the range 40–150 ppb. Long term exposures of poplar in The Netherlands to ozone concentrations close to ambient caused much larger leaf fall than on controls in clean air. It therefore appears likely that ozone in Europe reaches concentrations that damage sensitive trees directly by gaseous uptake.

7. Work in progress includes exposure of trees to SO_2, NO_2 and ozone singly and in mixture, pollutant gases and other stresses and acid mist and ozone, but the results of most of these experiments are not yet available. There are indications from several sources that ozone can increase leaching of nutrients which, if substantiated could have serious long-term consequences in nutrient-deficient ecosystems.

8. Experiments with simulated acid precipitation have produced conflicting results to date. This may be due in part to the technical limitations of the methods used but also reflects the difficulty of conducting experiments on trees, especially mature forms.

EFFECTS OF NATURAL AND SEMI-NATURAL ECOSYSTEMS

8.1 FIELD OBSERVATIONS

Natural vegetation in the UK has been largely modified by removal of woodland cover in prehistoric and historic time. Vegetation relatively unaffected by human activity is more accurately termed semi-natural and is mainly moorland and heathland composed of heather, bracken and associated species. Grasses and clovers are also important constituents of semi-natural ecosystems and effects of acid deposition on these species are reviewed in Chapter 5. Semi-natural ecosystems cover only a very small proportion of the land surface in the south and east, but these contain the most diverse plant and animal communities of these regions and are thus of high amenity value. In the north and west, semi-natural ecosystems are more extensive and also have high amenity value, but overall remarkably little attention has been paid so far to the effects of acid deposition on these little disturbed ecosystems in the UK. In Europe and North America, damage to forests attributed to acid deposition is a serious problem and has attracted considerable research interest, but even in these regions damage to other semi-natural vegetation types, if present, has largely been ignored.

Most field observations that have been made are purely descriptive and effects of acid deposition have been largely inferred from correlations with known concentrations of pollutants. Nowhere is this more true than in the study of lichens, species of which are important components of many semi-natural plant communities. A correlation between atmospheric pollution and the demise of lichens was first reported in Manchester by Grindon (1859). The sensitivity of lichens to sulphur pollution in the Newcastle area was documented by Gilbert (1965), and lichen distribution in the UK was mapped by Hawksworth and Rose (1970, 1976). These lichen maps matched lichen distribution with mean winter concentrations of SO_2, although lichens are also sensitive to other pollutants which may accompany SO_2. Fry and Cooke (1984) indicated that the 'lichen deserts' of Hawksworth and Rose (1976) are closely associated with high emission zones of sulphur dioxide (Barrett et al., 1983) (Figure 8.1), and the areas with unspoilt lichen communities correlate with a low dry deposition rate of sulphur (<2 tonnes S $Km^{-2}y^{-1}$). The decline in urban SO_2 concentrations in recent years has been correlated with a re-invasion by some lichen species of previous 'lichen deserts' (Seaward, 1982).

8.1   (a) **The relationship between lichen deserts and zones where there are large emissions of sulphur; _ _ _ _ _ _ lichen deserts; ———— emission zones of sulphur >12.5 tonnes S/km²/year.**

(b) **The relationship between prime lichen areas and areas with low dry deposition of sulphur; _ _ _ _ _ _ easterly or southerly limits of prime lichen areas, ———— areas with dry deposition of sulphur <2 tonnes/km²/year.**

(Data from Hawksworth and Rose, 1976; Barret et al., 1983. Reproduced from Fry and Cooke 1984 by permission of the Nature Conservancy Council). Note that the published lichen maps do not extend to the remainder of Scotland.

Apparent effects of wet acid deposition on lichens have been less well documented. Gilbert (1986) presented the results of a long term field survey in northern England. He showed that *Lobaria pulmonaria* has declined to extinction over 15 years in an old oak wood in Northumberland. Oak bark is known to be susceptible to leaching by wet acidic deposition, being poorly buffered and during the observation period oak bark pH declined from pH 5.2 to 4.5–5.0. An investigation of *L. pulmonaria* in oak-dominated forests of south west Norway (Gauslaa, 1985) concluded that the lichen was vulnerable to acid precipitation because it required a tree bark of pH 5.0 for growth. The selective survival of *L. pulmonaria* on the more basic bark of ash and elm compared with oak has been widely noted in remote areas of the UK.

A major reason for the apparent sensitivity of lichens to atmospheric pollution is that many species are adapted to utilise the atmospheric source of nutrient elements for growth. This is a characteristic that they share with many mosses and liverworts (bryophytes), and Gilbert (1968) also related the distribution of bryophytes to sulphur pollution in Newcastle-upon-Tyne. In British vegetation, bryophytes differ from lichens in that some species are able to achieve dominance. On mountain summits, *Racomitrium lanuginosum* may form extensive heaths, and in mires the bog mosses (*Sphagnum* species) are the major peat forming plants. The rain-fed or ombrotrophic mires cover large areas in parts of the north and west of Britain, and plants of these mires depend entirely on an atmospheric supply of essential elements for growth. These plants, particularly the *Sphagnum* species, are adapted to intercept directly and utilise this supply. It could be expected therefore that these species would be particularly sensitive to change in the atmospheric supply as the result of atmospheric pollution. The southern Pennine hills are covered by extensive blanket mires (extending to >50,000 hectares), and these hills are surrounded by towns which were early centres of the Industrial Revolution. The region has thus been exposed to high levels of acidic deposition for two centuries. Although historical records and surveys provide some evidence for vegetation change in the region (see eg. Press *et al.*, 1983), much firmer data are provided by examination of the blanket bog peat profiles. The disappearance of the peat-forming *Sphagnum* species, once dominant in these mires, is associated with the appearance of soot particles in the peat profile (Tallis, 1964), and this can be demonstrated from profiles throughout the region. (Soot and SO_2 were probably co-occurring pollutants from the start of the industrial revolution until the Clean Air Acts of the 1950s (see Chapter 1)). Tallis (1964) also reported from field surveys that of the eighteen species of *Sphagnum* reported in the region in 1913, only five were recorded in 1964, and of those only *Sphagnum recurvum* is at all common to-day (Press *et al.*, 1983). This minerotrophic species, not normally found in rain-fed mires, but typical of springs and flushes draining acidic rocks, may have a higher tolerance of dissolved salts than ombrotrophic species. Thus there is firm evidence that the decline and demise of ombrotrophic *Sphagnum* species in the region is correlated with atmospheric pollution. A similar apparent sensitivity of ombrotrophic *Sphagnum* species to atmospheric pollution has also been demonstrated near Sudbury, Canada where there are major sources of SO_2 (Gignac and Beckett, 1986).

Although certain *Sphagnum* species may be particularly susceptible to atmospheric pollution, other plant species may also have been directly or indirectly affected in the southern Pennines. The mires are now dominated by cotton grass (*Eriophorum vaginatum*), with crowberry (*Empetrum nigrum*) and bilberry (*Vaccinium myrtillus*) in the drier areas. Species such as bog myrtle (*Myrica gale*), the sundews (*Drosera* sp.), lesser twayblade (*Listera cordata*) and bog rosemary (*Andromeda polifolia*) have been eliminated or become extremely scarce in the last two centuries (Press *et al.*, 1983). Some of this decline may have resulted from changes in the hydrology of the mires as the result of the loss of the *Sphagnum* carpet, a process which may also have accelerated peat erosion. Similarly deliberate drainage and burning of the mires over this period may have adversely affected the growth of some plants. Thus an explanation involving atmospheric pollution as the causal factor for the loss of species in the absence of experimentation cannot be sustained, but it is extremely unlikely that the almost total elimination of *Sphagnum* species over such a large area can be explained without some involvement of atmospheric pollution.

Species from other habitats in the southern Pennines may also have declined since the Industrial Revolution. Some species are rarer in the region than might be expected from a knowledge of the soils, eg. acidic grassland plants such as Stag's-horn clubmoss (*Lycopodium clavatum*), alpine clubmoss (*Diphasiastrum alpinum*) and common tormentil (*Potentilla erecta*). Similarly Juniper (*Juniperus communis*) is absent, although it is locally abundant on a wide range of soils in many other parts of Britain. Again land-use may provide an explanation, but attempts have been made to explain the decline of certain herbaceous species in The Netherlands in terms of both habitat destruction *and* air pollution (van Dam *et al.*, 1986). A two-factor model was made in which decline was accounted for by habitat destruction, assessed from topographic maps, and air pollution, measured as the 95-percentile of SO_2 concentration (the concentration which is exceeded 5% of the time) recorded over the winter period 1978/79. Despite large yearly and seasonal variation in SO_2 concentration, the spatial pattern of concentration was considered to be sufficiently constant for the use of concentration measurements from one season as a relative measure of pollution. The decline of certain species, including some which are relatively uncommon in the southern Pennines, was found to be significantly correlated with air pollution. However, it must be remembered that correlation is *not* proof of a causal relationship. Experimental investigations are required to substantiate the validity of such relationships.

8.2 EXPERIMENTAL EVIDENCE

In Britain, the most extensive experimental evidence for effects of acidic deposition on semi-natural ecosystems comes from studies of the southern Pennine blanket mires. Most ombrotrophic *Sphagnum* species tested were shown to be markedly reduced in growth by SO_2 at 49 ppb (Ferguson *et al.*, 1978), an annual mean concentration which was probably equalled or exceeded in many parts of the southern Pennines for at least several decades (Ferguson and Lee, 1983a). In contrast the only species widespread in the southern Pennines today, *Sphagnum recurvum*, was relatively less affected by SO_2 or its solution products under experimental conditions. More recently, Lee *et al.* (1988) have demonstrated that the only surviving small relict populations of the ombrotrophic species *Sphagnum cuspidatum* in the southern Pennines are more tolerant of bisulphite ions than populations from North Wales and the northern Pennines. These data support the view that, in the past, the prevalence of SO_2 in the southern Pennines has resulted in a widespread vegetation change by removing the *Sphagnum* carpet from many thousand of hectares of mire surface. In addition, the very low activity of the soil enzyme arylsulphatase (important in the mineralisation of sulphate) in the most grossly polluted southern Pennine peats suggests that atmospheric pollution has affected not only the living *Sphagnum* carpet, but also microbial acitivity in the peat (Press *et al.*, 1985).

Mean annual concentrations of SO_2 in the southern Pennines have declined since at least 1952 (Figure 8.2), but there has been no marked recovery of *Sphagnum* cover. This is not simply the result of an absence of propagules since plants transplanted from a remote 'clean' mire site to the southern Pennines showed poor growth in five out of six species, and only the minerotrophic species *S. recurvum* survived (Ferguson and Lee, 1983b). This points to an inhibition caused by the interaction of present-day pollutants with the legacies of previous pollutants accumulated in the peat. Emissions of the gases NO and NO_2 which accompany SO_2 have increased in recent years and, as a result nitrate concentrations now account for one third of the acidity of precipitation in the southern Pennines. In contrast, data recorded by Smith (1872) show a ratio of sulphuric to nitric acid in Manchester rainfall of 1868–9 of 43.3:1. Thus nitrogen pollutants may be particularly important in determining the poor growth of *Sphagnum* species in the southern Pennines today. Nitrogen dioxide concentrations and volume weighted mean concentration of nitrate ions in bulk precipitation in the southern Pennines are more than twice those found in comparable areas of North Wales (more remote from

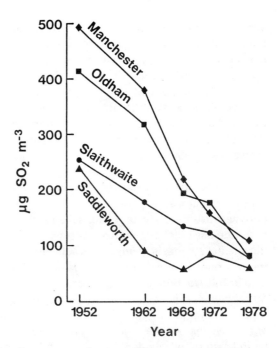

8.2   Some annual mean SO_2 concentrations (μg m^{-3}) in south Pennine towns in the period 1952–78. 1 μg SO_2 m^{-3} = 2.66 ppb SO_2. (Reproduced from Ferguson and Lee, 1983).

urbanization), and the difference in ammonium supply is even greater (Press *et al.*, 1986). The importance of the present atmospheric nitrogen supply as a factor affecting southern Pennine mires has been demonstrated by transplanting the aquatic *Sphagnum cuspidatum* from 'clean' Welsh sites into the southern Pennines. When the plants are grown in artificial bog pools isolated from the peat and receiving only atmospheric deposition, they rapidly accumulate tissue nitrogen (Figure 8.3) strongly

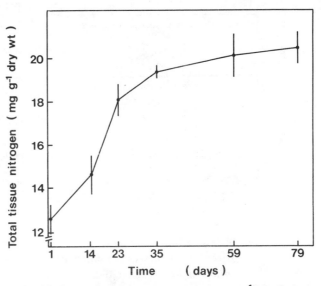

8.3   Total nitrogen concentration (mg g^{-1}) in Sphagnum moss (*Sphagnum cuspidatum*) transplanted from North Wales to the southern Pennines during March to June 1985. Vertical bars are standard errors. (Reproduced from Press *et al.*, 1986).

suggesting that the current atmospheric supply is supra-optimal to the growth of ombrotrophic species. This fact is supported by the presence of relatively high concentrations of tissue nitrogen in the relict southern Pennine *S. cuspidatum* populations and by the inhibition of *Sphagnum* growth in laboratory experiments by both nitrate and ammonium ions within the range of concentrations observed in precipitation in the southern Pennines (Press *et al.*, 1986).

The input of nitrate creates a special opportunity to measure physiological responses of plants to acidic deposition, because the enzyme responsible for the initial step of nitrate assimilation, nitrate reductase, is substrate inducible (ie. synthesis of enzyme is activated by the substrate, nitrate). In unpolluted areas, using this technique, it is possible to demonstrate a very close coupling of *Sphagnum* species to their atmospheric environment. In field experiments in an extremely remote site in sub-arctic Sweden, nitrate reductase acitivity was shown to be induced by nitrate additions to the mire surface, but more importantly was induced by natural precipitation events (Figure 8.4) with activity being proportional to ni-

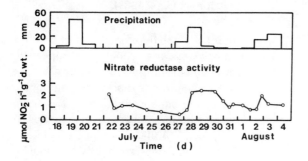

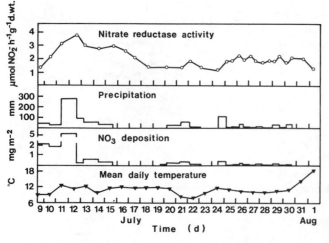

8.4 (a) Nitrate reductase activity in *Sphagnum fuscum* in relation to natural rainfall (mm), during a period in July/August 1983.

(b) Nitrate reductase activity in *Sphagnum fuscum* in relation to natural rainfall (mm), nitrate deposition (mg m^{-2}) and mean daily temperature (°C) during a period in July/August 1984. (Reproduced from Woodin *et al.*, 1985).

trate deposition. These data may suggest that many bryophyte and lichen species have a very close coupling with the atmospheric deposition to which, unlike higher plants, their photosynthetic tissues are directly and continuously exposed, and this may further help to explain their greater sensitivity to atmospheric pollutants. When *Sphagnum* species are transplanted from 'clean' Welsh sites to polluted sites in the southern Pennines this coupling of nitrate assimilation to the atmospheric supply is rapidly lost (Figure 8.5), and the southern Pennine relict

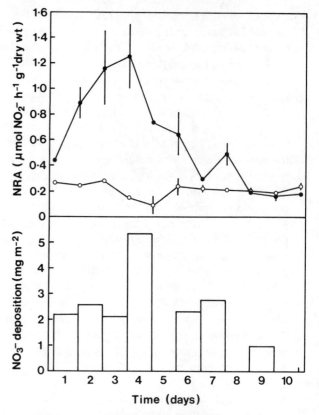

8.5 Nitrate reductase activity (NRA) in *Sphagnum cuspidatum* indigenous to the southern Pennines (O———O) and transplanted to the southern Pennines from an 'unpolluted' region (●———●) in relation to NO$_3^-$ deposition (mg m^{-2}) during a period in November 1984. Vertical bars are standard errors. (Reproduced from Lee *et al.*, 1987).

Sphagnum cuspidatum population, with its extremely high tissue nitrogen concentration, shows no response to nitrate deposition. This uncoupling is probably an attempt by the plant to prevent the assimilation of nitrogen to toxic concentration. The role of ammonium and even organic nitrogen (shown to represent as much as 36% of total nitrogen deposition in rain by Press *et al*, (1983)) should not be ignored as contributors to supra-optimal supplies of combined nitrogen.

Wet deposition is responsible for most of the nitrogen present in bulk precipitation samples and is the predominant form of deposition in most ombrotrophic mires. Deposition is often monitored in rain collected over 1 or 2 weeks, thus missing the episodic nature of precipitation. Even daily sampling can mask changes in solute concentration and deposition rates. In a comparison of half hourly and 24-hourly collections made in Manchester (Woodin, 1986), peak concentrations of nitrate and ammonium in the half hourly samples were far greater than those of daily samples. Solute concentrations within an event, in this study and elsewhere, are inversely related to rainfall rate (Asman and Slanina, 1980; Raynor and Hays 1982), probably due to less efficient scavenging by larger, faster falling raindrops. Peaks of nitrogen concentration tended to occur at the start and finish of rain events. Events ending in a light drizzle may leave a concentrated solution of nitrate and ammonium on the leaf surface which may be further concentrated by evaporation, possibly imposing physiological 'stress' on the photosynthetic tissue of plants such as mosses which lack cuticles. Concentrations of nitrate and ammonium in half hourly samples were highly correlated, emphasising that plants subject to a very high concentration of one are likely to be simultaneously subjected to a very high concentration of the other.

The southern Pennines not only have a high rainfall but are frequently covered by cloud and mist. The latter have been shown by various workers (Dollard *et al.*, 1983; Lovett *et al.*, 1982) to contribute considerably to total chemical deposition in areas of high elevation, although occult precipitation is not collected efficiently by conventional gauges. Lysimeters containing *Sphagnum capillifolium* from North Wales were placed on the bog surface of the southern Pennines next to bulk deposition collectors. Analysis of throughflow and bulk deposition showed that the moss immobilised most of the nitrate and ammonium, but sulphate and chloride passed through in amounts greatly in excess of bulk deposition almost every day (Table 8.1). The volume of the throughflow also exceeded precipitation on eight of the

thirteen wet days, most probably because of efficient trapping of occult precipitation. But to account for all the excess solute in throughflow occult precipitation must also have contained higher solute concentrations than bulk precipitation. Some evidence of the efficiency of *Sphagnum* in trapping occult deposition was provided by Woodin and Lee (1987) in experiments carried out on *S. fuscum* in Sweden. Nitrate solutions were applied to plots (0.3 m × 0.3 m) of *S. fuscum* in known volumes of distilled water and in different droplet sizes to give a received amount of 0.05 mM per plot. The nitrate reductase acitivity was measured during the 12 hours following treatment. Induction was found to be greater in all comparable treatments when the solution was applied as a fine spray (Figure 8.6). This evidence of the efficiency of

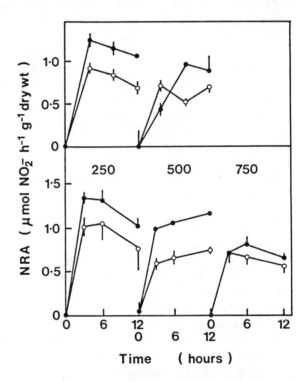

8.6 Nitrate reductase activity (NRA) in *Sphagnum fuscum* during 12 hours after fine mist (——●——) or large droplet (——○——) application of 250 cm³, 500 cm³ or 750 cm³ distilled water containing 0.05 mmoles of nitrate to plots of moss (0.3 m × 0.3 m). (Reproduced from Woodin *et al.*, in press).

Sphagnum in trapping mist droplets when combined with the fact that this form of deposition contains high concentrations of solutes suggests that polluted occult deposition may be particularly damaging to bryophytes. This may also help to explain the marked decline of *Racomitrium lanuginosum* which is a dominant species on mountain summits in other parts of Britain. This species also occurs in the drier parts of ombrotrophic mires, but like *Sphagnum* it has disappeared from this habitat in the southern Pennines since the Industrial Revolution (Tallis, 1987).

Table 8.1 Amounts of precipitation and solutes passing through *Sphagnum capillifolium* mats in the southern Pennines in relation to amounts collected in a bulk deposition gauge

	Ratio of 'throughflow' to 'bulk deposition'	
	Total (during 15 days)	Range (for daily samples)
Volume	1.45	0.42–3.26
SO_4^{2-}	3.79	0.91–13.01
Cl^-	1.95	0.41–5.47
NH_4^+	0.19	0.03–0.54
NO_3^-	0.13	0.03–0.53

Mountain summit vegetation in general may be particularly sensitive to the increasing atmospheric nitrogen supply. Higher plants in these communities are adapted to growth in cold, skeletal soils in which nitrogen mineralisation and nitrification are poor and where this element often limits plant growth. The increasing nitrogen supply could lower the frost resistance of some species, which would be particularly damaging in this habitat. No studies to substantiate this yet exist.

Experimental evidence for the effects of atmospheric pollutants on other British semi-natural vegetation is generally lacking, although Bell and his co-workers (see Grasslands section) have provided evidence for the evolution of tolerance to SO_2 in grass species from areas including the southern Pennines, suggesting the past importance of this gas as an ecological factor in ecosystems other than bogs. The small number of different plant species found in permanent grassland and woodland in the southern Pennine region may well reflect the sensitivity of the missing plant species to high concentrations of this gas. Pollutant exclusion and fumigation experiments in British semi-natural vegetation have been lacking. However fumigation experiments in German woodland (Steubing, et al., 1986) and a knowledge of past SO_2 concentrations suggest that this gas has been important in affecting the growth of plants beneath the trees in British woodlands close to urban and industrial centres.

The potential importance of NO_x and ozone on semi-natural communities must be inferred from either fumigation studies or from exclusion experiments in other countries. Growth in many boreal plant communities is limited by nitrogen supply, but few attempts have been made to assess whether the increase in atmospheric nitrogen supply is affecting plant growth, reproduction and survival. The effects on semi-natural communities of nitrogen from ammonia emissions from agricultural practices must also be assessed.

On the basis of extensive screening tests, Ashmore (1984) listed plant families in order of sensitivity to ozone. Papilionaceae proved most sensitive, Graminae and Brassicae intermediate and Compositae fairly resistant. Work is currently being carried out at Imperial College to identify relationships between susceptibility to ozone damage and type of habitat. Plants from calcareous and cultivated habitats appear to be more susceptible to acute doses of ozone than those from acid, nutrient-poor ones.

As described in Chapter 11, ozone pollution has been implicated in the forest decline of central Europe and is undoubtedly one of the causes of forest damage in both western and eastern USA. The effects of ozone on the forest ecosystem indigenous to the Blue Ridge Mountains of Virginia, USA, have been studied since the early 1970's (Duchelle et al., 1983). Open-top chambers have

been used in the Shenandoah National Park to show that ozone induced reductions in the height growth of native forest tree species and reduced foliar biomass growth of indigenous grasses, sedges and forbs mostly without visible injury symptoms. Several ozone episodes occurred each year lasting 1–3 days during which peak hourly ozone concentrations ranged from 80–100 ppb. Some species showed foliar symptoms, and a selection of these species were inspected in 1982 at twenty-four sites in Shenandoah National Park. A positive correlation between site elevation and vegetation injury was observed (Figure 8.7), consistent with the measurement of higher

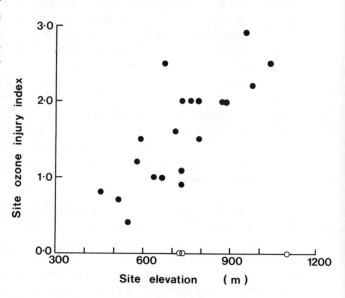

8.7   The relationship between site elevation and an index of foliar ozone-induced injury for 7 native species in the Shenandoah National Park of Virginia, USA (__O__ small sample). (Reproduced from Skelly et al., 1983).

ozone concentrations at high elevation sites (Unpublished Report 1983, cited in Skelly et al., 1983). Higher ozone concentrations at high altitude have been observed in West Germany and it is possible that these affect both productivity and diversity of plant species other than trees in these areas. In the UK ozone concentrations tend to be lower than those shown to affect plant growth in Virginia, USA (see Pollution Climate section), but the detection of ozone damage on sensitive crop cultivars in some recent summers by the workers at Imperial College (see section 5.4.3), raises the possibility that this gas may be affecting plants of similar sensitivity in some semi-natural ecosystems. This prospect is made all the more plausible when mixtures of gases are considered. Mooi (1984), in a fumigation study involving a mixture of NO_2, SO_2 and ozone at 20–30 ppb, showed marked reductions in the growth of the plantain Plantago major, whereas mixtures of NO_2 and ozone, and NO_2 and SO_2 caused only small reductions over the clean air controls. Exposure of the campion (Silene cucubalus) to

35 ppb ozone and to a mixture of 35 ppb ozone and 60 ppb SO_2 for 4 weeks resulted in reduced biomass and flowering (Ernst *et al.*, 1985). Allocation of photosynthates was strongly affected, undoubtedly leading to the inhibition of flowering. In further experiments, however, on five populations of campion (Dueck *et al.*, 1986), biomass was not reduced when NO_x (~60 ppb) was added to a mixture of ozone and SO_2 (~30 ppb) and exceeded that of the control in some populations. Much more investigation of British vegetation using exclusion experiments, fumigation experiments involving mixtures of pollutants (particularly NO_2, SO_2 and ozone), and interaction investigations between pollutant and physical (frost and drought) and biotic (insect damage) 'stresses' is required before generalisations on the effects of the changing nature of acidic deposition on most British semi-natural vegetation can be made.

8.3 CONCLUSIONS

1. In north and west Britain, semi-natural communities cover a large proportion of the total land surface. In south and east Britain, the areas of these communities are smaller, but they contain a rich range of species and therefore are of major conservation interest.

2. There has been speculation that changes in certain semi-natural communities are related to acid deposition, but only in studies of the southern Pennine blanket bogs has the role of acid deposition been tested experimentally in the field.

3. Blanket bogs are dominated by *Sphagnum* mosses which rely almost entirely on the atmospheric supply of elements for their growth. These bogs have shown to be particularly susceptible to the increased sulphur and nitrogen deposition that has occurred since the onset of the Industrial Revolution.

4. Apart from key studies on blanket bogs, little is known of the effects of increasing supply of the different forms of nitrogen including ammonia, on upland ecosystems. In many upland plant communities, growth is limited by the availability of nitrogen, but it is not clear whether the increase in atmospheric deposition of nitrogen compounds is affecting plant growth, reproduction, competition and survival.

5. In laboratory experiments, SO_2 concentrations comparable to urban winter concentrations suppressed yield of commercial grass varieties but had no effect on grasses from indigenous populations. The sensitivity of a wide range of native British plants to ozone has been investigated, showing that species differ markedly in tolerance to this gas.

9.1 INTRODUCTION

The protection of agricultural crops, horticultural produce and trees for amenity use and wood production from attack by pests and pathogens requires considerable financial resources. There is also pressure to minimise the impact of pesticides on non-target organisms in the natural environment. Consequently, effects of acid deposition and its related pollutants on plant pests and pathogens may have important economic and environmental consequences. This chapter reviews evidence of such effects. Evidence of effects of pollutants on vertebrate animals that consume vegetation is also surveyed.

9.2 EFFECTS ON FUNGI, BACTERIA AND VIRUSES

9.2.1 Fungi

Field observations

Many field observations have indicated that there are differences between the abundance of pathogenic fungi on vegetation in polluted and clean areas. In most cases, the observations were made around point sources of SO_2, where this pollutant is often accompanied by other phytotoxic gases and/or particulates. The evidence suggests that biotrophic pathogens are reduced or eliminated under such circumstances. For example, Scheffer and Hedgcock (1955) noted the absence of *Melampsorella cerastii, Melampsora albortensis*, and *Peridermium coloradense* from conifers around smelters in the USA, while Kock (1935) observed the absence of *Microsphaera alni* on oak (*Quercus* spp.) near point sources of pollution in Germany. There is also field evidence that urban air affects non-biotrophic pathogens, such as blackspot (*Diplocarpon rosae*), of rose (*Rosa* species) which was absent from urban areas of the UK in the past. Saunders (1966) showed by means of fumigation experiments that infection of rose plants by this pathogen was reduced when they were subjected to about 40 ppb SO_2 for 14 days immediately after inoculation of the host. With falling SO_2 levels in UK cities, blackspot has invaded urban areas, even appearing in central London. Other non-biotrophs, on the other hand, have been observed to be more abundant in SO_2-polluted areas, such as *Fusarium oxysporum* on pea, (*Pisum sativum*) (Szerszen, 1981) and the tree pathogens, honey fungus (*Armillaria mellea*), and white rot of pine (*Heterobasidion annosum*) (Grzywacz and Waxny, 1973). Non-pathogenic phylloplane yeasts have also been studied in the field in relation to SO_2 pollution, with both decreased (Dowding and Carvill, 1980) and increased (Lettl, 1983) incidence being observed.

In the case of ozone, field studies on fungi are extremely limited, probably because of the difficulty of establishing correlations with levels of an episodic pollutant which is not usually associated with individual point sources. However, increased infection has been observed in the field, by white rot of pine, on ozone-injured Ponderosa pine (*Pinus ponderosa*) (James et al., 1980), and by *Botrytis cinerea* on ozone-injured leaves of potato (*Solanum tuberosum*) (Manning et al., 1969). In both cases, similar results were found in controlled laboratory fumigation experiments.

Chamber filtration studies

Reports on the influence of ambient air pollution on fungal pathogens using chamber filtration studies are surprisingly limited. Information may be concealed in the unpublished observations of the numerous research workers who have carried out this type of experiment. However it is probable that in most cases fungicides were applied at an early stage of infection in order to minimise any possible confounding effects in experiments designed primarily to determine the impact of air pollution on the growth and yield of healthy plants. In addition, certain fungicides (eg. benomyl) are known to modify the effects of ozone on plants (see 10.6.3).

Controlled exposure experiments

There is a reasonably large number of reports of the effects of experimental fumigations on fungi (Heagle, 1973, 1982; Kvist, 1986; Shriner, 1980; Manning, 1975; Laurence et al., 1983; Saunders, 1973; Smith, 1976; and Babich and Stotzky, 1974). Almost without exception these were carried out in North America on pathogen-host systems which are of major importance there, although some of the diseases, eg. mildew (*Erysiphe graminis*) on barley, (*Hordeum vulgare*); grey mould (*Botrytis* species) on broad bean (*Vicia faba*); and crown rust (*Puccinia coronata*) on oat (*Avena sativa*) are a problem in the UK as well. In the case of SO_2 nearly all fumigations used high concentrations over short periods of time, so caution must be exercised in extrapolating these to ambient conditions in this country. For ozone, the situation is much more satisfactory, with experiments having been performed with concentrations as low as 100 ppb. When designing fumigation experiments, many workers have endeavoured to separate out direct effects on the fungus from indirect effects mediated via the host, by exposing plants to pollutants before and/or after inoculation. In a limited number of cases effects of pollutants on spore germination, mycelial growth and sporulation have been determined by means of *in vitro* experiments.

The response of biotrophic fungal pathogens to experimental fumigation with SO_2, or ozone has in nearly all cases been manifested as a reduced performance, whether it is assessed on the basis of decreased lesion numbers, hyphal growth, sporulation, or spore germination (eg. Laurence *et al.*, 1979; Hibben & Taylor, 1975). However, recent (unpublished) work at Imperial College has shown an increase in sporulation of mildew (*Erysiphe graminis*) on barley fumigated before and after inoculation with 22 ppb SO_2. In some cases, a greater effect was observed when the fumigation was done before inoculation, as in the work on SO_2 on bean rust (*Uromyces phaseoli*) of dwarf bean (*Phaseolus vulgaris*) (Weinstein *et al.*, 1975). This implies that the pollutant can act indirectly on the pathogen via the host, a phenomenon which Heagle (1973) believed was responsible for SO_2 reducing the incidence of fungal disease in the field. The complexity of field studies, where pollutant/pathogen interactions are also influenced by the weather, is discussed later in this section.

Unfortunately, it is not possible to make the same generalisations concerning the effects of air pollutants on non-biotrophic fungi. At one time, it was suggested that air pollution stimulated infection by non-biotrophs by providing sites for infection in the form of necrotic areas on the foliage. However, with increasing information from fumigation experiments, it is apparent that the situation is not so simple, with both inhibitory and stimulatory effects being observed. Thus SO_2 has been shown to decrease infection by blackspot on rose (Saunders, 1966), and southern corn leafblight (*Helminthosporium maydis*) on maize (*Zea mays*), (Laurence *et al.*, 1979), while it has resulted in an increased number of lesions caused by brown spot needle blight (*Scirrhia acicola*) on Scots pine, (*Pinus sylvestris*) (Weidensaul and Darling, 1979). Similarly, both types of effect are reported in the case of ozone, with a very confused picture being presented. Thus James *et al.* (1980) showed increased infestation and colonisation by white rot of pine, of ozone-fumigated Ponderosa pine and Jeffrey pine (*Pinus jeffreyi*) seedlings, but a decreased mycelial growth rate when the pathogen was subjected to a much lower ozone dose *in vitro*. Heagle (1977) showed that ozone-fumigation of maize before inoculation increased sporulation of southern corn leaf blight, but the reverse effect occurred when the ozone was administered under the same conditions after inoculation. The potential for ozone to affect the incidence of disease by direct effects on the pathogen has been shown by Hibben and Stotzky (1969) who found reduced germination of *Fusarium oxysporum*, *Verticillium albo-atrum*, and *V. dahliae* small hyaline cells after an *in vitro* fumigation, while Krause and Weidensaul (1978) found the same effect on the conidia of grey mould (*Botrytis cinerea*) on geranium, (*Pelargonium hortorum*) followed by decreased infection, when the ozone had been administered during sporulation. Currently, there is concern about reports from Germany that fungal pathogens that have been previously regarded as minor have increased in importance, apparently in parallel to the increase in ozone. Fehrmann

et al., (1986) have demonstrated experimentally that some of these (eg. *Fusarium nivale* and *Drechslera sorokiniana*) showed enhanced infection of wheat and barley that was previously fumigated with ozone.

There are some reports of yeasts and other non-pathogenic fungi of leaf surfaces being adversely affected by air pollutants, an example from the British Isles being pink leaf-surface yeast, (*Sporobolomyces roseus*) on ash (*Fraxinus excelsior*) whose colony numbers were negatively correlated with pollution levels in Dublin (Dowding and Carvill, 1980). Very recently, McLeod (1987) reported reduction in the growth of yeasts and in the germination and subsequent development of spores of other leaf-surface fungi, following fumigation *in vitro* with 50–200 ppb SO_2 for 24 hours. He postulated that such effects might be important in the field by altering the competitive balance with pathogenic fungi, which could explain changes in infection by the latter in response to SO_2 in open-air fumigation systems. Support for this view is provided by the demonstration by Hibben and Taylor (1975) that the non-pathogenic leaf surface fungus (*Hyalodendron album*) was less sensitive to either SO_2 or ozone than the biotrophic pathogen, powdery mildew (*Microsphaera alni*), to which it is antagonistic when growing on the foliage of lilac (*Syringa vulgaris*). Such interactions could have important economic implications and require further research.

9.2.2 Bacteria

There are only a few reports of the effects of air pollution on bacterial pathogens of plants (eg. Laurence and Aluisio, 1981; Laurence and Reynolds, 1982). These are all concerned with non-biotrophs, but in this case they consistently show reductions in the incidence of the disease. As in the case of fungal pathogens, indirect effects occur via the host tissues, as inhibition of diseases can occur on plants fumigated before inoculation. However, there is also evidence that the timing of the exposure to the pollutant is important, as SO_2 has been shown to have a greater effect on lesion enlargement of *Corynebacterium nebraskense* on maize when fumigated after inoculation (Laurence and Aluisio, 1981), while ozone caused a greater decrease in lesion numbers of *Xanthomonas fragariae* on strawberry (*Fragaria virginiana*) after a pre-inoculation fumigation. In the case of the symbiotic nitrogen-fixing bacteria, there is a report of reductions in their numbers in the nodules of legume roots, following ozone-fumigation of the shoots (Blum and Tingey, 1977).

Fungi, bacteria and acid rain

Until recently there were very few reports on the effects of simulated acid rain on fungi or bacteria. There now appears to be an upsurge in such research activity, as a result of the growing concern over the potential impacts of wet deposited pollutants. Interestingly, the limited number of experiments on fungal biotrophs have consistently shown inhibitory effects, and have been demonstrated for a foliar pathogen and two mycorrhizal species (Shriner, 1978; Feicht, 1981; Brewer and Heagle, 1983). In the case of non-biotrophic pathogenic fungi, acid rain has had an adverse effect in both *in vitro* and *in vivo* experiments (Campbell *et al.*, 1985; Martin *et al.*, 1985; Shafer *et al.*, 1985). As with gaseous pollutants, there is evidence that timing of the exposure is important for bacterial diseases. Shriner (1978) showed increased incidence of halo blight (*Pseudomonas phaseolicola*) on dwarf bean, (*Phaseolus vulgaris*) leaves when sprayed with acid rain before inoculation, but a decrease when the application was made after inoculation. However Bisessar *et al.* (1984) found a greater inhibition by acid rain, of development of bacterial speck (*Pseudomonas tomata*) on tomato (*Lycopersicon esculentum*) with post-than pre-inoculation treatments. It should be noted that in general, effects of acid rain have only been observed below pH 4.0, but in some cases the short duration of the treatments may result in these experiments being reasonably applicable to field conditions.

9.2.3 Viruses

The effect of SO_2 and ozone, separately, has been studied on a number of plant viruses (eg. Laurence *et al.*, 1981; Vargo *et al.*, 1978). A consistent pattern has been observed of different viruses protecting, partially or completely, a range of crop plants against ozone injury, although the mechanism for this is unknown. On the other hand, southern bean mosaic virus on dwarf bean and maize dwarf mosaic virus on maize, have been stimulated in their incidence on plants exposed to SO_2, either before or after inoculation (Laurence *et al.*, 1981).

9.2.4 Uncertainties

It is extremely difficult on the basis of current knowledge to make any definitive statement concerning the importance of effects of air pollution on fungi, bacteria, and viruses in the field. In his review of 1973, Heagle made the somewhat tautologous statement that 'little is known; much remains to be discovered'. Nine years later, a further review (Heagle, 1982) demonstrated an increased output of results from controlled fumigations which permitted him to make a number of generalisations on the subject, with some degree of confidence. Nevertheless, Heagle's original statement still stands, with enormous areas of ignorance remaining. In particular, many of the more important European plant diseases have not been studied. Furthermore, there is serious lack of knowledge of the impacts of prolonged chronic fumigations with the various ambient mixes of pollutants experienced in the UK, either post- or pre-fumigation. Indeed, there do not appear to be any reports on the effects of NO_x, either on its own or in combination with other pollutants. The mechanisms by which pollutants affect fungi, bacteria, and viruses are poorly understood

while almost nothing is known of interactions between the organisms themselves, environmental factors, and invertebrate pests. It would be valuable to study changes in the incidence of different types of pathogenic disease in relation to temporal and spatial changes in the concentration of various air pollutants.

9.3 EFFECTS ON PESTS

The effects of air pollution on insects and other invertebrates have received very little attention in most countries and, until recently, none at all in the United Kingdom. This is surprising in view of the enormous economic losses that occur to agriculture, horticulture, and forestry as a result of infestation by insect pests. Any effect, either positive or negative, of pollutants on such pests potentially has considerable economic significance. The available information has been reviewed in recent years by Alstad *et al.* (1982), Newman and Schreiber (1984), and Laurence *et al.* (1983).

9.3.1 Field observations

Evidence of changes in populations of invertebrates at polluted locations has been known for some time. For example, Wentzel (1965) reported a decrease in the population density of sawflies on Norway spruce (*Picea abies*) around point sources of pollution, while Wiackowski (1978) observed high populations of aphids around an SO_2 source in Poland. Both negative and positive changes have been observed at a single location, according to the species concerned. For example, Hillman (1972) found a decrease in numbers of parasitic Hymenoptera but an increase in aphid numbers around a source of SO_2 pollution. Villemant (1981) observed increases in some aphid species and decreases in others, with increasing levels of SO_2 and hydrogen fluoride in a Scots pine forest in France. In the case of these field observations, it has not been possible to relate changes in invertebrate populations to prevailing air pollution levels with any degree of precision because of the lack of reliable pollutant monitoring. In addition, other environmental factors may have a confounding influence. However, André *et al.* (1982) were able to show a positive correlation between the mortality of the mite (*Humerobates rostrolamellatus*) and winter ambient SO_2 levels at different sites in Brussels. Evidence that this was a causal relationship was, in this case, subsequently produced by André *et al.* (1984) who showed increasing mortality of the mite with increasing concentrations of SO_2 between 0 and 1600 ppb in fumigation experiments. In many cases it is extremely difficult to attribute effects observed on pests in the field directly to a particular pollutant or mixture of pollutants, as vegetation under any type of stress may be rendered more susceptible to insect attack. Furthermore, the mechanisms by which pollution might affect plant–invertebrate relationships are potentially very complex. They include changes in the attractiveness of plants to the animals, changes in plant food value or defence systems and direct impacts on the insects themselves or on their predators and parasitoids.

A number of field studies have been made on the incidence of various insects in relation to the proximity of major roads. These have produced evidence of increased abundance of aphids (Flückiger et al., 1978; Przybylski, 1979), leaf hoppers (Port, 1981), and Lepidoptera (Port and Thompson, 1980) near the carriageway. In this situation, it is particularly difficult to identify causal agents as a mixture of air pollutants is present, including nitrogen oxides, hydrocarbons, dusts, and lead, while other stresses occur such as turbulence from passing vehicles, deicing salt, and microclimatic changes associated with the presence of the road surface. However, studies in Switzerland on the performance of aphids in chambers located next to a motorway and ventilated with filtered or ambient air have shown a marked stimulation caused by the prevailing air pollution, in the number of Aphis fabae on Guelder rose (Viburnum species) (Braun and Flückiger, 1985). Nevertheless, it is still uncertain as to which pollutant(s) is/are responsible for these effects as the filter (charcoal and Purafil) effectively removed all phytotoxic gases, including NO and ethylene (C_2H_4).

9.3.2 Chamber filtration studies

So far as is known, there are only two published chamber filtration studies on the effects of ambient air on invertebrates, other than in the rather special case of motorway verges. These were performed with Aphis fabae on broad bean (Vicia faba) (Dohmen et al., 1984) and Macrosiphon rosi on rose (Dohmen, 1985) in London and Munich, respectively. In both cases, ambient summertime air, containing low concentrations of pollutants, significantly increased the performance of the aphids compared with those living in charcoal-filtered air. There is a clear requirement for further such studies in locations with different pollution climates, backed up by parallel fumigation experiments designed to elucidate the relative importance of the different pollutants in the ambient mix.

9.3.3 Controlled exposure experiments

The effects of air pollutants on invertebrates and the mechanisms responsible for these, can only be determined with certainty by controlled fumigation experiments. Such experiments have now been performed with SO_2, $SO_2 + NO_2$, ozone, $SO_2 +$ ozone and hydrogen fluoride. In most cases, herbivores have been studied, although there are a limited number of fumigations of other types of invertebrate, eg. ozone on house-flies (Beard, 1965; Levy et al., 1972).

The majority of experiments used pollutant concentrations which are above the long-term mean for rural and most urban areas of the UK, although the generally short duration of the experiments means they are reasonably relevant to conditions that can occur for short periods in the field. Both chewing and sucking organisms have been studied, in particular Mexican bean beetle (Epilachna varivestis) which is sensitive to several different pollutants when placed on previously fumigated foliage, thereby indicating that the effects are mediated via the plant itself. Sulphur dioxide produced increased feeding preference of larvae on dwarf bean (Phaseolus vulgaris) (Hughes et al., 1981) and soybean (Glycine max) (Hughes et al., 1982) as well as increasing growth rates and fecundity (Hughes et al., 1982; Hughes et al., 1983). In the case of hydrogen fluoride-fumigated dwarf bean plants, the results are contradictory, with both positive (Benepal et al., 1982) and negative (Weinstein et al., 1975) effects observed. Recently published work shows preferential feeding on soybean foliage previously fumigated with ozone (Endress and Post, 1985) but Hughes et al. (1985) have demonstrated that a short-term fumigation (24 h) of 24 ppb SO_2 had no effect on the weight gain of Mexican bean beetle larvae subsequently fed on the foliage. However, above this concentration there was an increasing weight gain up to 295 ppb SO_2 but this effect was diminished at still higher concentrations.

An increasing number of studies is being carried out into the effects of air pollution on British horticultural, agricultural and forestry aphid pests, with most of the evidence indicating an indirect effect via the plant rather than any direct impact on the insect itself. The results of these investigations are so far remarkably consistent, with increased growth rates observed after fumigation with SO_2 or NO_2 within a range of 18–260 ppb (Dohmen et al., 1984; McNeill et al., 1986; Warrington, 1987; Aminu-Kano and McNeill, 1988) but with reductions at higher concentrations or doses (Warrington, 1987). A concentration-dependent differential response has also been observed for gypsy moth (Lymantria dispar) whose larvae showed decreased feeding preference for white oak (Quercus alba) leaves previously fumigated with 90 ppb O_3, but increased preference at 150 ppb (Jeffords and Endress, 1984). A very recent experiment has shown a remarkably large effect on green spruce aphid with a very low SO_2 dose: Aminu-Kano and McNeill (1987) found a significant stimulation in mean relative growth rate when the aphids were placed on Norway spruce foliage previously fumigated with 99 ppb SO_2 for only 30 minutes. This suggests that infrequent, short-term incidents of SO_2 that occur in rural areas could have a marked impact on a pest. In this respect, it should be noted that the unexplained 'bent-top' disease of Sitka spruce, which is particularly prevalent in the South Wales coalfield, is normally accompanied by severe outbreaks of green spruce aphid. This adds weight to suggestions that air pollution may be involved in this phenomenon.

From studies on effects of low concentrations of ozone on bush bean (*Phaseolus vulgaris*), Rosen and Runeckles (1976) demonstrated a synergistic interaction between injury from ozone and greenhouse whitefly (*Trialeurodes vaporariorum*). Daily exposure (6 hours a day) of the bean plants to 20 ppb ozone produced no visible symptoms of injury but in the presence of whitefly, severe chlorotic symptoms were produced after 6 days. Plants similarly infested with whitefly but maintained in charcoal-filtered air showed no signs of injury (Figure 9.1).

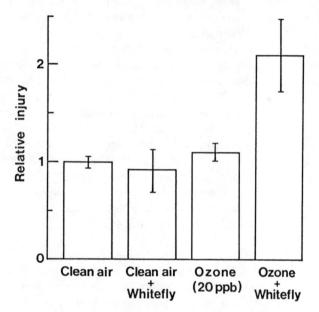

9.1 Leaf injury (relative to clean-air controls) on bush bean (*Phaseolus vulgaris* L. cv. Pure Gold Wax) exposed to ozone, whitefly and ozone and whitefly together (redrawn from data of Rosen and Runeckles, 1976). Injury was measured by a spectral reflectance method sensitive to chlorosis.

This interaction was observed at concentrations of ozone frequently found in ambient air. Thus damage to plants attributed to insect attack may be in part a response to low concentrations of pollutants such as ozone.

A few studies have been made on interactions between air pollutants and various nematode species. Shew *et al.*, (1982) fumigated tomato (*Lycopersicon esculentum*) infested with *Pratylenchus penetrans* and found that the nematode created some protection against reductions in shoot and root growth caused by 196 ppb ozone + 215 ppb SO_2. In the presence of the same concentration of ozone + 858 ppb SO_2 it increased the adverse effect of the pollutant on leaf growth, but decreased the pollutant-induced reduction in axillary shoot production. Other work has demonstrated both positive and negative effects of ozone and ozone + SO_2 on the performance of five different nematode species (Weber *et al.*, 1979). A particularly interesting study on the effects of nematodes as well as a number of other types

of invertebrate was carried out during the duration of the ZAPS (Zonal Air Pollution System) outdoor SO_2 fumigation programme. In this case a grassland in Montana was fumigated with a range of SO_2 concentrations up to 80 ppb over several growing seasons and changes in various components of the ecosystem were measured. In most cases, increasing SO_2 levels decreased the number of invertebrates, including tardigrades and non-stylet nematodes (Leetham, *et al.*, 1982), beetles, thrips, and Collembola (Leetham *et al.*, 1984), and grasshoppers (McNary *et al.*, 1981).

9.3.4 Pests and predators

Although there are some field data suggesting that parasitic insects may increase in the proximity of a source of SO_2 pollution (Hillman, 1972), there is almost no reliable information on effects of pollutants on parasitoids or predators which play an important role in regulating the population of potential insect pests. McNeill *et al.* (1986) and Aminu-Kano and McNeill (1988) have shown that increasing population numbers and growth rates of two grain aphids along a gradient of increasing SO_2 concentration in a field fumigation, was not associated with effects on predators or parasitoids. Nevertheless, it is vital to determine the interaction between pollutants, insect pests and their predators and parasitoids in order to understand the economic significance of air pollution for crop protection. In the case of organisms which have a very short generation time, even a small stimulation in performance may result in a pest escaping the control of its natural enemies (Lawton and McNeill, 1979). Furthermore, the effects of all these changes on final crop yield remain to be determined.

9.4 EFFECTS ON HERBIVORES

The pollutant that has been most thoroughly investigated with respect to vertebrates is fluoride. This is because for almost a century, point sources of gaseous and particulate fluorides, notably brick, steel, glass and phosphate works, potteries and aluminium smelters have presented a serious problem to dairy and beef farming. There are many reviews of the effects of fluorides available including the following: NAS (1974), Shupe *et al.*, (1983), and Wheeler and Fell (1983). In this review effects on man are specifically excluded.

Except in industrial environments, direct effects of fluoride on vertebrates other than man caused by inhalation are extremely unlikely to occur because the quantity taken in through the nose and retained is so small (WHO, 1984; Davison, in press). In the UK, most of the fluoride intake of vertebrates is obtained by ingestion of food. Thus the group at greatest risk is chewing herbivores such as cattle. Small quantities cause no harm, and may be beneficial, but an excess intake may cause symptoms that vary in severity from cosmetic effects on teeth to painful stiffness and lameness. If uncorrected, fluorosis may lead to serious economic loss. The symptoms and treatment are well known and fluorosis is preventable, by a combination of monitoring and good husbandry. It is largely reversible, but at some economic cost.

A survey of England in the 1960s (Burns and Allcroft, 1964) showed that there were very large areas of Yorkshire, Bedfordshire and Staffordshire where fluorosis made dairy farming impossible. Since then, the situation has undoubtedly changed and probably improved, because of industrial contraction, change in fuels and improved control technology, but there has not been a more recent survey to reassess the situation.

In contrast to the large amount of information on the effects of fluoride on farm animals, there is little on wild animals. Most publications report increased concentrations of fluoride in mammal bones (Kay et al., 1975a, b; Wright et al., 1978; EPA, 1980; Andrews et al., 1982; Walton, 1984, 1985, 1986) collected near sources, but none provide evidence of effects on populations or on species diversity. Moreover, there are few authentic reports of the characteristic symptoms of fluorosis in wild vertebrates, though recently Walton (1986 and in press) recorded typical effects on the teeth of moles trapped near an aluminium smelter.

Apart from fluoride, almost nothing is known about the significance of air pollution for terrestrial vertebrates other than man. Various studies in heavily polluted areas have resulted in observations on changes in the patterns of energy pathways through the vertebrate components of terrestrial ecosystems, eg. the extensive programme carried out in a forest in Poland, reported by Grodzinski et al. (1984). However, in such cases a whole range of pollutants was present, including heavy metals and it is impossible to make any meaningful statement about the importance of individual pollutants to extrapolate to polluted ecosystems elsewhere. The only long-term, controlled experiment on this topic was the ZAPS open air fumigation programme at Colstrip, Montana, where investigations were made into the responses of small mammals inhabiting a grassland exposed to a gradient of SO_2 (Chilgren, 1979), and of the potential impact of the latter on ruminants via changes in plant quality (Leetham et al., 1984). Trapping experiments over two summers showed that deer mouse (Peromyscus maniculatus) apparently responded to SO_2 treatment. Larger numbers of adults were trapped and greater animal activity was observed on the control plots, compared with plots in which mean SO_2 concentrations ranged between 34 and 133 ppb. In contrast, no conclusive results were obtained for prairie voles (Microtus ochrogaster), the other common small mammal present. The mechanisms by which SO_2 may have caused changes in the behaviour of the deer mouse remain obscure, but Chilgren (1979) suggested that irritation of the respiratory system may have taken place, particularly as a result of higher concentrations occurring during nocturnal temperature inversions.

Leetham et al. (1984) considered the results of the ZAPS investigations in terms of possible impact on wild and domesticated ruminants which are ecologically and economically important on the local grasslands. They noted that increased levels of sulphur in forage can interfere with the digestion of ruminants via toxic effects on rumen micro-organisms, although the latter can also be stimulated under circumstances when they utilise the sulphur for amino-acid synthesis. However, over 3 years of exposure, the elevated sulphur levels in couch-grass (Agropyron smithii) arising from the ZAPS fumigations did not affect its digestibility for ruminants. A further secondary effect of changes in plant chemistry was a reduction in selenium uptake at high SO_2 levels, leading to the possibility of deficiencies of selenium in ruminants. High sulphur concentrations in forage may also lead to copper deficiency in ruminants (Suttle, 1974). Leetham et al. (1984) pointed out that increased rates of leaf senescence caused by SO_2 may reduce the nutritional value of forage as the proportion of dead-to-green material rises.

9.5 CONCLUSIONS

1. Considerable resources are spent on the control of pests and pathogens in agriculture and forestry. Consequently any interactions between those organisms and pollutants are a matter of concern.

2. Primary plant pathogens were previously thought to be affected only by large concentrations of pollutants but recent work (eg. on field exposure of cereals) has shown that prolonged exposure to concentrations commonly found in rural areas may decrease the incidence of some pathogens. In contrast, decreases in urban pollution concentrations have led to the appearance of diseases such as black spot of roses, which were formerly controlled by the presence of SO_2.

3. Controlled exposure to ambient concentrations of SO_2 and/or NO_2 in the field and laboratory has been shown to stimulate some plant pests such as aphids. In controlled exposure experiments, growth rates of pests are significantly increased by very low concentrations of gaseous pollutants and by brief exposures at higher concentrations. Both types of exposure are likely in the field, and so these responses may be of considerable importance for influencing the occurrence of pest damage.

4. Little is known of the effects of pollutants on predators and parasites that have an important natural role in controlling pest population.

5. The hazards that fluoride deposition on grass poses to grazing cattle are well known, but pathways of fluoride into wild animals are still unclear. Apart from studies of fluoride, very little is known of the significance of air pollution to terrestrial vertebrates, excluding man.

INTERACTIONS BETWEEN AIR POLLU-TANTS AND OTHER ENVIRONMENTAL FACTORS 10

10.1 INTRODUCTION

In nature, plants live in a taxing and constantly varying environment. They must compete with other individuals for essential space, light, nutrients and water and contend with drought, frost, wind and the ravages of pests and diseases as well as air pollution. Chapter 4 emphasised the importance of the study of biochemical and physiological effects of pollutants in understanding the overall plant response to pollutant exposure (cf. Figure 4.1) and touched on the interactions which may occur between pollutant and other stresses. Chapter 9 showed how exposure to pollutants can alter the incidence of plant pests and pathogens, stress factors of considerable importance. This chapter reviews the effects of exposure to pollutants on plant responses to other environmental factors and the ways in which these factors may modify plant responses to pollutant exposure. A schematic representation is shown in Figure 10.1. Some environmental factors may modify the absorption of pollutants into the leaf whereas others modify the response of the plant to the absorbed pollutant. Conversely, sensitivity to stresses such as drought, frost, nutrient deficiency and metal mobility (increased by effects of pollutants on soil) may be modified by pollution-induced changes in the plants. Such changes may also predispose the plant to damaging effects of biotic stresses such as pests, pathogens, grazing and trampling. The modifying effects of winter stress, light, water and agricultural chemicals are described in some detail below.

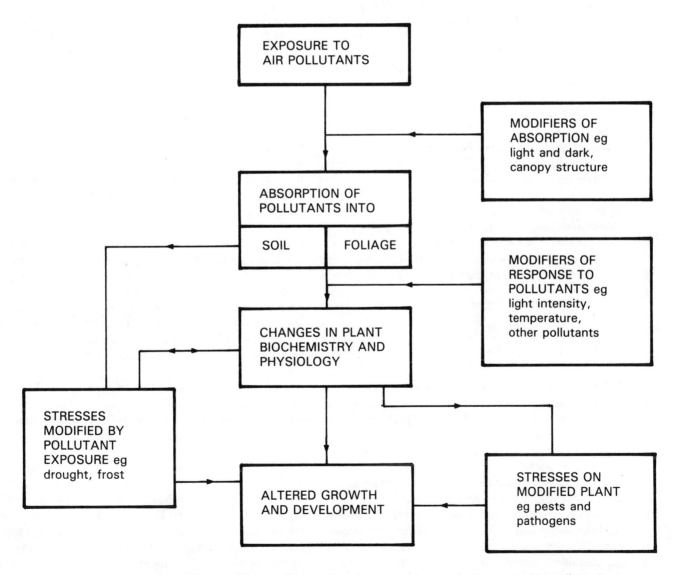

10.1 Scheme to show possible modifying effects of various stresses on plants exposed to pollutants.

10.2 MINERAL NUTRIENTS

Plants require a balanced supply of over a dozen essential elements in varying quantities during their life-cycle in order to survive, grow and reproduce. The soil, which is the source of these nutrients for most plants, may also contain elements that are potentially toxic, such as aluminium (see Chapter 3.1). In areas where the land is intensively managed, fertilisers and liming are used to optimise nutrient concentrations so variation in the supply to the crop is minimised. However, the major part of the land mass of the UK is not fertilised annually, if ever, so the nutrient supply is much lower and very variable. This area includes land of major amenity and scenic value, most of the nature reserves, hedgerows and woodland. In many instances, the whole character of the vegetation of such 'unimproved' areas depends upon the fact that levels of the major nutrients are low. Addition of even small quantities of a major nutrient (eg. nitrogen) may cause dramatic changes in the floristic composition.

Variation in the supply of nutrients may either increase or decrease the direct effects of gaseous pollutants, depending upon the nutrient in question and the circumstances. Conversely, wet and dry deposition of SO_2 and NO_x leads to an increase in soil sulphur and nitrogen. It also alters soil acidity, mineralisation processes and leaching of nutrients from canopies, effects which are most significant in the agriculturally 'unimproved', or wilderness areas. To complicate the position further, pollutants and mineral nutrition both affect survival of plants exposed to frost and drought and they modify plant relations with pests and diseases.

As the complex interactions between pollution and mineral nutrition impinge on so many aspects of this review and in order to avoid repetition, they are discussed at appropriate points in this and other chapters (see Chapters 3, 8, 11) rather than in greater detail in this section.

10.3 WINTER STRESS

10.3.1 The nature of winter stress

The stresses experienced during winter by most natural ecosystems and many crops are important factors limiting species distribution and agricultural productivity. Native species have various degrees of resistance to these stresses and crops are selected or bred for resistance to extend their useful geographical or altitudinal range. Nevertheless, severe winters or out-of-season frosts may cause transient changes in photosynthesis, water deficit, loss of reserves, or disruption of cell membranes. These may then lead to short-term loss of yield or biomass, leaf necrosis or the death of the plant. Cereals, pasture grasses, ornamental species, and fruit or forest trees may all be affected to various degrees.

Frost injury is brought about by the formation of extracellular ice, which may result in leakage of solutes, loss of turgor, denaturation of proteins and cell death. Membrane damage is believed to be a primary event in frost injury. This is of great significance because all the major pollutants and free radicals generated during their metabolism, are known to injure specific components of membranes (see Chapter 4). In particular, pollutants affect the proteins (Tingey and Taylor, 1982; Mudd et al., 1984) which play an essential role in the transport of ions and solutes and in osmotic regulation. The unsaturated fatty acids within membranes are also affected (Mudd, 1982) and this might be expected to alter frost resistance because changes in these components are considered to be important in cold acclimation (Cossins, 1983).

Pollutants may have other effects by disturbing the normal seasonal rhythm of 'hardening', dormancy and growth that is essential for survival and maximum productivity of crops, or by altering the partitioning of reserves. Hardening involves radical changes in metabolism and in membrane properties. A pollutant-induced reduction in photosynthesis, with its consequent effects on carbohydrate metabolism and concentrations of compatible solutes, together with an increased 'stress' respiration (Huttunen et al., 1983) would be expected to reduce frost hardiness (Alden and Hermann, 1971). It has recently been shown that cells of grass leaves are considerably larger in plants exposed to SO_2 and NO_2, and that they have stiffer walls and lower solute concentrations (Mansfield et al., 1986). This combination would be expected to affect survival adversely in winter. In addition, the short days and low irradiance in winter reduce resistance to pollutants (Bell et al., 1979; Jones and Mansfield, 1982).

In the long term, increased nitrogen input from wet and dry deposition might be of significance to winter survival. High nitrogen, particularly if applied late in the season, and coupled with low potassium, can seriously reduce the frost resistance of both grasses and trees, by apparently prolonging growth and so delaying the induction of frost hardiness or dormancy (Treshow, 1970; Koskela, 1970; Soikkeli and Karenlampi, 1984).

Where evergreens are concerned, winter desiccation is as important a facet of winter injury as frost injury. With a decrease in temperature the mobility of water decreases because of higher viscosity and lower cytoplasmic permeability. Thus low temperature in the soil or conducting tissues may lead to reduced transport or interruption of the supply of water, and eventually to a water deficit. Desiccation occurs frequently when there are cold, drying winds and when there are rapid changes in air temperature. Such injury is frequently seen in evergreen plants that are not covered by snow but it also occurs in deciduous species. The most recent large scale winter desiccation event in the UK occurred in 1986 when a period of cold winds in February caused severe damage to frost-hardy conifers such as yew and spruce. Herbaceous crops were unaffected. Resistance to winter desiccation resides largely in closure of the stomata and low conductance of the cuticle. In spruce, there is a decrease in stomatal conductance during the winter that reduces transpiration to a fraction of summer-time values (Tranquillini, 1982). Cuticle characteristics are therefore vitally important in determining resistance to winter desiccation. It is well established that pollutants impair stomatal function (Black, 1982; see Chapter 4) and accelerate the weathering of cuticular waxes (Fowler et al., 1980; Huttunen and Laine, 1981; Cape and Fowler, 1981) and it is therefore possible that in polluted atmospheres, resistance to winter desiccation is decreased.

Bleaching of the leaves is common in some conifers during the winter (Linder, 1972). This appears to be due to low temperature and high irradiance leading to photodestruction of chlorophyll by free radicals generated by 'over-excited' chloroplast membranes. Any pollutant taken up in winter would be expected to exacerbate this destruction of photosynthetic pigments. It has been suggested that this might be a contributory factor in the chlorosis of the upper surfaces of spruce shoots which is a symptom shown by declining forest trees in West Germany (Davison and Barnes, 1986).

10.3.2 Field observations relating to pollutants and winter injury

There have been many reports in the last twenty years of field observations pertaining to the effects of pollution in winter. Some of the first were those of Materna and Kohut (1963), and Materna (1974) who concluded that exposure of Norway spruce to long-term mean concentrations greater than 7 ppb SO_2 increased the susceptibility to frost damage and led to die-back. Sensitivity increased with altitude and he postulated that the injury was an integrated effect of air pollution and other stresses. Materna's results may have been influenced by the occurrence of large peaks of SO_2 concentration from time to time and by the possible presence of other pollutants. Consequently they may not be applicable to the UK situation.

In Finland, winter and pollution injury have been closely examined in conifers growing around industrialised towns where there is a complex mixture of pollutants. Visible injury of conifers was noticed where there were emissions of SO_2, NO_x and hydrogen flouride, (Havas, 1971; Havas and Huttunen, 1972) and it was observed that chronic damage which became visible in spring, originated in winter. The most detrimental damage occurred after hard winters (Havas and Huttunen, 1980). Parts of trees which were covered by snow did not develop symptoms (Huttunen, 1978). Measurements of osmotic potential, pH, buffering capacity, conductivity and sugar content of spruce showed that pollution affected physiological characteristics associated with frost resistance (Huttunen, et al., 1981). Some combinations of SO_2, NO_x and hydogen flouride appeared, therefore, to reduce resistance to winter stress. Finnish workers have also shown from recordings of water content, transpiration and water potential in pine needles, that more intense winter water stress occurred in polluted areas (Huttunen, Havas and Laine, 1981). The stress was ascribed to effects of pollutants on stomatal function and to erosion of wax (Huttunen et al., 1981; Huttunen, 1973, 1975; Huttunen and Laine, 1981). Accelerated erosion of needle surfaces in polluted atmospheres has been shown by other workers for a variety of species. Although pollutant-winter injury of this type has been described mostly in evergreen species, Huttunen (1974) observed damage in buds of deciduous trees.

There are few observations of the reaction of herbaceous species to ambient air pollution in the winter, other than old reports from heavily polluted conurbations that are not very relevant to present day conditions. However, Bleasdale (1952) showed that plants grown overwinter in Manchester were smaller in polluted areas and implied that pollution affected winter hardiness. In the 1970's Matthews (1981) and Young and Matthews (1981) used pot-grown peas (Pisum sativum cv. Alaska) placed at different sites for a standard period to study seasonal variation in the effects of air pollution in north-east England. There was great variation in the extent of visible injury both between sites and at different seasons. The symptoms were identical to those produced by fumigation with SO_2. It was concluded that the injury was primarily caused by SO_2 and that there was a complex temperature interaction. Between October and April severe necrosis was produced within two weeks of exposure at all of the polluted sites, but in summer there was no necrosis, even though SO_2 concentrations were similar to those in winter. At the least polluted site, plants withstood a frost of $-10°C$ without injury. Recent filtration experiments at Ascot, Berkshire and Kew, London have shown that frost sensitivity can be increased by ambient air pollution (Ashmore et al., 1988). During February, 1986 low temperature ($-12°C$) resulted in frost damage to clover (Trifolium pratense). Plants growing in chambers with unfiltered air had significantly more frost damage than those in filtered air chambers.

Forest decline is discussed in detail elsewhere in this review but the involvement of winter stress is also appropriately discussed here. It has been suggested that forest decline is caused by combinations of stress factors (see Chapter 11) with ozone playing a major role in the syndrome. Physical stresses in the form of drought and frost feature prominently in these theories. The evidence for an involvement of physical stress is compelling, as the die-back has coincided with a decade or more of drought years and harsh winters and at high altitudes there is generally greater winter stress. The decline spread following harsh frosts in 1980 and 1983, which often occurred after mild weather (Rehfuess, 1986). Further evidence for the involvement of frost is provided by Rehfuess and his colleagues who have observed that frost injury in an affected stand in spring was restricted to branches that were chlorotic (*ibid*). Needles of spruce showing the characteristic chlorosis exhibit lower raffinose and starch content which might reduce frost resistance (Bosch *et al.*, 1983). Support for an involvement of gaseous pollutants and winter stress also comes from the fact that in forest damage areas it is only the trees that appear to be affected. Injury has not been reported in shrubs and herbaceous species that are beneath the snow in winter, even though some are known to be pollution sensitive (Prinz, *et al.*, 1985).

Similar ideas are being expressed in the USA in relation to forest decline in the eastern states. Puckett (1982), using dendroecological methods to analyse several species in New York, found that the response to temperature and precipitation was greater in recent years than in the past. The suggestion was made that the added stress of air pollution caused this change in response to climate. Recently it was reported (Friedland *et al.*, 1984) that needles of red spruce (*Picea rubens*) in the Green Mountains are prone to browning and defoliation due to frost or winter desiccation. The authors concluded that winter stress contributes to the later stages of the decline of the species. Furthermore, the authors suggested that, because foliar nitrogen concentrations and mortality increase with altitude (Johnson and Siccama, 1983, 1984), deposited nitrogen may have initially prolonged growth, thus delaying cuticle development and carbohydrate conversion so that the trees were not fully hardened. However, Johnson and Siccama (1984) showed that there was little or no difference between the nitrogen content of fine roots or needles of red spruce in 'poor' and 'good' condition. Whether rates of nitrogen deposition are sufficiently high to reduce resistance to winter stress significantly remains an open question.

10.3.3 Controlled exposure to pollutants

Comparatively few controlled exposure experiments have been done during the winter months or have involved exposure of plants to pollutants and low temperature. Most of the authors who have fumigated grasses or trees over the winter months in chambers that attempt to simulate ambient conditions have reported effects on growth, but none mention winter injury or an effect on survival during the winter (reviewed in Davison and Barnes, 1986). However, this is not evidence that interactions do not occur, because the temperature in most of the chambers was elevated by at least 1°C and much of the work was done in areas of Britain with a mild climate.

Keller (1978a, b; 1981) was one of the first to demonstrate that fumigation with a pollutant may reduce frost

resistance. He exposed young spruce to SO_2 in cabinets out of doors and found increased frost sensitivity in spring (Figure 10.2). This was confirmed by Feiler *et al.*,

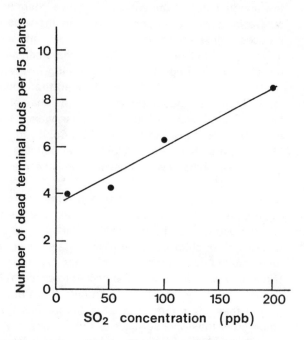

10.2 Numbers of dead terminal buds after exposure of dormant seedlings of beech (*Fagus sylvatica*) to different concentrations of SO_2 from December to April. (Reproduced from Keller, 1978).

(1981) who showed that SO_2 led to greater electrolyte leakage and concluded that SO_2-treated spruce were unable to regulate membrane permeability. Davison and Bailey (1982) working with ryegrass (*Lolium perenne*) similarly found that exposure to 94 ppb SO_2 predisposed plants to freezing injury (Figure 10.3). The effect depended on the nutritional status of the plants, being greatest with high nitrogen and sulphur in the soil. Subsequently, the same team showed (in Davison and Barnes, 1986) that freezing resistance was reduced by exposure to SO_2 for only two weeks during the hardening phase of the experiment and that one of the effects of the pollutants was to increase potassium leakage from the tissues. In the same experiment there was an interactive effect of sub-zero temperature and SO_2 on post-freezing growth of the roots. The effect of SO_2 on root growth, but not shoot growth, was greater at the higher sub-zero temperatures. Winter wheat (*Triticum aestivum* cv. Bounty) has also been shown to be more susceptible to frost when exposed to SO_2 (Baker *et al.*, 1982). In an experiment in which it was exposed throughout its growth in an open field system, severe leaf injury appeared in exposed plants after a period when temperatures fell to −9.2°C following a mild spell. The authors concluded that the damage was due to a reduction in frost resistance caused by the pollutant.

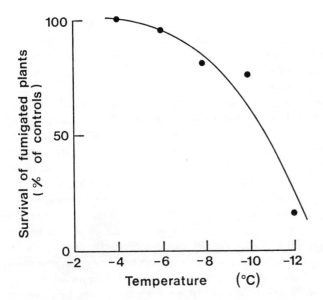

10.3 Survival of SO₂-treated ryegrass (*Lolium perenne*) after exposure to sub-zero temperatures. Pre-fumigation with 87 ppb SO₂ lasted for 5 weeks. (Reproduced from Davison and Bailey, 1982. Reprinted by permission from Nature, Vol. 297, pp 400–402. Copyright © Macmillan Magazines Limited).

Evidence for an interaction between cold stress and ozone in Norway spruce has recently been produced (Brown *et al.*, 1987). Following a November frost, visible injury occurred on the older needles of three clones which had been continuously exposed to 100 ppb ozone during the summer, 47 days previously. These results provide some evidence to support the hypothesis that forest decline may be caused by an ozone enhancement of frost sensitivity (see Chapter 11).

10.3.4 The significance of interactions between pollution and winter injury

Taking into consideration the known effects of pollutants on the physiological and morphological attributes of plants that contribute to winter hardiness, the many field observations in Europe and the few experimental investigations that have been reported, there is good evidence that pollutants may affect plant response to winter stress. However, the significance of such an interaction will differ with different crops. For example, there are three features of annual crops such as cereals that suggest that pollution effects on their hardiness may be less important than for some others.

i) Because the leaves are ephemeral, effects on the cuticle and cuticular transpiration may be relatively unimportant.

ii) It is known that cereals can compensate for injury if it occurs early in the season so that no effect may be discernible at harvest.

iii) There is the practical point that cereal cultivars are continuously replaced because of the breeding of higher yielding or more disease resistant types. New cultivars are tested rigorously in different parts of Europe, many of which are polluted and cold, so the testing may inadvertently select in favour of varieties with resistance to the combined stresses.

Pasture species may be protected during some of the winter by snow cover but they are still exposed in autumn and spring, the most dangerous times of the year for frost effects. Most forage grasses are obligate outbreeders so cultivars exhibit a broad range of genetic variation. Consequently, natural selection occurs in response to the prevailing environmental conditions, including air pollution (Roose *et al.*, 1982). Davison and Bailey (1982) suggested that a frost-pollution interaction might result in sensitive individuals being killed during the winter, therefore promoting selection. Similarly, Wilson and Bell (1985) suggested that rapid selection for acute SO₂ tolerance in grasses in a Manchester park may have been due to an SO₂/frost interaction. If selection is rapid, then the effects of pollution on grass performance may be transient but much more needs to be learned about the interplay between atmospheric pollution on competition and the community dynamics of swards. Few of the experiments on pasture species have used combinations of species or had realistic management regimes in the form of cutting or grazing. None have involved two- or three-year-old swards. Because they affect resource allocation and the physical structure of swards, these factors affect the ability of plants to withstand winter stress and probably pollution. For example, the winter hardiness of ryegrass is affected by spacing and the height and density of the sward in autumn so the timing of the last cut could alter the effects of environmental stresses.

Perennial, evergreen species that are exposed above snow are at greatest risk from the combined effects of pollution and winter stress. Trees are particularly vulnerable because, even when there is genetic variation within the population, the longevity of the individuals and the long juvenile period before seed is produced result in there being little chance of the population adapting to circumstances that change rapidly. For this reason, there should be some concentration of research effort on effects of interactions between pollutants and winter stress on trees.

10.4 LIGHT

Light quantity and duration appear to be important modifiers of plant responses to stress imposed by a number of pollutants, with light regimes prior to and during fumigation having the capacity to influence plant sensitivity. Research has identified this interaction at various levels of organisation, not only in short term exposure to pollutants in controlled environments designed to examine physiological and biochemical effects (Black 1982) but also in longer term laboratory and field experiments to elucidate effects of pollutants on growth and yield (Mansfield *et al.*, 1986). Despite evidence that light may increase and decrease plant sensitivity to pollutants, its modes of interaction are not well understood. In addition, exposure to low concentrations of pollutants which elicit no visible plant response may predispose plants to subsequent environmental stresses.

Several hypotheses have been proposed to explain light induced modification of plant responses to pollutants, involving stomatal, respiratory and carbon fixation and allocation processes. A major theory is that light may modify plant sensitivity to pollutants by influencing stomatal behaviour and thus pollutant uptake by the plant. It is generally accepted, for example, that plants are more sensitive to SO_2 and ozone when stomata are open as compared to closed and that the degree of stomatal opening influences the responses observed. For example, Coyne and Bingham (1982) reported greater visible damage to pine trees when these were polluted with ozone in high light as distinct from low light, an effect they attributed to larger stomatal conductances of high light plants. In contrast, this type of interaction was not observed in shaded and unshaded soybeans (*Glycine max*) polluted with ozone in open top chambers in the field (Heagle and Letchworth, 1982). These apparently conflicting observations may not be incompatible. Guderian (1985) suggested that while high light intensity during exposure may result in enhanced injury in the short term, subsequent sensitivity may be reduced in longer exposures, an example of the complex and dynamic nature of plant:pollutant:environment interactions. Thus although it is accepted that stomata may modify plant responses, their role in determining plant sensitivity to long term exposures has not been satisfactorily elucidated.

Additional evidence for the complex nature of the modifying influence of light was provided by Dugger *et al.* (1962), who observed that light regimes prior to exposure could have a significant effect on the susceptibility of tobacco (*Nicotiana tabacum*) plants to ozone and Menser *et al.* (1963) who found that conditions of high light during growth reduced plant sensitivity to this pollutant. In addition, Davis and Wood (1973) found that a pre-exposure treatment with 24 hours of light protected plants from visible injury, but post-exposure light treatment damaged polluted plants.

Although SO_2 and ozone may have greater physical effects when irradiances are high and stomatal conductances and pollutants fluxes are maximal, modification of plant responses to pollutants cannot be explained purely by short term changes in stomatal aperture. This conclu-

sion is particularly applicable to NO_x which has the capacity to enter leaves via the cuticle, a pathway not subject to stomatal control (Lendzian, 1984). Thus, although stomatal closure in response to light may reduce NO_x flux into the plant, damage or injury may not be precluded. Indeed, plants polluted with NO_x in the dark may exhibit a greater sensitivity than those polluted in the light (Amundson *et al.*, 1982). Zeevaart (1976) proposed that this differential sensitivity may result from the formation of different conversion products of NO_x under the two light regimes. In the light, NO_x may be converted to useful amino acids and proteins, whereas in the dark, products such as nitrous and nitric acids may be produced, leading to greater damage and sensitivity. Such observations would indicate that light:pollutant interactions are complex and are not mediated solely by stomatal behaviour, but also by factors such as the requirement for ATP or reducing power to drive the enzymatic processes of nitrogen metabolism (Lea and Miflin, 1974, also see Chapter 4).

An alternative hypothesis is that environmental conditions prior to and during exposure may predispose plants to pollutant stress via modification of the amounts of metabolic intermediates which are vital to the processes which repair pollutant damage. For example, Mansfield and Jones (1985) and Jones and Mansfield (1982b) have proposed that enhanced sensitivity shown by plants exposed to pollutants in low light or short photoperiods may result from low photosynthetic rates, a reduced store of carbohydrates and thus a reduction in repair capacity. This reduction may be reflected by the observed lack of respiratory stimulation in plants exposed to SO_2 in low light as compared with higher light intensities.

Other workers (eg. Koziol and Jordan, 1978) have also implicated carbohydrates in the sensitivity of plants to pollutants, but these workers have observed that loading of leaves with carbohydrates, either artificially or via a long light treatment, enhanced damage on exposure to pollutants. However, these conclusions were based on responses of plants to pollutants under conditions where light was limiting but temperatures were relatively high. Clearly, to examine plant responses to winter stress, plants need to be polluted under conditions of high and low irradiance but at low temperatures.

Further illustration of the difficulties involved in the interpretation light:pollutant interactions was provided by Carlson (1979). He observed that foliar injury was exhibited by ash (*Fraxinus* species) and maple (*Acer* species) trees only when these were polluted with combinations of SO_2 and ozone under high light, whereas photosynthetic reductions were observed at high and low but not intermediate intensities, suggesting that maximum physiological damage may occur at two contrasting light regimes. Carlson and Bazzaz (1985) hypothesised that these responses were due to multiple action of pollutants on plants. Low irradiance damage could result from reduced energy for repair, while at high irradiance, enhanced damage could be mediated via an increased production of reactive oxygen species. Carlson's work also illustrates that the degree of plant sensitivity depended on the process under investigation and that effects on physiological processes may not necessarily be reflected in growth or injury.

There is good evidence that increased sensitivity to pollutants is observed in plants, in particular grasses grown under conditions of limited growth, such as winter (Bell et al., 1979), low light or short period (eg. Jones and Mansfield, 1982b; Mansfield and Jones, 1985). The enhanced responses to pollution that these workers observed under these environmental conditions have been attributed to low reducing power and reduced ability to detoxify SO_2 (Davies, 1980). Mansfield et al., (1986) concluded that if rates of photosynthesis are limited by light and are insufficient to provide the respiratory substrate necessary, repair does not take place and photosynthesis and possibly growth are reduced. They do propose, however, that if plants can compensate following stress, effects on growth and yield need not necessarily result. Indeed these workers have observed compensation by polluted plants via investment in photosynthetic material such that specific leaf area and leaf ratio increase at the expense of root growth. This strategy is sound only as long as water or nutrients are not limiting.

A similar alteration in resource allocation under light limited and polluted environments has been shown for birch (Betula species) trees (Freer-Smith, 1985). By virtue of their long life span and their prolonged exposure to pollutants, trees are likely to exhibit effects of reduced root growth, especially when grown on nutrient poor, shallow or dry soils. Indeed light:pollutant interactions have been implicated in the 'light and air' theory of forest decline (Prinz et al., 1982, 1985) in which high light intensity is considered to act as a trigger factor, leading to the development of chlorosis on the upper surface of branches and needles of trees growing at altitude in Europe. It is thought that ozone in the presence of high light leads to the production of toxic free radicals, photooxidation of chlorophyll and damage to membranes and cuticles. These effects are thought to be exacerbated by the action of acid mists, prevalent at altitude, which leach out vital nutrients, resulting in a decline in vigour and an increased susceptibility to disease and cold. An alternative explanation for the observed yellowing of the upper surface of needles has been proposed by Mies and Zöttl (1985) who believe that these symptoms need not arise from the direct action of pollutants on chlorophyll photo oxidation but via an indirect chain of events. They propose that exposure to pollutants results in a reduction in magnesium and chlorophyll content, leading to nutrient and chlorophyll deficiency in older needles when magnesium is preferentially allocated and translocated to younger leaves. This deficiency enhances sensitivity to high light intensity in the upper portions of older leaves. If trees which are damaged by these high light:pollutant interactions also exhibit changes in resource allocation when conditions are light limited, significant adverse consequences must result.

These observed interactions between plant responses to pollutants and the light environment are of great relevance to the British climate. Combinations of pollutants and light stress occur commonly in winter when many of our major crops are at the young seedling stage and many of our trees are still in leaf. In addition, other stresses such as chilling or freezing are prevalent at this time of year. Clearly, research must be extended to define the interaction between plant responses and combinations of environmental and pollution stresses naturally occurring in the field.

10.5 WATER STRESS AND FLOODING

Plant responses to pollutants may be modified by several facets of water stress: water content of the atmosphere, soil water deficit and soil water surfeit. Exposure of plants under these conditions may result in changes in stomatal behaviour and thus pollutant uptake and also alterations in cellular components, both of which may lead to altered plant responses to pollutants. Alternatively, the imposition of a pollutant stress may modify the plant's response to water stress whether it be of atmospheric or soil origin.

That water stress:pollutant interactions exist has been observed for many years, but the complexity of these interactions and their implications for growth and yield has only recently been appreciated (Mansfield et al., 1986). For example, it is well documented that the relative humidity of the atmosphere plays an important role in determining plant responses to pollutants, although the mechanisms involved are less well understood. It is known that humidity may influence pollutant uptake by plants, either on to external surfaces or into leaves via stomata. A good sink for dry deposition of SO_2 is provided via formation of dew on surfaces such as leaves (Fowler and Unsworth, 1979). Enhanced deposition on to wet surfaces may explain the observations of Murdy and Ragsdale (1980) who found that exposure of geraniums to SO_2 for 7 hours resulted in damage to sexual reproduction, measured as percentage seed set, only when the relative humidity was 80% or above. In addition, increased sensitivity to SO_2 injury has been observed in meadow grass (Poa pratensis) which was subjected to a light misting (Elkiey and Ormrod, 1981).

Since the relative water content of the atmosphere may modify stomatal conductance in many species, it may also affect pollutant uptake and plant sensitivity. For example, it is well established that plants exposed to pollutants under high humidity show greater injury than those polluted under low humidity (Davis and Wood, 1973; Norby and Kozlowksi, 1981; Black, 1985). These differential responses may be attributed to changes in pollutant fluxes (Srivastava et al., 1975; McLaughlin and Taylor, 1985). However, unlike the interactions between pollutants and some other environmental variables, the humidity regime in which plants are maintained before and after exposure to ozone, SO_2 or NO_x does not seem to affect the severity of visible damage (Davis and Wood, 1973).

Alternatively, pollutants themselves may modify stomatal behaviour, with concommitant changes in CO_2 uptake, pollutant flux and rates of water loss. For example, enhanced stomatal opening may result from low concentrations of SO_2, whereas exposure to ozone or high concentrations of SO_2 can lead to reduced stomatal apertures (see Chapter 4 and Black, 1985 for review). Starkey et al., (1981) found that exposure to PAN (peroxyacetyl nitrate) could lead to a stimulation of water loss of bean (Phaseolus species) plants which led to the earlier development of symptoms of water stress compared with unpolluted plants. However, this pollutant does not appear to be a general problem in the UK (UK PORG, 1987). Relationships between stomatal behaviour and pollutants may be complex. For example, when relative humidity of the atmosphere is low, the opening response observed during exposure to low concentrations of SO_2 may be replaced by enhanced closure (Majernik and Mansfield, 1971). These modifications of stomatal behaviour have implications for water use economy, plant growth and productivity, especially if water is limiting in the soil. Clearly it is important to understand plant responses to combinations of pollutants such as ozone, SO_2 and NO_x which are prevalent during periods of the year when water stress may be frequent.

Several investigations have been carried out in the field and laboratory to study interactions between soil moisture, pollution stress and plant responses and to elucidate the processes involved. The relationships between soil moisture and the sensitivity of plants to pollutants have been reasonably well established for a range of species. Soil water deficits, through their action on plant water relations and stomatal behaviour, have been shown both to enhance and depress plant responses to SO_2 (Unsworth et al., 1982; Olszyk and Tibbits, 1981) and ozone (Rich and Turner, 1972). Under optimum soil water conditions, leaf turgor is maximal, stomatal conductances are large and uptake of pollutants is facilitated (Kozlowski and Pallardy, 1979). In the field these conditions are more likely to exist early in the day and would explain the observations that exposure of field plants to pollutants in the morning is often more injurious than later in the day when soil and leaf water deficits may

have developed. However, although stomatal closure in times of water stress may be beneficial in reducing water loss and pollutant uptake, photosynthesis and nutrient uptake will also be reduced. In addition, under certain circumstances such as high light environments experienced at high altitude, the light reaction of photosynthesis will be overloaded which may result in physiological and/or visible damage and reduced growth.

Differential sensitivity to pollutants has been found also in plants growing in flooded and non-flooded soils. Norby and Kozlowski (1983) found that injury and growth inhibition in birch (Betula nigra) seedlings exposed to 350 ppb SO_2 were significantly lower in flooded versus non-flooded plants, responses attributable to reduced stomatal conductances and SO_2 uptake in flooded plants. However, when studies were carried out using another variety of birch (Norby and Kozlowski, 1982), the results indicated that stomatal aperture was not solely responsible for controlling plant responses to pollutants.

Heggestad et al. (1985) were not able to explain greater reduction in yield of soybeans polluted with ozone under low (more negative) soil water potential in terms of modification of stomatal behaviour. Instead they observed that ozone treated plants exhibited a reduction in root growth. Such reductions in root growth have also been reported in plants exposed to SO_2 and NO_x both singly and in combination (Jones and Mansfield, 1982a; Freer-Smith, 1985; Mansfield et al., 1986) and to ozone (Walmsley et al., 1980, Kress et al., 1986). Indeed Kress et al. (1986) have proposed that ozone may act via the suppression of stimulation of root growth that occurs frequently in response to drought. In addition reductions in root growth have been shown to be accompanied by an increase in specific leaf area and thus transpiring area when plants are exposed to mixtures of SO_2 and NO_x (Mansfield and Jones, 1986). These workers propose that enhanced sensitivity to water stress is likely to result from such modifications of root:shoot ratios.

The basis for interactions between pollutants and water stress seems to lie therefore at the cellular as well as stomatal level, although the two are intricately linked. This complexity was demonstrated recently when Mansfield et al. (1986) found that leaves polluted with SO_2 and NO_2 not only exhibited reductions in dry weight but also increases in specific leaf area and water content. The apparently conflicting observations could be explained by thicker leaves and enlarged but loosely packed mesophyll cells. In association with these anatomical changes were alterations in cell water relations, ie. less negative solute potentials and similar leaf water potentials resulting in a small but consistent reduction in the turgor of polluted leaves. The decline in turgor was associated with the loss of plasticity of cell walls. These workers suggest that the changes were of considerable physiological significance and would render plants less able to resist drought or develop drought hardiness.

The difficulties of turgor maintenance will be further exacerbated if plants also exhibit reduced capacity to control transpiration when polluted. Such responses have been observed in leaves of birch leaves polluted with mixtures of 20 ppb SO_2 and 20 ppb NO_2 and above (Wright *et al.*, 1988), and in excised leaves of timothy grass previously grown for 33 days in 10 ppb SO_2 and 10 ppb NO_2 and above (P.W. Lucas and T.A. Mansfield, pers. comm.) (Figure 10.4). Such concentrations of these pollutants are found in the UK in some urban and rural areas. These workers attribute this enhanced water loss to an increase in the permeability of leaf cuticles.

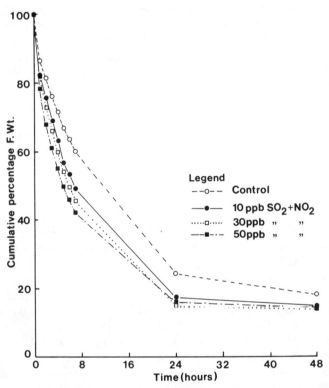

10.4 Decline in fresh weight over time of excised leaves of timothy (*Phleum pratense*) previously grown for 33 days in SO_2 + NO_2 or clean air. Each point represents the mean of nine replicate leaves taken from individual plants. The difference in initial rate of water loss between control leaves and those exposed to 10 ppb SO_2 + 10 ppb NO_2 was statistically significant at P <0.01. (P.W. Lucas pers. comm.).

This work exemplifies the complex and often subtle effects of air pollutants on plants and the subsequent responses to other stresses and in particular, water stress. For example, it can be hypothesised that the pollutant may act on the leaf tissue resulting in changes in leaf morphology and physiology, resource allocation and root growth. These factors may only appear detrimental

after the plant is subjected to additional environmental stress. The complexity of response and problems of interpreting plant pollutant interactions has also been identified by work from the NCLAN programme in the USA. Kress *et al.*, (1986) have shown that roots and shoots of soybeans may respond differently to ozone depending on the presence or absence of water stress. When plants were irrigated, the aerial parts of plants proved to be more sensitive to ozone whereas in non-irrigated plants, exposure to ozone resulted in reduced root growth. These reports highlight the problems involved in elucidating plant responses to pollutants when subsequent responses may be observed in a different organ or time scale from that of the initial direct action of the pollutant.

It is vital to understand these complex interactions, not only to define the mechanisms involved in the modification of plant responses to pollutants but also permit the correct interpretation of responses of plants polluted in laboratory chambers, or open top/open air systems in the field. In Britain, field crops, trees and natural vegetation are regularly subjected to transient or even prolonged atmospheric or soil water stress at times when atmospheric loadings of pollutants such as O_3, NO_x and SO_2, may be high. However, as yet, we have insufficient understanding of the degree of modification of plant responses, especially for trees, to pollutants singly or in combination by water stress or *vice versa*.

10.6 AGRICULTURAL CHEMICALS

The last twenty-five years have seen a significant increase in the use of pesticides and herbicides in agriculture and forestry but in spite of the quantity and range of agrochemicals now in use, very little work has been published on how they may interact with air pollutants. There are, however, several ways in which these chemicals might have direct or indirect effects on pollutant response.

Applied chemicals may have a direct influence on plant response by altering uptake and accumulation of pollutants. For gaseous pollutants this mechanism could operate where the chemical, or its products within the plant, influence stomatal aperture, or where they alter the solubility of the pollutants on mesophyll cell walls. Similarly, an agrochemical with an effect on cuticle properties might alter the effective dose of pollutants deposited on the plant surfaces. Chemicals that are persistent in the soil may modify the action of airborne pollutants on the roots.

Where pollutants and agrochemicals have a common mode of physiological action within the plant then interaction would be expected. Here, a knowledge of the biochemical mode of action is therefore essential in assessing the potential interactions of the two groups of chemicals. Direct interactions of this type would appear to be more likely in the case of chemicals designed to act on the plant such as herbicides, plant growth regulators and anti-transpirants rather than with pesticides. Indirect interactions are also possible, though they can only be the subject of speculation at present. For example, where plant production is limited by an insect pest, its removal by a pesticide might then reveal pollution as a previously hidden limiting factor.

10.6.1 Herbicides and plant growth regulators

The discovery of the herbicidal activity of non-toxic concentrations of the organic molecules 2,4-dichloro-phenoxyacetic acid (2,4-D) and 4-chloro-2-methyl-phenoxyacetic acid (MCPA) in the mid 1940s revolutionised the techniques of weed control and led to the development of the wide range of herbicides now available. These phenoxyalkanoic acids are active as herbicides because they are persistent synthetic auxins which interfere with the fluctuations in endogenous auxins required for normal growth. Sherwood and Rolph (1970) have shown that 2,4-D and ozone have antagonistic effects on the growth of tomato, zinnia and elm, and Ordin et al. (1972) found that 2,4-D reduced the inhibitory effect of PAN on the growth of oat coleoptiles. However, greater than additive interactions in the effects of ozone and a number of herbicides have also been reported (Carney et al., 1973). In recent field fumigations, Baker and Full-wood (1986) identified a strong interaction in the effects of SO_2 exposure and application of a mixture of two herbicides ('Methoxone' and 'Deloxil'), a fungicide and a plant growth regulator to winter barley. The use of such mixtures is common practice but, in this experiment, they were sprayed simultaneously in April. Scorching of the young leaves developed which was positively associated with the concentration of ambient SO_2. As there were ground frosts following the spray application, there may also have been an effect on frost sensitivity. Baker and Fullwood went on to conduct a spray component trial in which both herbicides produced injury at high SO_2 concentration. The damage was greatest when a plant growth regulator was also present. The authors suggested that as the surfactant in the regulator formulation increased penetration of the herbicides, these may have interacted with SO_2 to give enhanced cold sensitivity. It is possible that applications of herbicides and surfactants during cold periods coinciding with unusually large ambient SO_2 concentrations may cause leaf damage to cereal crops.

The effects of wet deposition on the uptake and impact of a small number of herbicides have been specifically investigated in recent years (Lokke, 1984). Larsen (1985) exposed dicotyledonous crop species and two cereals to a range of sub-lethal concentrations of the chlorinated phenoxyacid 2,4DP ('Dichlorprop') and also sprayed with simulated acid rain (NH_4NO_3 aq.) adjusted to three pH values: 5.6, 4.3 and 3.3. 'Dichlorprop' caused epinasty of the leaves and stem, accelerated senescence, chlorosis, stunted growth and wounding of the stem. These symptoms occurred at smaller herbicide concentrations when more acidic rain was applied to the plants, with swede (Brassica napus), radish (Raphanus sativus) and garden cress (Lepidium sativum) showing particularly severe symptoms in response to combinations of 2,4-DP and simulated acid rain of pH 3.3. In similar experiments with swede and mustard (Sinapis alba), symptoms of injury from 2,4-D were shown to occur when plants were exposed to artificial rain of pH 3.3 (Lokke, 1984). It is suggested by these authors that the interactions between effects of acid rain and herbicides may result from changes to the cuticles of foliage, due to pollutant exposure, which facilitate the penetration of chemicals. It is well established that polluted atmospheres cause changes to epicuticular wax and the known effects of acid rain and mist on nutrient loss from foliage tend to support this as a likely mechanism for interacting effects.

10.6.2 Plant growth regulators

Over the last ten years, plant growth regulators (PGRs) have been introduced and increasingly used in agriculture. The endogenous plant hormones abscisic acid (ABA) and indol-3-ylacetic acid (IAA) are known to be involved in the regulation of stomatal responses to CO_2 (Raschke, 1975; Snaith and Mansfield, 1982), and there is some evidence for an interaction between ABA and SO_2 (Black, 1982). Controlled exposures using large concentrations of SO_2 (2000 ppb) suggest that this pollutant or its products within the plant may amplify ABA-induced closure of stomata. Many herbicidal auxins, such as napth-2-yloxyacetic acid (NOXA) and napth-1-ylacetic acid (NAA), either inhibit opening or induce the closure of stomata (Pemadasa, 1979; Cox et al., 1985). Although the inhibition of photosynthesis by most herbicides is attributed to their direct interference with the light reactions, some inhibit transpiration and photosynthesis through their effect on stomatal conductance. The non-selective herbicide glyphosate ('Roundup') can cause stomatal closure prior to its effect on CO_2 uptake (Brecke and Duke, 1980) and is also known to induce cyclical opening and closing of stomata (Shaner and Lyon, 1979). Two types of PGRs are increasingly used on cereal crops as antilodging agents. Ethephon-based compounds applied during stem elongation decompose to release the plant hormone ethylene, while chromequats are applied during tillering and act by inhibiting gibberellin biosynthesis (Lang, 1970). As these compounds shorten the internodes of cereals, while exposure to SO_2 and NO_2 has been shown to increase stem height of barley (H. vulgare) (Pande and Mansfield, 1985b), there is a potential for interacting effects. There is also evidence that ethylene derived from ethephon may cause stomatal closure and plants exposed to SO_2 and ozone are also known to show enhanced ethylene production (Peiser and Yang, 1979). Stomatal closure would restrict pollutant uptake and affect water-use economy.

10.6.3 Antitranspirants and fungicides

Antitranspirants and film-forming coatings are likely to decrease pollutant uptake by plants. A range of commercially available antitranspirants and sticker-spreaders has recently been shown to decrease the accumulation of airborne heavy metals by lichen thalli (Garty et al., 1985). A similar compound based on di-l-p methane and used to give persistence of chemicals on cereal crops and to prevent pod shatter in oilseed rape and peas, has recently been found to influence the sensitivity of coniferous trees to acute pollutant injury from SO_2 and $SO_2 + NO_2$ mixtures (Freer-Smith and Lucas, 1987). In the three controlled fumigations of Sitka spruce (*Picea sitchensis*) the polymeric coating decreased the extent of acute pollutant injury and, in the third experiment, statistically significant interactions in the effects of 400 ppb SO_2 and of the coating were identified. Analysis of variance of the plant dry weights at the end of a six week fumigation also showed antagonistic interactions in the effects of the two treatments, with the treatment combinations SO_2 + coating causing substantially smaller decreases of dry weight than would have been given by summing the individual effects of coating and of SO_2.

The fungicide benomyl and other known or postulated antioxidants can protect crops against injury by ozone. The fungicidal activity of benomyl (a benzimidazolecarbamate) is attributed to its effect on DNA synthesis, but protection from ozone probably occurs at the membrane level since treatment with benzimidazole increases the cholesterol content of bean leaves (*Phaseolus vulgaris*) and sterols are known to be effective membrane stabilisers (Spotts et al., 1975).

10.7 CONCLUSIONS

1. Plants in natural and man-made ecosystems are naturally subject to a wide range of biotic and abiotic stresses. The various stresses not only influence plant growth, but may also modify the response of plants to pollutants. These modifiers vary in intensity from season to season and year to year.

2. A dry atmosphere or soil may change stomatal behaviour and alter pollutant uptake. Plants exposed to pollutants in a very humid atmosphere are often more susceptible to injury than plants exposed in a less humid atmosphere. However, wet or waterlogged soils have been shown to reduce pollutant injury in some species. Pollutants can directly affect stomatal behaviour and thus modify the water status and photosynthetic efficiency of the plant; they may also reduce root growth leading to increased sensitivity to water stress.

3. Some pollutants may act as nutrients (eg. sulphur or nitrogen) when absorbed through leaves or taken up by roots. However, these supplies are not necessarily beneficial. For example, exposure to NO_2 may stimulate plant growth but decrease tolerance to drought and frost and increase the palatability of foliage to leaf-eating insects. The significance of these effects may be greatest in plants growing in semi-natural situations where nutrient levels are normally low.

4. Some plants are more sensitive to pollutants in winter than at other times of the year because they are growing slowly eg. in low light intensities. Exposure to pollutants in summer, autumn or winter may reduce resistance to winter stresses such as desiccation and freezing.

5. Agricultural chemicals such as pesticides, fungicides, etc. are a normal part of agricultural practice yet their effect on pollutant response has been neglected until recently. There is evidence that fungicides alter responses to ozone and recent results show that the surfactants in many sprays may increase pollutant penetration of the leaf.

FOREST DECLINE

11.1 INTRODUCTION

There have long been extensive, and often severe, problems of tree health and survival in parts of Poland, East Germany and, in particular, Czechoslovakia. It is generally accepted that such problems are caused by the large concentrations of SO_2 (and probably other pollutants) emitted from local coal combustion (see Chapter 7). Similarly, damage to forests in the San Bernadino Mountains of California has been attributed to oxidants generated photochemically from motor vehicle exhausts in the Los Angeles area.

During the mid-1970s concern grew in Germany over the health of Silver fir (*Abies alba*) and Norway spruce (*Picea abies*), a concern that has since extended to Scots pine (*Pinus sylvestris*) beech (*Fagus sylvatica*) and oak species (*Quercus* spp.). A wide variety of symptoms (discussed later) have been described in affected trees. Although some symptoms are similar to those seen in earlier declines, the scales and progress of the current damage do not seem to match previous reports. For this reason the decline in health is frequently referred to in the German language as the "Neuartige Waldschäden" (the new type of forest damage). It has been widely suggested that the decline is associated with air pollution, but there is at present no scientific *proof* linking the two, either directly or indirectly. In this chapter various hypotheses are suggested to explain forest decline and attempts are made to evaluate them in terms of known responses of trees to air pollution and other stresses.

There are reports of local decline of Silver fir in central Europe dating back to the 18th and 19th centuries (Wachter 1978). However decline on the scale observed since about 1972 appears to be unprecedented. Although the damage symptoms have remained rather ill-defined, the problem particularly as manifest by needle loss in Norway spruce has now been identified from northern Italy, through Austria and Switzerland, along the northern half of the eastern boundary of France, through Germany, eastern Belgium, The Netherlands (which also has further particular problems as will be discussed later) and into southern Sweden. There are also reports of damage in Norway. Needle loss on Norway spruce in Britain increased substantially between 1984 and 1987 so that the health of the trees surveyed can only be described as 'moderate' (Innes, 1987). Symptoms of decline bearing some resemblance to the European problem have been reported on red spruce in the eastern USA and there is also concern over widespread declines of sugar maple and southern pines in North America.

11.2 SYMPTOMS OF DAMAGE

A range of symptoms associated with the new type of forest damage have been suggested, with none being uniquely specific to the decline phenomenon. Furthermore, different combinations of symptoms are seen in different areas, and the symptoms differ between species, and may even differ in intensity (and sometimes in form) between individual trees within a stand. As most work has centred on Norway spruce this can be taken as the prime model.

11.2.1 Norway spruce

Needle loss Defoliation is the most widely reported phenomenon. In German surveys, more than half of the Norway spruce stands initially classified as diseased had foliage losses not exceeding 10% in 1985. Crown thinning is frequently, but not invariably, most pronounced in the immediate sub-top region of the tree, with the branches above and below being more heavily foliated. Crown thinning may be accompanied by the presence of green needles in fresh litterfall.

Altered branching habit Pattern of branching has also been variously considered to be important. At one stage the existence of very pendulous secondary branches was suggested to be significant, particularly if combined with needle loss to produce the lametta or 'tinsel' damage. However, pendulous secondary branching is a widely known and natural feature that has long been described and is a genetic variant most common in spruce populations from snowy areas. Other aspects of branching must also be considered, because differences, presumed genetic, in the angle and length of primary and secondary branches can give the appearance of differences in foliage density (Pollanschutz *et al.*, 1985, Binns *et al.*, 1986).

Much play has been made of the development of adventitious shoots ('fear twigs') on the upper side of primary branches suffering defoliation. However, the growth from adventitious buds embedded in bark is a common reaction to defoliation brought about by insect or fungal attack, foliage damage by frost or, rarely, fire.

Chlorotic and discoloured foliage Various discolourations of foliage are also reported, there being two, perhaps three, distinct groups of symptoms. The least common symptom, but the best defined, is chlorosis typical of magnesium deficiency (Bosch *et al.*, 1983) but potassium problems have also been suggested (Zottl, pers. comm.). Some of the chlorosis has been shown to be reversible by the addition of an appropriate fertiliser. Nevertheless there is a clear impression that certainly magnesium deficiency, and perhaps also potassium deficiency, has become much more common in recent years (Hüttl, 1986).

A deficiency of magesium produces a hard golden-yellow colour of the tips of older needles, the colour progressively extending to the entire needle which finally turns brown and falls off. Potassium deficiency is similarly found on older and inner needles but is softer in colour, sometimes tinged with pink and is evident on the entire needle from the outset. Again, as the condition advances, needle shedding may occur. Under certain circumstances potassium deficiency can bear a superficial resemblance to frost damage. Diagnosis of nutrient deficiency can be aided by foliar analysis but can only be confirmed if addition of fertiliser eliminates the symptom. By contrast to the yellow chlorosis typical of nutrient deficiencies is a reddening of foliage, followed by needle shedding, that has been reported to be associated with forest decline of Norway spruce in certain parts of Germany particularly in the Bavarian Alps. The affected needles are of the older age classes in the inner portion of the crown and frequently become infected with the needle cast fungi *Lophodermium picea* and *Rhizosphaera Kalkhoffii*. Infected needles are shed during windy conditions in November or December leading to the loss of almost all but the current needles from secondary branches.

The needle reddening associated with needle cast disease can be found on almost all soil types in southern Germany, and seems to have no association with a particular pollution climate. Further north, in forests in the Fichtelgebirge from which lichens are lacking (presumably indicating higher levels of SO_2), a spasmodic browning and loss of needles, particularly from the lower crown, has been observed and apparently is eliminated by growing trees in filtered air (Mengel, pers. comm.). The nature of the browning, however, is far from specific and can be seen on the lower and heavily shaded portion of the crowns of spruce growing well in unpolluted regions. This symptom, therefore, requires more research in relation to Forest Decline and meanwhile must be treated with some caution.

Symptoms caused by air pollutants Acute injury to foliage as a result of exposure to high concentrations of SO_2, ozone or hydrogen fluoride produces symptoms that are well defined, but at lower concentrations the symptoms of chronic injury are less specific. Severe damage to Norway spruce by SO_2 (and probably associated pollutants) occurs in parts of western Czechoslovakia, parts of Poland and in small 'hot-spots' throughout the industrial world. This problem is also found in north eastern Bavaria close to the border with Czechoslovakia and East Germany. Damage is most severe on exposed ridges and plateaux and usually leads to death of evergreen conifers, but the deciduous coniferous and broad-leaved species survive.

Over the extent of Europe where the new forest damage is reported, symptoms of acute injury to spruce by gaseous pollutants have not been widely observed. Symptoms of chronic injury by air pollutants include needle loss, chlorosis and altered growth, all of which

are reported symptoms of the decline and so it is not possible to exclude the possibility that air pollution is a cause of decline on the basis of symptomology.

11.2.2 Other conifers

Silver fir has always been a difficult species to grow successfully and records of damage, often with symptoms similar to those now ascribed to acid rain, can be found going back a century or more. Typically there is a loss of apical dominance leading to a flattened tree top below which there is a region of pronounced loss of needles and even branch dieback, a symptom graphically described as a 'storks nest'. Silver fir may also show magnesium deficient foliage similar to that found on Norway spruce, and foliage reddening may occur.

Scots pine shows less well defined symptoms and generally seems to be more resistant than spruce or fir to whatever is causing the damage. However, both magnesium deficient foliage and crown thinning are not unusual in central Europe. High atmospheric concentrations of ammonia from intensive farming are believed to be causing chlorosis in some localities, particularly in The Netherlands.

11.2.3 Beech

Concern over beech has been fairly recent (Roeloffs *et al.*, 1985). Premature loss of foliage is reported as the primary symptom, the shed leaves sometimes being green. In addition there is a change in the pattern of branching with long shoot growth being limited to branch apices which otherwise are clothed only in short shoots, giving the branch an extended 'spiky' appearance (Schutt and Summerer, 1983). Affected beech stands, which are usually over 60 years of age, are often reported to show high incidence of pathogenic fungi such as *Armillaria mellia*, *Nectria coccinea* etc., (Binns and Redfern, 1983; Flückiger *et al.*, 1986).

11.3 HYPOTHESES

The Forest Decline syndrome is characterised by a range of symptoms which show similarities across species (eg. premature needle loss), but also differ substantially in their extent, progression and, frequently, in the details of the ways in which the symptoms are expressed (type of discolouration etc.). Few, if any, of the symptoms are unique or specific to the decline phenomenon, most being general indicators of stress which can be caused by a wide range of environmental conditions. From the examination of symptoms, therefore, it is impossible to determine the causal agency. Similarly, the monitoring of environmental conditions is unsatisfactory for establishing causal relationships. There appears to be no single factor present at stressful levels in all the various areas which show Forest Decline. However, a large number of features, ranging from the biochemical to the ecological, have been studied in one or more of these areas and as a result, many differing hypotheses have been put forward. In examining these, it is important to appreciate that some are broad in concept, incorporating the conclusions and opinions resulting from a number of studies at different sites, whereas others are more narrowly based. Furthermore, the hypotheses are not mutually exclusive. The particular combination of biotic and abiotic factors which occur, and which may result in Forest Decline, will clearly differ on the basis of geography and climate. A schematic representation of the main proposed mechanisms of forest damage which may lead to growth decline and dieback is shown in Figure 11.1.

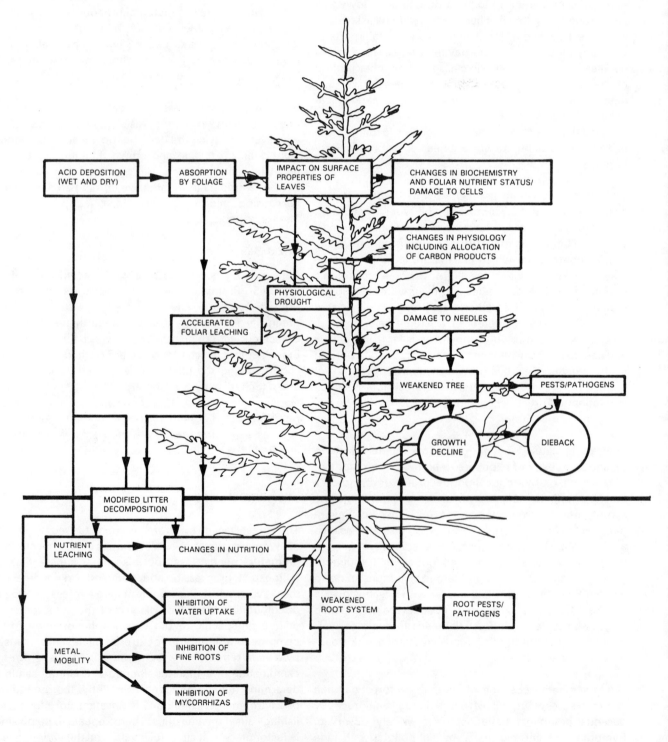

11.1 Proposed mechanisms of forest damage leading to growth decline and dieback.

11.3.1 Acidification, soil leaching, aluminium mobilisation and toxicity

This hypothesis was first proposed by Ulrich as a result of studies of nutrient and pollutant flux in the beech forests of the Solling near Gottingen, and has been continually refined as new information becomes available. Ulrich et al. (1980) attributed the decline of beech stands to the combination of acid rainfall, acidification from the dry deposition of SO_2 and other acidic gases, and heavy metal pollution. Soil acidification leached Ca^{2+} and Mg^{2+} from the mineral layers of soils by cation exchange and mobilised aluminium as Al^{3+}. Ulrich postulated that aluminium concentrations in the soil were sufficient to damage the fine roots of trees. Furthermore, it was suggested that in warm years the soil humus that had been progressively accumulating would decompose with unusual rapidity, the nitrogen mineralising through to nitrate to create additional acidity to add to that introduced as pollutants. The addition of high pollution inputs to high natural production of acidity would lead, it was suggested, to aluminium concentrations capable of causing root death, with consequent nutritional and water problems for the tree that would then become more liable to attack by other agents including wood rotting fungi.

On the basis of this hypothesis, soils over-lying thin glacial till or granite bedrock as in areas of Scandinavia, Canada and parts of central Europe would be at greatest risk from acidic deposition. It is therefore difficult to explain why forest decline is seen on a wide range of soil types, some of which are well-buffered against acidification. Moreover, studies carried out in Norway, Sweden, Scotland and Canada have indicated clearly that the roots of conifers are able to withstand aluminium concentrations well in excess of those encountered in even the most acidic soils. It remains possible that mycorrhizal fungi associated with tree roots (and important for forest nutrition) may be damaged at a lower concentration of aluminium. However, should the effect be through mycorrhizal association the major response by the tree would be a deficiency of phosphorus, or less likely nitrogen. Effects on the uptake of other nutrients such as magnesium and potassium should not however be ruled out. The high elevation forests exhibiting damage in the eastern USA are mostly found on organic soils. Research into causes is focussing on shoot mediated processes, rather than aluminium toxicity.

11.3.2 Pollutant gases and mist or rain

As doubts have arisen over the ability of the acidification/aluminium hypothesis to account for the various effects observed, the idea that gaseous air pollutants, and particularly ozone, may have a major role in forest decline has become increasingly favoured. For most workers in the field the hypothesis that has attracted most attention is presently that put forward by Bosch et al. (1983) and Rehfuess and Bosch (1986). Essentially, they suggest that at upper elevations below which a temperature inversion layer often exists, high concentrations of photochemical ozone may build up and eventually damage the integrity of leaf membranes making them more permeable to cations. Acidic cloud water, which commonly occurs in mountainous regions may then leach out magnesium at rates that the tree cannot replenish. The loss of magnesium may be a symptom rather than a cause of the problem, which may be a straightforward destruction of chloroplasts, which contain magnesium, by abnormal concentrations of photo-oxidants.

This hypothesis, developed by Rehfuess and by Prinz, Krause and their colleagues working in North-Rhine Westphalia, has a number of attractive features. Ozone damage to forests was studied extensively in the San Bernadino Mountains downwind of Los Angeles in the 1970s. The ozone induced foliar injury, premature needle fall and decreased growth. These responses weakened trees and seemed to increase susceptibility to pine beetles and root rot which ultimately may have caused death. In Eastern USA and in Canada (Ontario and Quebec) there are fourteen major study sites where a range of forest species show oxidant injury (EPRI, 1986). Most of the soils in these areas are naturally acidic and nutrient poor, but it is thought that ozone exposure combined with acid mist or fog increases nutrient leaching, thus exacerbating the poor soil conditions, and leading to foliar deficiencies (Mg and Ca) and decreasing biomass production. Despite species differences, intraspecific variability and site peculiarities, there appear to be some similarities in the macroscopic and microscopic symptoms found on the foliage of damaged trees known to be exposed to ozone in the US and those showing new type forest damage in Europe.

The Photo-oxidant Review Group recently concluded (UK PORG, 1987), that there is some evidence to suggest a 2-fold increase in background ozone concentrations in Europe over the last 100 years. There are episodes of photochemical ozone in much of Europe which reach concentrations known to be damaging to trees in North America. There is also evidence that ozone concentrations increase with altitude and remain large for longer periods, facts that are consistent with the initial appearance of decline symptoms at between 600–800 m in Germany and with the observed greater damage to red spruce at high altitude in the US.

However, a number of aspects of the hypothesis are apparently not consistent with observed decline. Potentially damaging ozone episodes occur less frequently in much of Europe than in the US but decline is much greater in Europe. Damage has spread to lower altitudes where there is less ozone and no acid mist and is found on species such as beech and oak which are thought to be relatively ozone-tolerant. The importance of the ozone/acid mist interaction is unclear. There are apparently conflicting results from controlled ozone/mist experiments in different laboratories, and symptoms produced in laboratory exposures to ozone and acid mist do not match those found in the field. Some of these inconsistencies may be due to differences in the sensitivities of seedlings and mature trees, or to the interacting influence of soil nutrition. There may also be an involvement of frost and winter stress (see Chapter 10 and 11.3.3.). Recent experiments have suggested that Norway spruce, Sitka spruce and red spruce seedlings were less frost hardy in autumn after they had been exposed to ozone during the previous summer (Brown et al., 1987; D. Cottam and E. Wright, pers comm.). A similar effect was found with Red spruce seedlings exposed to simulated acid mist (zd. Fowler, pers comm.).

11.3.3 Environmental stress and interactions between pollution and environmental stress

Forest decline could be the result of a combination of natural and pollutant stresses occurring concurrently (eg. drought and ozone) or sequentially (summer pollution and winter frost). Such initial stresses are often followed by attack by biotic agents such as bark beetles or wood rotting fungi that may finally be responsible for the death of trees. The general correlation between severe winter weather, unusually dry summers and the worst increases in the extent of forest decline in Europe (Federal Ministry of Food, Agriculture and Forestry Report, 1982) is usually cited as evidence for the interaction theory. For agricultural crops, a number of natural environmental factors have been identified which show strong interactions with the effects of mixtures of air pollutants (see Chapters 9 and 10 and the report of the 2nd CEC/COST Workshop, 1986). For forests, scientific opinion favours interactions between the effects of winter injury from low temperatures and the effects of gaseous air pollutants (ozone, NO_x and SO_2) and acid mist and between the effects of summer drought and ozone. However metals cannot be ruled out, particularly in heavily polluted areas (see the report of the 3rd CEC/COST Workshop, 1988). Much of the work in the north eastern USA implicates similar combinations of unfavourable environmental conditions (eg. Johnson and Siccama, 1983; Johnson et al., 1986). Impacts of such combinations of factors on the main symptoms of decline (yellowing, nutrient loss, needle cast, death of fine roots etc.) can usually be demonstrated in controlled experiments. With increasing experimental and observational evidence that there is no single cause of forest decline, the involvement of complex interactions between wet and dry deposition and other environmental stresses, which may be both root- and shoot-mediated, seems increasingly likely.

11.3.4 Pathogens, pests and viruses

The involvement of insect attack, particularly of fir and spruce aphid, fir moth, bark beetle, scale insects and sawflies in forest decline has been documented for some stands in Europe and in the USA (Flückiger et al. 1978; Wachter, 1978; Fuhrer, 1983 (see Chapter 9)). For both fungal and insect pathogens, interactions, usually complex, with air pollutants are well known and have been investigated in some detail for agricultural crops (see Chapter 9). It should be pointed out that some symptoms of Forest Decline are very similar to those resulting from insect attack. On Scots pine, for example, green aphid (*Eulachnus agilis*) induces yellowing, early senescence and needle loss. Although at many sites it is clear that insect attack has an important role, the possibility of predisposing stress resulting from pollution must be kept in mind.

As well as their direct involvement, insects may act as carriers of fungal and viral infection. As a result of histological investigations, Fink and Braun (1978) suggested that viruses may play a decisive part in fir decline, and it has also been suggested that viruses may increase sensitivity to drought and frost. However, no serious study of the involvement of viruses in the die-back syndrome has yet been made.

Fungi such as *Armillaria, Lophodermium* and *Sclerophoma* are often observed on declining and on otherwise healthy conifer stands throughout Europe and can be regarded as weakening agents which, in combination with the abiotic causes of Forest Decline, may ultimately cause death.

11.3.5 Trialkyl lead and heavy metals

Faulstich and Stournaras (1985) have recently speculated from limited data that trialkyl lead released from motor vehicles may be contributing to European forest damage. Their results are not widely accepted at present.

The release or relocation of Al^{3+} and probably also of other heavy metals in ground water has been an integral part of the 'Acidification' hypothesis (11.3.1) since it was first proposed. Evidence that the heavy metal loads of trees and soils are related to forest decline is generally lacking in Europe. From the data which have been reported, heavy metals cannot be excluded as being a contributing factor in forest decline in certain localities but they seem very unlikely to be a universal cause.

11.3.6 Other chemicals

It has recently been postulated that traces of organic compounds present in air may be responsible for some of the growth alterations associated with forest decline, and some attempts have been made to measure the airborne organic compounds at two sites near Regensburg in West German (Figge, 1988). Hydrogen peroxide generated by photochemical reactions has been measured in air, rain and cloudwater in Europe and North America, at concentrations known from laboratory experiments to be near damage thresholds for some plants. Although these compounds are present at small concentrations, some are persistent in the atmosphere and some are highly reactive. The atmospheric concentrations of some of these compounds may have increased over the last ten years (Frank and Frank, 1985). These authors and others have suggested that organic compounds are involved in photochemical reactions in the atmosphere and that highly reactive molecular species are formed and may enter leaves where they then interfere with physiological processes.

11.3.7 Ammonia

A totally different form of damage may result from exposure to high concentrations of ammonium sulphate, the ammonia being derived from manure or other animal slurry spread on fields. This damage is reported to be common in parts of The Netherlands where the intensive rearing of livestock is practised. The symptoms consist of increased susceptibility to winter damage and reduced concentrations of potassium and magnesium in older foliage with consequent chlorosis. The damage is limited to isolated trees and small forests in areas of intense livestock rearing (including poultry).

11.4 SURVEYS

The monitoring of the development of forest decline and the surveying of its extent is bedevilled by the lack of specific symptoms. Needle loss is a particularly difficult criterion on which to judge damage because so many other factors can reduce the needle numbers. A recent British study has shown crown needle density in spruce declines linearly with tree age, there being no identifiable geographical component (Innes et al. 1986).

Thus needle-loss is non-specific as a symptom and has no simple relation to growth. Furthermore, visual estimates of the thinness of the crown are difficult to standardise because the precision of any assessment lies not only in the skill of the observer but also in the ability to define a norm against which comparisons can be made. Different perceptions of the norm may be responsible for some of the reported regional differences and it is likely that the norm drifts with time and even suffers occasional marked shifts eg. following the introduction of standard photographs for comparison purposes. In Britain and West Germany there has also been the realisation that, with repeated surveys, observers have become increasingly more ready to classify as damaged those trees that they would previously have regarded as unremarkable.

11.4.1 Classification of damage

Because foliar discolouration does not seem to be an inevitable aspect of the symptomology of the various conditions that might encompass forest decline, loss of foliage assessed as the thinness of the crown has been accepted by the UNECE as the only possible common criterion and the basis of the standard survey technique. The recommended method divides the defoliation categories used in early German surveys into nine classes of which category 9 is 91–100% defoliated. To aid in assessment, photographs of trees with full foliage are issued to provide standards. Other features that are recorded are: branch habit, defoliation type, extent of browning or yellowing, needle life in years. It is further recommended that foliage samples be taken for chemical analysis.

11.4.2 Surveys elsewhere in Europe

On the basis of this method, Forest Decline has been reported, inter alia, in northeastern France, eastern Belgium, The Netherlands, Austria, Switzerland, northern Italy, southern Sweden and, of course, West Germany, with extension into eastern countries including Czechoslovakia, East Germany and Poland. However, not all authorities, particularly those on the fringes of this area, are agreed that the appearance of the trees represents a new syndrome or that pollution is necessarily involved. As pointed out elsewhere, there are undoubtedly various damaging factors with different distributions in space and time. Thus, much of the damage to pine in The Netherlands is probably caused by high local concentrations of atmospheric ammonia (see section 11.3.7).

11.4.3 British surveys

Surveys, according to the UNECE protocol, have been carried out by the Forestry Commission for coniferous trees in Britain since 1984. The surveys cover stands of Sitka spruce, Norway spruce and Scots pine planted between 1941 and 1955. Stands of these species were stratified in six zones across the country, each zone representing a different pollution environment. Norway spruce and Scots pine were chosen because there are numerous descriptions of the symptomology on these European species, whilst Sitka spruce was included because it is the most widely planted species in Britain. The age range was chosen to ensure that crops would not be due for felling before completion of the envisaged period of monitoring. Aspects of the survey design, in particular the limited age range used (damage in continental Europe is worst on old trees), attracted some criticism. In consequence, in the 1986 survey, a further 33 plots of Norway spruce were included extending the maximum age from 50 to 106 years (Innes et al., 1986). In 1987 older Scots pine and Sitka spruce were added and an additional inventory based on a 16 km by 16 km grid was set up, based on an EEC regulation, to provide comparable data for all countries within the Community (Innes and Boswell, 1987).

Table 11.1 Surveys of needle loss in the UK and West Germany in 1983–87, according to the German 5-category classification. UK values are the percentage of trees surveyed that fitted into the damage classes; FRG values are the percentage of species area within each damage class. (From Innes *et al.* 1986, Innes 1987, Innes and Boswell 1987 and BML 1987).

Damage class % Needle loss Year	0 0–10					1 11–25					2 26–60					3 + 4 61–100				
	83	84	85	86	87	83	84	85	86	87	83	84	85	86	87	83	84	85	86	87
UK																				
Sitka spruce	—	65	83	45	20	—	28	13	34	41	—	6	4	15	38	—	1	0	1	1
Scots pine	—	50	71	24	17	—	29	20	42	37	—	16	8	32	44	—	5	1	2	2
Norway spruce (<50 years)	—	73	83	52	31	—	26	16	37	41	—	2	1	11	28	—	0	0	0	0
Norway spruce (>50 years)	—	—	—	11	8	—	—	—	34	30	—	—	—	53	57	—	—	—	0	5
West Germany																				
Norway spruce	59	49	48	46	51	30	31	28	32	32	10	19	21	20	16	1	2	3	2	1
Pine	56	41	43	46	50	32	38	41	40	38	10	20	15	13	11	1	1	2	1	1
Silver fir	25	13	13	18	21	27	29	21	22	27	41	45	50	49	44	8	13	16	11	8

A summary of the results of the main UK conifer survey is given in Table 11.1, which also shows results from West Germany. In the UK, there was a large increase between 1985 and 1986 in the percentage of trees judged to shown medium to serious needle loss (26–60%), and the 1987 survey confirmed the trend of increasing needle loss. In West Germany, the damage on spruce and pine increased substantially between 1983 and 1984 but in general the health of conifers seems to have changed little in recent years. It is difficult to compare absolute values between countries because of differences in the selection of trees and in the timing and scale of assessments. However on the basis of needle loss the health of Norway spruce and Scots pine on the sample plots in Britain is only moderate and is similar to the situation in West Germany. The extent of yellowing of needles observed in Britain is also similar to that in West Germany (Innes and Boswell, 1987). The Forestry Commission have emphasised (Innes, 1987) that the sample plots in their main survey are not representative of the total population of trees in the country and that, because of changes in the survey design and procedure, trends must be interpreted with caution. Nevertheless, there must be concern at the findings of such a decline in crown density and there is considerable effort aimed at identifying the causes.

As already discussed, needle loss may be caused by a wide range of factors, many of which occur naturally. In 1984 and 1985 the scale of needle loss in the UK surveys did not appear unusual and it was concluded that there was 'no evidence of any new form of forest damage'. In 1986, when damage increased, there had been a period of low winter temperatures and drying winds which, on past experience, was expected to cause damage to spruce.

Many pine were damaged by the needle-cast fungus (*Lophodermium seditosum*). There was no clear correlation between damage and estimated sulphur or nitrogen deposition, but pH, ozone and exposure to wind were possible damaging factors that could not be assessed in the 1986 analysis. At the time of writing, the 1987 analysis of factors which may correlate with damage has not been completed.

Surveys of other tree species have also been made. The health of beech in West Germany has been of concern, with many authorities believing that symptoms indicated a totally new form of damage that increased from about 1984 onwards. A survey organised by the UK Friends of the Earth (FoE) (Rose and Neville, 1985) reported on 1638 beech and 1546 yew trees in Britain, assessing them into four health categories, based on symptoms such as foliar loss, tinselling, 'fear twigs' and altered branching habit (see 11.2). Of the yews inspected, 78% had signs of dieback, and 26% of these showed moderate or advanced damage. On the beech, 69% showed signs of damage, with 16% of these having advanced damage. The surveys, which were done by non-specialists, covered a large number of sites and generally selected isolated (and often old) trees. Even when experienced foresters assess trees for foliar damage there is considerable variation between observers, a problem that has encouraged the development of intensive training of observers by the Forestry Commission and by survey agencies in other countries. Consequently there is uncertainty about the magnitude of damage reported by FoE, but their survey encouraged the Forestry Commission to expand their conifer survey to include older trees (up to 110 years old), and to initiate a survey of beech, starting in 1985. The Forestry Commission beech survey records symptoms including those associated with beech decline in West Germany (11.2.3). Early leaf yellowing, crown thinness, and abnormal branching were observed quite frequently, but the damage was not considered to be different from that observed on beech in the UK in the past (Lonsdale, 1986 a,b). Beech is known to be susceptible to drought and there were potentially damaging droughts in 1975, 1976, 1983 and 1984. However the possibility cannot be excluded that pollution was a cause of some of the symptoms, either directly, or by interacting with other stresses.

In 1986 the Department of the Environment and Forestry Commission commissioned work investigating the health of broadleaf hedgerow trees. Results are not yet available. A further survey funded by the Nature Conservancy Council and Forestry Commission is investigating beech and Scots pine in relation to air pollution at sites of conservation interest.

Although a number of carefully organised surveys of tree health in the UK have been completed, it is not possible to determine from them whether pollution is a cause of the symptoms observed in the UK, nor is it possible to exclude it. On the basis of evidence reviewed earlier (especially in Chapters 7, 9 and 10) it is possible that pollutants which have not been monitored in forest areas in the past could have damaged trees either directly through soil pathways, or by interacting with other stresses such as drought, cold, pests and pathogens. With such a potentially large range of pollutant stresses that could cause foliar loss or discoloration, in addition to a complex range of natural stresses, it is unlikely that causes of tree damage will be established unequivocally from statistical correlations between foliar loss, weather, pollution and other factors. Nevertheless, forest surveys are an important tool for monitoring the health of forests and the Review Group recommend that they are continued.

11.4.4 Early diagnosis of forest decline

Although the visual surveys previously described show the extent of current damage, they do not indicate the role of air pollution in the damage process nor its potential for future damage. A multi-national project has been established to develop a number of objective tests of the condition of tree foliage. These tests are intended to assess the health of trees before injury, during the phase of invisible or latent damage and after visible damage occurs. When validated, these tests will allow the early diagnosis of decline and the development a potential predictive capacity and the objective quantification of

forest decline. These tests are intended to assess the health of trees before injury during the phase of invisible or latent damage and after visible damage occurs. When validated, these tests will allow the early diagnosis of decline and lead to the development of a potential predictive capacity and the objective quantification of forest decline.

In a recent pilot survey (Cape et al., 1988) Norway spruce, Scots pine and beech were sampled in seven sites from south Germany to north-east Scotland and subjected to a range of diagnostic laboratory tests. These included leaf surface, nutritional status, biochemical, histological and physiological measurements. In a number of the tests, significant differences between sites were found for at least one tree species, with the UK sites at one end of the distribution and continental sites (especially those in regions where visible damage is observed) at the other end. Examples of these gradients in response were the measured amounts of surface wax on needles of Norway spruce and differences in the contact angles of water droplets on the needle surfaces (a measurement which correlates well with changes in wax structure). British sites also showed lower ethylene emission from needles (hydrocarbon emissions are general stress indicators in plants), larger buffering capacities in the range pH 7–10 for current-year needles and different proportions of carotenoid pigments. Gradients in the response of foliage to such diagnostic analysis indicate ultrastructural, biochemical and physiological differences across Europe. Work is currently being focused on whether these differences are related to pollutant exposure, to climatic factors or to both in combination. Research is needed to determine how these responses vary with age and genotype and the specificity of response to individual pollutants must be tested, since these factors are known to be modified by other stresses.

Diagnosis of true Forest Decline is not simple, requiring the use of a range of symptoms, examination of their development with time and suitable lateral thinking regarding likely causes in any one locality. That pollution is involved in both the ozone/magnesium damage and the foliage browning in high areas in Germany seems certain, although there may be climatic or other predisposing factors. Pollution and/or cold stress may also be precursors in the reddening and needle cast problems in southern Bavaria which have been attributed to fungal attack by some scientists. In Britain, localised SO_2 damage has considerably lessened over recent decades reflecting changes in the emissions and dispersal of this pollutant. However, soil acidification is known to be occurring in some areas and the possibility of ozone damage alone or in combination with frost or drought should be taken seriously. However the occurrence of such damage in Britain, where ozone episodes are less frequent than in central Europe and where the climate is endemically windy, is likely to be infrequent. Equally, there is substantial wet and dry deposition of sulphur and nitrogen to tree foliage in Britain and the possibility that these inputs disturb growth or interact with other stresses cannot be excluded.

11.6 CONCLUSIONS

1. There have long been problems of tree damage in relatively limited areas close to sources of industrial pollution. Such problems are probably caused by high concentrations of SO_2, perhaps exacerbated by other pollutants. In Europe, such damage is observed in parts of Czechoslovakia, Poland, East Germany and north eastern Bavaria.

2. During the mid-1970s concern grew in West Germany over a widespread decline in the health of silver fir and Norway spruce. This concern later extended to Scots pine, beech and oak. Symptoms of decline were: the premature loss of foliage, yellowing of foliage, decreased branch growth in broad leaved trees, and decreases in root growth.

3. These symptoms have been observed in many parts of West Germany, Northern Italy, Switzerland and France and as far north as Southern Sweden, regions in which there are different mixtures of pollutants. Forest damage on this scale appears unprecedented.

4. In the UK, annual surveys of Sitka spruce, Norway spruce and Scots pine have been carried out by the Forestry Commission since 1984 using internationally agreed protocols. In 1984 and 1985 the scale of needle loss did not seem unusual compared with past experience. In 1986 there was a large increase in the percentage of trees showing medium to severe crown thinning and older Norway spruce surveyed for the first time showed particularly poor crown density. The results of the 1987 survey confirmed the progress of crown thinning and showed that there was foliar yellowing on a similar scale to that found in West Germany. On the basis of the observed crown thinning, the health of the UK sample is now regarded as only 'moderate', and appears similar to the situation in West Germany.

5. A survey of the UK Friends of the Earth of beech and yew in 1984, concentrating on mainly isolated and old trees, drew attention to poor health in these species. Surveys of beech by the Forestry Commission since 1985 have not revealed any new evidence of decline but this species has been known to show damage after dry years.

6. None of the symptoms of forest decline can be attributed to a unique cause and consequently it is impossible to distinguish in surveys between damage caused by natural stresses and pollutants. A very large number of hypotheses (not mutually exclusive) have been proposed to explain the decline. The three most important appear to be:

   i) soil acidification leading to leaching of base cations and mobilisation of aluminium and other metals.

   ii) direct effects of atmospheric pollutants, particularly ozone and acid mist.

   iii) interactions between pollutant stresses and other stresses.

7. In the UK, a large increase in damage to conifers in 1986 followed a harsh winter and attacks by fungi and insect pests. Such stresses alone may have caused the damage, but the possibilities that pollutants predisposed trees to natural stress or interacted with those stresses cannot be excluded. Similar conclusions apply to the health of beech which appears to decline after dry years.

8. Surveys of foliage density and discoloration cannot establish causes. This has led to the investigation of a number of diagnostic tests indicative of pollutant stress. These include measurements of leaf surface, biochemical and physiological factors. A recent multinational pilot survey in Europe has shown that some of these tests can identify significant differences between trees growing at different sites across Europe which experience a range of pollution climates. This approach merits further development.

9. Although no relationships between forest decline and acid deposition have yet been proved in UK surveys, there is no cause for complacency. At least three of the damage mechanisms that have been proposed for pollution damage to forests could apply in the UK. Soil acidification is known to be occurring in some areas, episodes of ozone are observed in summer, especially in southern Britain and there is increasing evidence from UK experiments of interactions between air pollution and natural stresses.

RECOMMENDATIONS 12

Policy

1. Until recently there has been little information available on the differing mixtures of acidic pollutants occurring across much of rural Britain (pollution climate). Results from the new monitoring networks will improve this situation. As an aid to policy making, it is recommended that the concept of pollution climate be further developed. A comparison of the pollution climates of Britain and other parts of Europe could be facilitated by developing numerical models and standardised data bases for European observations. This approach is also likely to identify additional pollutants that need to be monitored and to allow adequate inter comparisons between countries.

2. Results from pollutant monitoring should be combined with information on land use in the UK to assist in identifying areas at risk and species requiring further study. This approach would also be useful for modelling the potential impact of air pollutants including acid deposition when land use changes are contemplated. As an example, the potential exists for long term changes in the soils of upland areas as a consequence of acid deposition. Alterations in land use, eg. from moorland to forestry are likely to further influence the rates of change of soils.

3. Although there has been much research in the UK into the effects of air pollutants on plants, there has been little emphasis in deriving dose–response relationships which would be useful for decision making on pollution control. It is recommended that the balance of research be kept under regular review by the sponsoring organisations to ensure that there is a satisfactory integration of work of direct relevance to policy makers and work to understand the basic mechanisms of response to pollutants. Both are necessary if we are to protect existing ecosystems, identify new threats, and translate the results of research into policy decisions.

4. This review has concentrated on the effects of acid deposition and related pollutants. However, other products of man's activities, such as carbon dioxide, also have environmental impacts. Over the next 50–100 years many scientists believe that there will be significant climatic changes resulting from manmade pollution. In addition to considering the direct consequences of climatic change, it will be necessary to consider how the responses of terrestrial ecosystems to pollutants such as acid deposition might differ in the changed climates of the future.

Research

1. Pollutants rarely occur singly. They usually occur in mixtures. It is known that atmospheric loads of pollutants differ in different parts of the UK. But much more information is required in order that the mixtures of pollutants, 'pollution climates', and their geographical limits can be defined with greater precision. This information is needed for the design and interpretation of studies of the effects of pollutants on crops, trees and semi-natural vegetation growing in the UK.

2. Special attention should be paid to the occurrences of
   (i) ozone,
   (ii) the chemistry of mists and low cloud, and
   (iii) ammonia and oxides of nitrogen whose concentrations are increasing in some parts of the UK.
   The increases of ammonia are largely attributable to slurries from animal husbandry and those of nitrogen oxides to increasing numbers of motor vehicles.

3. Better knowledge of the ambient mixtures of pollutants should be paralleled by an improved understanding of the processes controlling the transfer of pollutants, individually and in combinations to plant and soil surfaces. These studies must take account of diurnal changes in plant function, notably photosynthesis, which influence deposition on and uptake by plants. For the future, responses should be related to amounts of pollutants taken up by plants instead of, as at present, atmospheric concentrations.

4. Although in the past there have been suggestions that acid deposition is unlikely to significantly affect soil properties, results from Sweden, Germany and the UK suggest that the acidity of some soils have been changed appreciably. Studies, including historical assessments of the effects of atmospheric pollutants should be made on selected soils in the UK, taking note of the altered movement of heavy metals.

5. Studies of the effects of atmospheric pollutants on soils should be concerned with physical, chemical and biological aspects of nutrient cycling, including the microbiological decomposition of litter and the occurrence of mycorrhizas.

6. When studying the impacts of atmospheric pollutants on soils it is necessary to clarify the role of maritime-derived sulphate. At sites where there is substantial sulphate deposition, aluminium may be

mobilised into soil solution and drainage water, where it may be toxic to plants and animals.

7. The application of lime in upland areas has decreased over recent years, largely because of withdrawal of subsidies for this practice. Liming experiments in the UK and elsewhere indicate that reintroduction of liming may help to counteract the acidifying effects of pollutants on soils but may also lead to changes in species composition and soil biology of upland ecosystems. These complex effects require investigation and for these reasons it may be appropriate to include such studies within designated Environmentally Sensitive Areas.

8. So that estimates can be made of the plants and crops that are at risk, it is essential to improve knowledge of their sensitivity/tolerance to the combinations of pollutants occurring in different pollution climates. A screening programme for major economic and amenity species is necessary. These studies could be of particular importance if trees, as a result of changes in agricultural policy, are grown in locations previously devoted to agricultural crops.

9. To gain an improved understanding of plant responses in conditions that occur naturally, it is necessary to widen the scope of existing field based experiments being done in the UK. These should include the study of effects of a range of pollutant climates on agricultural crops, forest species and semi-natural vegetation.

10. Very little is known of the sensitivity of major UK agricultural crops to ozone, although potentially damaging episodes of ozone are known to occur almost every summer. A research programme into crop responses to ozone is necessary and should take into account the known co-occurrences of ozone with other gaseous pollutants.

11. Crops and semi-natural vegetation are subject to a variety of stresses, such as drought and unseasonally early or late frosts, which can restrict growth and cause economic losses. There is evidence to suggest that these stresses may affect the responses of plants to atmospheric pollutants. Conversely exposure to atmospheric pollutants may affect the sensitivity of plants to drought, frost etc. These interactions need to be critically examined. They may explain why a mixture of pollutants may be damaging in some circumstances and not in others. This programme should be widened to include interactions with pests and pathogens.

12. Because it is not known whether the responses of young and mature trees to atmospheric pollutants are the same, it is necessary to augment present studies on young trees with experiments on mature trees. These experiments should be of sufficient duration (5–10 years) to determine whether continuing exposures to relatively small concentrations of pollutants may prove to be harmful.

13. Mists and low cloud have been found to be more 'acidic' than rain. As they occur commonly in the uplands where there has been much forest planting, it is necessary to study the effects of acid mists (and other pollutants known to be common in the uplands), on trees and other upland vegetation.

14. Plant pollution research has traditionally been concerned with growth and yield, but has become increasingly sophisticated in recent years. Nevertheless, the range of observations of effects of pollutants still needs to be widened to take account of flowering, fruiting and the quality of the harvested products (whether silage, hay, vegetables, grain, fruit or timber).

15. Most research into pollution effects on plants has been concentrated upon the responses of foliage to atmospheric pollutants. But because it has been shown that roots can be affected more adversely than foliage, knowledge of events below ground needs to be improved. Changes in roots can affect their ability to gain water and nutrients and to form beneficial associations with mycorrhizal fungi which colonise woody and herbaceous plants.

16. Surveys of the health of British trees have been substantially increased in scope and range since 1984. Results suggest that there has been a significant decline in the health of conifers since 1985 and the health of other species is not good. It is important that surveys of forests, amenity trees and hedgerow trees continue, as they represent a standardised method of detecting changes. It seems unlikely that surveys alone will identify causes of poor health. Consequently it is necessary that close liaison is encouraged between those researching the responses of trees to controlled stresses and those assessing tree health in the field.

17. It is also desirable to encourage the development of tests that identify the early stages of specific pollutant damage in trees and to test their use in the field.

18. In the field, plant responses are often confounded with effects of other environmental factors. To explain and predict possibly damaging effects of pollutants, it is essential to maintain parallel programmes of basic biochemical and cellular research to identify mechanisms of plant response. Only with such fundamental knowledge are we likely to be able to understand plant responses to the complex mixtures of stresses that commonly occur.

ACKNOWLEDGEMENTS

The review group wishes to thank the many individuals and organisations who have contributed to this report, in particular Dr M.R. Ashmore, Dr J. Barnes, Dr R. Derwent, Dr D. Fowler, Dr J. Irwin, Dr A. Martin, Dr A.R. Mcleod and Dr A.R. Wellburn.

We also wish to thank Dr E. Wright and Dr K. Oates for providing Plate 2 and Dr S. McNeill and Dr J.N. Cape for providing Plates 6 and 9 respectively.

Finally, we are indebted to Mr R. Wilson for preparing the figures and cover, Dr A. Crossley for photographic work and the secretarial staff of ITE Edinburgh for their help in preparing this report.

REFERENCES

Abrahamsen, G. 1984. Effects of acidic deposition on forest soil and vegetation. *Phil. Trans. R. Soc. Lond. Ser. B*, **305**, 369–82.

Abrahamsen, G., Horntvedt, R. & Tveite, B. 1977. Impacts of acid precipitation on coniferous forest ecosystems. *Wat. Air & Soil Pollut.*, **8**, 57–73.

Alexander, M. 1980. Effects of acid precipitation on biochemical activities in soil. In: *Ecological Impact of Acid Precipitation – Proceedings of an International Conference*, edited by D. Drabløs and A. Tollan, 47–53. SNSF Project, Norway.

Alden, J. & Hermann, R.K. 1971. Aspects of the cold hardiness mechanisms in plants. *Bot. Rev.*, **37**, 37–143.

Alscher, R. 1984. Effects of SO_2 on light-modulated enzyme reactions. *Gaseous Air Pollutants and Plant Metabolism*, edited by M.J. Koziol and F. Whatley, 181–200. Butterworths, London.

Alstad, D.N., Edmunds, G.F. & Weinstein, L.H. 1982. Effects of air pollutants on insect populations. *A. Rev. Ent.*, **27**, 369–84.

Aminu-Kano, T. & McNeill, S. 1988. Air pollution and insect pests (abstract). In: *Acid Rain and Britain's Natural Ecosystems*, edited by M.R. Ashmore, J.N.B. Bell and C. Garretty. Imperial College Centre for Environmental Technology, London.

Amundson, R.G. & Maclean, D.C., 1982. Influence of oxides of nitrogen on crop growth and yield: an overview. In: *Air Pollution by Nitrogen Oxides*, edited by T. Schneider and L. Grant, 501–10. Elsevier, Amsterdam.

Amundson, R.G., Weinstein, L.H., Van Lenken, P. & Colavito, L.J. 1982. Joint action of HF and NO_2 on growth, fluorine accumulation and leaf resistance in Marcross Sweetcorn. *Env. exp. Bot.*, **22**, 49–55.

Anderson, L.S. & Mansfield, T.A. 1979. The effects of nitric oxide pollution on the growth of tomato. *Environ. Pollut.*, **20**, 113–21.

André, H.M., Bolly, C. & Lebrun, Ph. 1982. Monitoring and mapping air pollution through an animal indicator: a new and quick method. *J. appl. Ecol.*, **19**, 107–11.

André, H.M., Lebrun, Ph, Masson M. & Sarton, F. 1984. On the use of *Humerobates rostrolamellatus* (Acari) as an air pollution bioassay monitor. The incidence of SO_2–NO_2 synergism and of winter temperature. *Sci. Tot. Environ.*, **39**, 177–87.

Andrews, S.M., Cooke, J.A. & Johnson, M.S.. 1982. Fluoride in small mammals and their potential food sources in contaminated grasslands. *Fluoride*, **15**, 56–62.

Arovaara, H., Hari, P. & Kuusela, K. 1984. Possible effect of changes in atmospheric composition and acid rain on tree growth. *Comm. Inst. Forest. Fenn.*, **122**, 1–16.

Asada, K. 1980. Formation and scavenging of superoxide in chloroplasts, with relation to injury by sulfur dioxide. In: *Research Report from the National Institute for Environmental Studies, Japan (1980).*, 165–79.

Asada, K. & Kiso, K. 1973. Initiation of aerobic oxidation of sulfite by illuminated spinach chloroplasts. *Eur. J. Biochem.*, **33**, 253–7.

Ashenden, T.W. 1979. The effects of long-term exposure to SO_2 and NO_2 pollution on the growth of *Dactylis glomerata L.* and *Poa pratensis L. Environ. Pollut.*, **18**, 249–58.

Ashenden, T.W. & Mansfield, T.A. 1978. Extreme pollution sensitivity of grasses when SO_2 and NO_2 are present in the atmosphere together. *Nature, Lond.*, **273**, 142–3.

Ashenden, T.W. & Williams, I.A.D. 1980. Growth reductions in *Lolium multiflorum* Lam. and *Phleum pratense* L. as a result of SO_2 and NO_2 pollution. *Environ. Pollut. Ser. A*, **21**, 131–9.

Ashmore, M.R. 1984. Effects of ozone on vegetation in the United Kingdom. In: *The Evaluation and Assessment of the Effects of Photochemical Oxidants on Human Health, Agricultural Crops, Forestry, Materials and Visibility*, edited by P. Grennfelt 92–104, Göteborg.

Ashmore, M.R., Bell, J.N.B. & Reilly, C.L. 1978. A survey of ozone levels in the British Isles using indicator plants. *Nature, Lond.*, **276**, 813–5.

Ashmore, M., Bell, J.N.B. & Rutter, J. 1985. The role of ozone in Forest Decline in West Germany. *Ambio*, **14**, 81–7.

Ashmore, M.R., Bell, J.N.B. & Rutter, A.J. 1988. Effects of acid rain on trees and higher plants. In: *Acid Rain and Britain's Natural Ecosystems*, edited by M.R. Ashmore, J.N.B. Bell and C. Garretty. Imperial College Centre for Environmental Technology, London.

Ashmore, M.R. & Dalpra, C. 1985. The effects of London's air on plant growth. *Lond. Environ. Bull.*, **3**, 4–5.

Ashmore, M.R., Mimmack, A., Mepstead, R. & Bell, J.N.B. 1987. Research at Imperial College with open-top chambers, 1976–86. Proceedings 2nd Open-top Chamber Workshop: Environmental Management in Open-top Chambers. CEC Brussels, (in press).

Ashmore, M.R. & Onal, M. 1984. Modification by SO_2 of the responses of *Hordeum vulgare* to ozone. *Environ. Pollut. Ser. A*, **36**, 31–43.

Ashmore, M.R. & Tickle, A.K. 1988. Effects of ozone on native plant species. In: *Acid Rain and Britain's Natural Ecosystems*, edited by M.R. Ashmore, J.N.B. Bell and C. Garretty, Imperial College Centre for Environmental Technology, London.

Asman, U.A.H. & Slanina, J. 1980. Meteorological interpretation of the chemical composition of precipitation and some results of sequential rain sampling. In: *Ecological Impact of Acid Precipitation*, edited by D. Drabløs and A. Tollan, 140–1, SNSF Project, Norway.

Awang, M.B. 1979. *The Effects of SO$_2$ Pollution on Plant Growth with Special Reference to Trifolium repens*. Ph.D. Thesis, University of Sheffield.

Ayazloo, M. & Bell, J.N.B. 1981. Studies on the tolerance to sulphur dioxide of grass populations in polluted areas. I. Identification of tolerant populations. *New Phytol.*, **88**, 203–22.

Babich, H. & Stotzky, G. 1974. Air pollution and microbial ecology. *Critic. Rev. Environ. Contr.*, **4**, 353–421.

Bache, B.W. & Scott, N.M. 1979. Sulphur emissions in relation to sulphur in soils and crops. In: *International Symposium on Sulphur Emissions in the Environment*, edited by F.F. Ross, Society for Chemical Industry, London.

Baker, C.K. & Fullwood, A.E. 1987. Leaf damage following crop spraying in winter barley exposed to sulphur dioxide. *Crop Prot.*, (In press).

Baker, C.K., Colls, J.J., Fullwood, A.E. & Seaton, G.G.R. 1986. Depression of growth and yield in winter barley exposed to sulphur dioxide in the field. *New Phytol.*, **104**, 233–41.

Baker, C.K., Unsworth, M.H. & Greenwood, P. 1982. Leaf injury on wheat plants exposed in the field in winter to SO$_2$. *Nature, Lond.*, **299**, 149–51.

Ballantyne, D.J. 1984. Phytotoxic air pollutants and oxidative phosphorylation. In: *Gaseous Air Pollutants and Plant Metabolism*, edited by M.J. Koziol and F.R. Whatley, 223–30, Butterworths, London.

Barnes, R.L. 1972. Effects of chronic exposure to ozone on photosynthesis and respiration of pines. *Environ. Pollut.*, **3**, 133–8.

Barrett, C.F., Atkinson, D.H.F., Cape, J.N., Fowler, D., Irwin, J.G., Kallend, A.S., Martin, A., Pitman, J.L., Scriven, R.A. & Tuck, A.F. 1983. *Acid Deposition in the United Kingdom*. UK Review Group on Acid Rain, WSL, Stevenage.

Beard, R.L. 1965. Observation on house flies on high ozone environments. *Ann. ent. Soc. Am.*, **58**, 404–5.

Beevers, L. & Hageman, R.H. 1980. Nitrate and nitrite reduction. In: *The Biochemistry of Plants vol. 5, Amino Acids and Derivatives*, edited by B.J. Miflin, 116–68. Academic Press, New York.

Bell, J.N.B. 1982. Sulphur dioxide and the growth of grasses. In: *Effects of Gaseous Air Pollution in Agriculture and Horticulture*, edited by M.H. Unsworth and D.P. Ormrod, 225–36, Butterworths, London.

Bell, J.N.B. 1984. Air pollution problems in western Europe. In: *Gaseous Air Pollutants and Plant Metabolism*, edited by M.J. Koziol and F.R. Whatley, 3–24, Butterworths, London.

Bell, J.N.B. 1985. SO$_2$ effects on the productivity of grass species. In: *Sulfur Dioxide and Vegetation, Physiology, Ecology and Policy Issues*, edited by W.E. Winner, H.A. Mooney and R.A. Goldstein, 209–26, Standford University Press, California, USA.

Bell, J.N.B. & Lane, P.L. 1984. The effects of simulated urban air pollution on grass yield: Part 1–Description and simulation of ambient pollution. *Environ. Pollut. Ser. B*, **8**, 245–63.

Bell, J.N.B. & Mudd, C.H. 1976. Sulphur dioxide resistance in plants: a case study of *Lolium perenne*. In: *Effects of Air Pollutants on Plants*, edited by T.A. Mansfield, 87–103. (Society for Experimental Biological Seminar Series, Volume 1) Cambridge University Press, Cambridge, London, New York.

Bell, J.N.B., Rutter, A.J. & Relton, J. 1979. Studies on the effects of low levels of sulphur dioxide on the growth of *Lolium perenne* L. *New Phytol.*, **83**, 627–43.

Benepal, P.S., Rangappa, M. & Dunning, J.A. 1982. Interaction between ozone and Mexican bean beetle feeding damage on leaves (Abstract). *Ann. Rep. of the Bean Improvement Cooperative*, **22**, 50.

Benoit, L.F., Skelly, J.M., Moore, L.D. & Dochinger, L.S. 1983. The influence of ozone on *Pinus strobus* L. pollen germination. *Can. J. For. Res.*, **13**, 184–7.

Bennett, J.H. & Hill, A.C. 1973. Inhibition of apparent photosynthesis by air pollutants. *J. environ. Qual.*, **2**, 526–30.

Bennett, J.P. & Runeckles, V.C. 1977a. Effects of low levels of ozone on plant competition. *J. appl. Ecol.*, **14**, 877–80.

Bennett, J.P. & Runeckles, V.C. 1977b. Effects of low levels of ozone on growth of crimson clover and annual ryegrass. *Crop Sci.*, **17**, 443–5.

Berry, C.R. 1973. The differential sensitivity of eastern white pine to three types of air pollution. *Can. J. For. Res.*, **3**, 543–7.

Bialobok, S., Karolweski, P. & Oleksyn, J. 1977. A comparison of the effects of sulphur dioxide, ozone and a mixture of the gases on the injuries to leaves of trees. *Third Ann. Rep. Inst. Dendrology, Kornik* (Poland).

Binns, W.O. & Redfern, D.B. 1983. *Acid rain and forest decline in Germany.* Res. and Dev. Paper No. 131, Forestry Commission, Edinburgh.

Binns. W.O., Redfern, D.B., Boswell, R. & Betts, A.J.A. 1986. *Forest health and air pollution.* Res. and Dev. Paper No. 147, Forestry Commission, Edinburgh.

Bisessar, S., Palmer, K.T., Kuja, A.L. & Linzon, S.N. 1984. Influence of simulated acidic rain on bacterial speck of tomato. *J. environ. Qual.*, **13**, 18–22.

Black, V.J. 1982. Effects of SO_2 on physiological processes in plants. In: *Effects of Gaseous Air Pollution in Agriculture and Horticulture*, edited by M.H. Unsworth and D.P. Ormrod, 76–91, Butterworths, London.

Black, V.J. 1985. SO_2 effects of stomatal behaviour. In: *Sulfur Dioxide and Vegetation*, edited by W.E. Winner, H.A. Mooney and R.A. Goldstein, 96–117, Standford University Press, California, USA.

Black, V.J., Ormrod, D.P. & Unsworth, M.H. 1982. Effects of low concentration of ozone, singly, and in combination with sulphur dioxide on net photosynthesis rates of *Vicia faba* L. *J. exp. Bot.*, **33**, 1302–11.

Black, V.J. & Unsworth, M.H. 1979. Effects of low concentrations of sulphur dioxide on net photosynthesis and dark respiration of *Vicia faba* L. *J. exp. Bot.*, **30**, 473–83.

Bleasdale, J.K.A. 1952. Atmospheric pollution and plant growth. *Nature Lond.*, **169**, 376–7.

Bleasdale, J.K.A. 1952. *Atmospheric Pollution and Plant Growth.* Ph.D. thesis, University of Manchester.

Bleasdale, J.K.A. 1973. Effects of coal–smoke pollution gases on the growth of ryegrass (*Lolium perenne* L.). *Environ. Pollut.*, **5**, 275–85.

Blum, U. & Tingey, D.T. 1977. A study of the potential ways in which ozone could reduce root growth and nodulation of soybean. *Atmos. Environ.*, **11**, 737–9.

Blum, U., Mrozek, E. & Johnson, E. 1983. Investigation of ozone (O_3) effects on ^{14}C distribution in ladino clover. *Environ. & exp. Bot.*, **23**, 369–78.

BML 1987. (Bundesministerium für Ernahrung, Landwirtschaft und Forsten), Waldschadenserhebung 1987, Bonn, 1–81.

Bolsinger, M. & Flückiger, W. 1984. Effect of air pollution at a motorway on the infestation of *Viburnum opulus* L. by *Aphis fabae*. Scop. *Eur. J. For. Path.*, **14**, 256–60.

Bonner, F.T. 1970. Oxygen exchange between NO and water. *Ing. Chem.*, **9**, 190–3.

Bonner, F.T. & Jordan, S. 1973. Simultaneous nitrogen and oxygen exchange between NO and aqueous solutions of nitrite. *Ing. Chem.*, **12**, 1363–9.

Bonte, J. 1977. Effects du SO_2 sur les vegetaux en plein champ, a faible concentration et applique d'une falcon permanente, Ministère de l'Agriculture de France, INRA, Morlaas.

Bonte, J., de Cormis, L. & Tisne, A. 1981. Etude des effets à long-terme d'une pollution chronique par SO_2, Ministère de l'Agriculture de France, INRA, Morlaas.

Bosch, C., Pfannkuch, E., Baum, U. & Rehfuess, K.E. 1983. Uber die Erkrankung der fichte (*Picea abies* [L.] Karst.) in den Hochlagen des Bayerischen Waldes. *Forstwiss. Cent Bl.*, **102**, 167–81.

Bosch, C., Pfannkuch, E., Rehfuess, K.E., Runkel, K.H., Schramel, P. & Senser, M. 1986. Einfluss einer Düngung mit Magnesium und Calcium, von Ozon und saurem Nebel auf Frosthärete, Ernährungszustand und Biomasseproduktion junger Fichten (*Picea abies* [L.] Karst.) *Forstwiss. Cent Bl.*, **105**, 218–29.

Bowen, H.J.M. 1977. Natural cycles of the elements and their perturbation by man. In: *Environment and Man. Volume 6. The Chemical Environment*, edited by J. Lenihan and W.W. Fletcher, 1–37, Blackie, Glasgow and London.

Bown, C.J. & Heslop, R.E.F. 1979. *The Soils of the Country round Stranraer and Wigtown.* Memoirs of the Soil Survey of Great Britain, Scotland, Macaulay Institute for Soil Research, Aberdeen.

Braun, S. & Flückiger, W. 1985. Increased population of the aphid *Aphis pomi* at a motorway. Part 3–The effect of exhaust gases. *Environ. Pollut. Ser. A*, **39**, 183–92.

Brecke, B.J. & Duke, W.B. 1980. Effects of glyphosate on intact bean plants (*Phaseolus vulgaris* L.) and isolated cells. *Pl. Physiol.*, **66**, 656–9.

van Breemen, N., Burrough, P.A., Velthorst, E.J., van Dobben, H.F., de Wet, T., Ridder, T.B. & Reijnders, H.F.R. 1982. Soil acidification from atmospheric ammonium sulphate in forest canopy throughfall. *Nature, Lond.*, **229**, 548–50.

van Breemen, N., Driscoll, C.T. & Mulder, J. 1984. Acidic deposition and internal proton sources in acidification of soils and waters. *Nature, Lond.*, **307**, 599–604.

van Breemen, N. & Jordens, E.R. 1983a. Effects of atmospheric ammonium sulphate on calcareous and non-calcareous soils of woodlands in The Netherlands. In: *Effects of Accumulation of Air Pollutants in Forest Ecosystems*, edited by B. Ulrich and J. Pankrath, 171–82, D. Reidel Publishing Co.

van Breemen, N., Mulder, J. & Driscoll, C.T. 1983b. Acidification and alkalinisation of soils. *Pl. Soil.*, **75**, 283–308.

Brewer, P.F. & Heagle, A.S. 1983. Interactions between *Glomus geosporum* and exposure of soybeans to ozone or simulated acid rain in the field. *Phytopathology*, **73**, 1035–40.

Briffa, K.R. 1984. *Tree-Climate Relationships and Dendroclimatological Reconstruction in the British Isles.* Ph.D. thesis, University of East Anglia.

Briffa, K.R., Jones, P.D., Wigley, T.M.L., Pilcher, J.R. & Baillie, M.G.L. 1983. Climate reconstruction from tree rings: Part 1, basic methodology and preliminary results for England. *J. Climatol.*, **3**, 233–42.

Brown, K.A. 1985a. *Formation of Organic sulphur in Anaerobic Peat,* Central Electricity Generating Board Report No. TPRD/L/2886/N85, Leatherhead, Surrey.

Brown, K.A. 1985b. Sulphur distribution and metabolism in waterlogged peat. *Soil Biol. & Biochem.*, **17**, 39–45.

Brown, K.A. 1985c. Acid deposition: effects of sulphuric acid at pH 3 on chemical and biochemical properties of bracken litter. *Soil Biol. & Biochem.*, **17**, 31–8.

Brown, K.A. & MacQueen, J.F. 1985. Sulphate uptake from surface water by peat. *Soil Biol. & Biochem.*, **17**, 411–20.

Brown, K.A., Roberts., T.M. & Blank, L.W. 1987. Interaction between ozone and cold sensitivity in Norway spruce: A factor contributing to the forest decline in Central Europe? *New Phytol.*, **105**, 149–55.

Buckenham, A.H., Parry, M.A. & Whittingham, C.P. 1982. Effects of aerial pollutants on the growth and yield of spring barley. *Ann. appl. Biol.*, **100**, 179–87.

Bunce, H.W.F. 1979. Fluoride emissions and forest growth. *J. Air Pollut. Control Ass.*, **29**, 642–3.

Burns, K.N. & Allcroft, R. 1964. Fluorosis in cattle, *Animal Disease Surveys Report No. 2, part 1.* Ministry of Agriculture Fisheries & Food, HMSO, London.

Campbell, L., Martin, S.P., Sinn, J.P. & Bruck, P.I. 1985. Germination of spores of *Leptosphaerulina briosiana* and *Phytophthora infestans* in simulated acid rain solutions. *Phytopathology*, **75**, 499.

Cape, J.N. 1984. The importance of solution equilibria in studying the effects of sulphite on plants. *Environ. Pollut. Ser. A*, **34**, 259–74.

Cape, J.N., Fink, S., Freer-Smith, P.H., Mehlhorn, H., Paterson, I.S., Wellburn, A.R. & Wolfenden, J. 1988. The early diagnosis of forest decline: results of a pilot survey, 1986. Grange-over-Sands, Cumbria: Institute of Terrestrial Ecology.

Cape, J.N. & Fowler, D. 1981. Changes in epicuticular wax of *Pinus sylvestris* exposed to polluted air. *Silva fenn.*, **15**, 457–8.

Capron, A.C. & Mansfield, T.A. 1976. Inhibition of net photosynthesis in tomato in air polluted with NO and NO_2. *J. exp. Bot.*, **27**, 1181–6.

Carlson, R.W. 1979. Reduction in the photosynthesis rate of *Acer, Quercus* and *Fraxinus* species caused by sulphur dioxide and ozone. *Environ. Pollut.*, **18**, 159–70.

Carlson, R.W. 1983. The effect of SO_2 on photosynthesis and leaf resistance at varying concentrations of CO_2. *Environ. Pollut., Ser. A*, **30**, 309–21.

Carlson, R.W. & Bazzaz, F.A. 1985. Plant response to SO_2 and CO_2. In: *Sulfur Dioxide and Vegetation*, edited by W.E. Winner, H.A. Mooney and R.A. Goldstein, 313–31, Standford University Press, California, USA.

Carney, A.W., Stephenson, G.R., Ormrod, D.P. & Ashton, G.C. 1973. Ozone-herbicide interactions in crop plants. *Weed Sci.*, **21**, 508–11.

CEC/COST Workshop proceedings (Risø and Copenhagen, Denmark). 1986. *How are the Effects of Air Pollutants on Agricultural Crops Influenced by the Interactions with Other Limiting Factors?* March 1986. (XII ENV/32/86 EAD.46.86) CEC, Brussels.

CEC/COST Workshop proceedings (Lokeberg, Sweden). 1988. *Direct Effects of Dry and Wet Deposition on Forest Ecosystems – in particular Canopy Interactions.* October 1986. (EAD.62/87) CEC, Brussels.

Cerović, Z.G., Kalezić, R. & Plesničar, M. 1983. The role of photophosphorylation in SO_2 and SO_3^{2-} inhibition of photosynthesis in isolated chloroplasts. *Planta*, **156**, 249–54.

Charlson, R.J. & Rodhe, H. 1982. Factors controlling the acidity of natural rainwater. *Nature, Lond.*, **295**, 683–5.

Chevone, B.I. & Yang, Y.S. 1985. CO_2 exchange rates and stomatal diffusive resistance in soybean exposed to O_3 and SO_2. *Can. J. Pl. Sci.*, **65**, 267–74.

Chilgren, J.D. 1979. Small mammal investigations at ZAPS: demographic studies and responses to gradient levels of SO_2. In: *The Bioenvironmental Impact of a Coal-fired Power Plant* edited by E.M. Preston and T.L. Gullett, 764–89, 4th Interim Report EPA-600/3-79-044. Environmental Protection Agency, Corvallis.

Cohen, J.B. & Ruston, A.G. 1925. *Smoke. A Study of Town Air.* Edward Arnold London.

Colvill, K.E., Bell, R.M., Roberts, T.M. & Bradshaw, A.D. 1983. The use of open-top chambers to study the effects of air pollutants, in particular sulphur dioxide, on the growth of ryegrass. *Lolium perenne* L. II. The long-term effect of filtering polluted urban air or adding SO_2 to rural air. *Environ. Pollut. Ser. A*, **31**, 35–55.

Colvill, K.E., Horsman, D.C., Roose, M.L., Roberts, T.M. & Bradshaw, A.D. 1985. Field trials on the influence of air pollutants, and SO_2 in particular, on the growth of Ryegrass *Lolium perenne L. Environ. Pollut. Ser. A*, **39**, 235–66.

Commission of The European Community. 1987. *The State of the Environment in the European Communities* 1986. 1–388. (Eur 10633) Luxembourg.

Cossins, A.R. 1983. The adaptation of membrane structure and function to changes in temperature. In: *Cellular Acclimatisation to Environmental Change*, edited by A.R. Cossins and P. Sheterline, Cambridge University Press.

Costonis, A.C. 1970. Acute foliar injury of eastern white pine induced by sulphur dioxide and ozone. *Phytopathology*, **60**, 994–9.

Costonis, A.C. 1973. Injury to Eastern White Pine by sulphur dioxide and ozone alone and in mixtures. *Eur. J. For. Path.*, **3**, 50–5.

Costonis, A.C. & Sinclair, W.A. 1969. Relationships of atmospheric ozone to needle blight of eastern white pine. *Phytopathology*, **59**, 1566–74.

Cowling, D.W., Jones, L.H.P. & Lockyer, D.R. 1973. Increased yield through correction of sulphur deficiency in ryegrass exposed to sulphur dioxide. *Nature, Lond.*, **243**, 479–80.

Cox, R.M. 1983. The sensitivity of forest plant reproduction to long-range transported air pollutants: *in vitro* sensitivity of pollen to acidity. *New Phytol.*, **95**, 269–76.

Cox, R.V., Snaith, P.J. & Mansfield, T.A. 1985. The significance of natural and synthetic auxins in the control of stomatal movements. *Acta Hort.*, **17**, 247–54.

Coyne, P.I. & Bingham, G.E. 1982. Variation in photosynthesis and stomatal conductance in an ozone-stressed ponderosa pine stand. *Forest Sci.*, **28**, 257–73.

Crampton, C.B. 1961. The evolution of soils on hills in South Wales, and factors affecting their distribution, and their past, present and potential use. *Welsh Soils Discussion Group Report No. 8*, 52–69.

Crawshaw, D.H. 1986. The effects of acidic runoff on streams in Cumbria. In *Pollution in Cumbria* edited by P. Ineson. (ITE Symposium No. 16) Grange-over-Sands, 1985.

Creasey, J. 1984. *The Geochemistry of a Small Upland Catchment in North-East Scotland*, Ph.D. Thesis, University of Aberdeen.

Cresser, M.S. & Edwards, A.C. 1987. *Acidification of Freshwaters*, Cambridge University Press, Cambridge.

Cresser, M.S., Edwards, A.C., Ingram, S., Skiba, U. & Peirson-Smith, T. 1986. Soil-acid deposition interactions and their possible effects on geochemical weathering rates in British uplands. *J. geol. Soc. Lond.*, **143**, 649–58.

Crittenden, P.D. & Read, D.J. 1978. The effects of air pollution on plant growth with special reference to sulphur dioxide. II. Growth studies with *Lolium perenne* L., *New Phytol.*, **80**, 49–65.

Crittenden, P.D. & Read, D.J. 1979. The effects of air pollution on plant growth with special reference to sulphur dioxide. III. Growth studies with *Lolium multiflorum* Lam. and *Dactylis glomerata* L., *New Phytol.*, **83**, 645–51.

Crowther, C. & Ruston, A.G. 1911. The nature, distribution and effects upon vegetation of atmospheric impurities in and near an industrial town. *J. agric. Sci.*, **4**, 25–55.

Cuttle, S.P. 1983. Chemical properties of upland peats influencing the retention of phosphate and potassium ions. *J. Soil Sci.*, **34**, 75–82.

van Dam, D., van Dobben, H.F. ter Braak, C.F.J. & de Wit, T. 1986. Air pollution as a possible cause for the decline of some phanerogamic species in The Netherlands. *Vegetatio.*, **65**, 47–52.

Darrall, N.M. 1986. The sensitivity of net photosynthesis in several plant species to short term fumigation with sulphur dioxide. *J. exp. Bot.*, 1313–22.

Darrall, N.M. 1987. Physiological Responses to Air Pollutants (in press).

Davis, D.D. & Wood, F.A. 1973. The influence of environmental factors on the sensitivity of Virginia Pine to ozone. *Phytopathology.*, **63**, 371–6.

Davies, T. 1980. Grasses more sensitive to SO_2 pollution in conditions of low irradiance and short days. *Nature, Lond.*, **284**, 483–5.

Davison, A.W. & Bailey, I.F. 1982. SO_2 pollution reduces the freezing resistance of ryegrass. *Nature, Lond.*, **297**, 400–2.

Davison, A.W. & Barnes, J.D. 1986. Effects of winter stress on pollutant responses. In: *How are the Effects of Air Pollution on Agricultural Crops Influenced by the Interaction with Other Limiting Factors?* 16–32. Proceedings of CEC/COST Workshop Risø and Copenhagen, Denmark. March 1986. (XII/ENV/32/86 EAD.46.86). CEC Brussels.

Department of the Environment. 1986. Effects of airborne sulphur compounds on forests and freshwater. *DOE Pollution Paper* 7, HMSO, London.

Dighton, J., Skeffington, R.A. & Brown, K.A. 1986. The effects of sulphuric acid (pH 3) on roots and mycorrhizas of *Pinus sylvestris*. In: *Mycorrhizae: Physiology and Genetics*, edited by V. Gianinazzi-Pearson & S. Gianinazzi, 739–43, INRA, Paris.

Dochinger, L.S., Bender, F.W., Fox, F.L. & Heck, W.W. 1970. Chlorotic dwarf of eastern white pine caused by an ozone and sulphur dioxide interaction. *Nature, Lond.*, **225**, 476.

Dohmen, G.P. 1985. Secondary effects of air pollution: enhanced aphid growth. *Environ. Pollut. Ser. A*, **39**, 227–34.

Dohmen, G.P., McNeill, S. & Bell, J.N.B. 1984. Air pollution increases *Aphis fabae* pest potential. *Nature, Lond.*, **307**, 52–3.

Dochinger, L.S. & Seliskar, C.E. 1970. Air pollution and the chlorotic dwarf disease of eastern white pine. *Forest Sci.*, **16**, 46–55.

Dollard, G.J., Unsworth, M.H. & Harvey, M.J. 1983. Pollutant transfer in upland regions by occult precipitation. *Nature, Lond.*, **302**, 241–3.

Dowding, P. & Carvill, P.H. 1980. A reduction of counts of *Sporobolymyces roseus* Kluyve on ash (*Fraxinus excelsior* L.) leaves in Dublin city. *Irish J. environ. Sci.*, **1**, 65–8.

Duchelle, S.F., Skelly, J.M. & Chevone, B.I. 1982. Oxidant effects on forest tree seedlings in the Appalachian Mountains. *J. Soil Wat. Air Pollut.*, **12**, 363–73.

Duchelle, S.F., Skelly, J.M., Sharick, T.L., Chevone, B.I., Yang, Y.-S. & Nellessen, J.E. 1983. Effects of ozone on the productivity of natural vegetation in a high meadow of the Shenandoah National Park of Virginia. *J. environ. Manage.*, **17**, 299–308.

Dueck, Th.A., Ernst, W.H.O., Mooi, J. & Pasman, F.J.M. 1986. Effects of SO_2, NO_x and O_3 in combination on the yield and reproduction of *Silene cucubalus* populations. *J. Pl. Physiol.*, **122**, 97–106.

Dugger, W.M., Taylor, O.C., Cardiff, E. & Thompson, C.R. 1962. Stomatal action in plants as related to damage from photochemical oxidants. *Pl. Physiol.*, **37**, 487–91.

Eaton, J.S., Likens, G.E. & Bormann, R.H. 1973. Throughfall and stemflow chemistry in a northern hardwood forest. *J. Ecol.*, **61**, 495–508.

Edwards, A.C., Creasey, J., Skiba, U., Peirson-Smith, T. & Cresser, M.S. 1985. Long term rates of acidification of UK upland acidic soils. *Soil Use & Manage.*, **1**, 61–5.

Elkiey, T. & Ormrod, D.P. 1981. Sulfur and nitrogen nutrition and misting effects on the response of blue grass to ozone, sulfur dioxide or their mixture. *Wat. Air & Soil Pollut.*, **16**, 177–86.

Endress, A.G. & Post, S.L. 1985. Altered feeding preference of Mexican bean beetle *Epilachna varivestis* for ozonated soybean foliage. *Environ. Pollut. Ser. A*, **9**, 9–16.

EPA. 1980. Reviews of the environmental effects of pollutants. IX. Fluoride Health Effects Research Laboratory, Environmental Protection Agency, Cincinatti, Ohio.

EPA. 1984. Air Quality Criteria for Ozone and Other Photochemical Oxidants. EPA/660/8-84-020A., Research Triangle Park. N.C., USA.

EPRI (USA). 1986. Forest health and acidic deposition. Special Report of Research project 5002.

Ernst, W.H.O., Tonneijck, A.E.G. & Pasman, F.J.M. 1985. Ecotypic response of *Silene cucubalus* to air pollutants (SO$_2$, O$_3$) *J. Pl. Physiol.*, **118**, 439–50.

Evans, L.S., Lewin, K.F. & Cunningham, E.A. 1982. Effects of simulated acidic rain on yields of field-grown radishes and garden beets. *Agric. Environ.*, **7**, 285–98.

Farrar, J.F., Relton, J. & Rutter, A.J. 1977. Sulphur dioxide and growth of *Pinus sylvestris. J. appl. Ecol.*, **14**, 861–75.

Faulstich, H. & Stournaras, C. 1985. Potentially toxic concentrations of triethyl lead in Black Forest rainwater. *Nature, Lond.*, **317**, 714–5.

Federal Ministry of Food, Agriculture and Forestry (F.R.G.) 1982. Forest damage due to air pollution – the situation in the F.R.G.

Fehrmann, H., von Tiedemann, A., Blank, L.W., Glashagen, B., Eisenmann, T. & Fabian, P. 1986. Predisposing influence of air'pollutants on fungal leaf attack in cereals and grape-vines. In: *How are the Effects of Air Pollution on Agricultural Crops Influenced by the Interaction with Other Limiting Factors?* 98–103. Proceedings of CEC/COST Workshop, Risø and Copenhagen, March 1986, (XII/ENV/32/86. EAD.46.86) CEC, Brussels.

Feicht, P.G. 1981. *Effect of ozone and simulated acidic rain on interactions between* **Glomus macrocarpus** *and soybeans*. MSc thesis, North Carolina State University, Raleigh, N.C.

Feiler, S. Michael, G., Ranft, H., Tesche, M. & Bellman, C. 1981. Zur Komplexwirkung von SO$_2$ und Frost auf Fichte (*Picea abies* L. Karst.) *Biol. Rdsch.*, **19**, 98–100.

Ferguson, N.P. & Lee, J.A. 1983a. Past and present sulphur pollution in the southern Pennines. *Atmos. Environ.*, **17**, 1131–7.

Ferguson, N.P. & Lee, J.A. 1983b. The growth of *Sphagnum* species in the southern Pennines. *J. Bryol.*, **12**, 579–86.

Fergurson, N.P., Lee, J.A. and Bell, J.N.B. 1978. Effects of sulphur pollutants on the growth of *Sphagnum* species *Environ. Pollut.*, **16**, 151–162.

Ferguson, N.P., Robinson, R.N., Press, M.C. & Lee, J.A. 1984. Element concentrations in five *Sphagnum* species in relation to atmospheric pollution. *J. Bryol.*, **13**, 107–14.

Figge, K. 1988. Organic trace compounds in the atmosphere and their effect on leaf organs. In: *Direct Effects of Dry and Wet Deposition on Forest Ecosystems – in particular Canopy Interactions.* Proceedings of CEC/COST Workshop, Lokeborg, Sweden. October 1986. (EAD.62/87) CEC, Brussels.

Fink, S. & Braun, H.J. 1978. Zur epidemischen erkrankung der Weisstanne, *Abies alba* Mill: I Untersuchungen zur symtomatik und formulierung einer Vivose-Hypothese. *Allg. Forst. und Jagdztg.*, **149**, 145–50.

Firestone, M.K., Killham, K.S. & McColl, J.G. 1983. Fungal toxicity of mobilised soil aluminium and manganese. *Appl. & environ. Microbiol.*, **46**, 758–61.

Firestone, M.K., McColl, J.G., Killham, K.S. & Brooks, P.D. 1984. Microbial response to acid deposition and effects on plant productivity. In: *Direct and Indirect Effects of Acid Deposition on Vegetation*, edited by R.A. Linthurst, Butterworth, Boston.

Flückiger, W., Braun, S., Leonardi, S., Asche, N. & Flücki-ger-Keller, H. 1986. Factors contributing to forest decline in northwestern Switzerland. *Tree Physiol.*, **1**, 177–84.

Flückiger, W., Oertli, J.J. & Baltensweiler, W. 1978. Observations of an aphid infestation on hawthorn in the vicinity of a motorway. *Naturwissenschaften*, **65**, 654–5.

Fowler, D., Cape, J.N., Nicholson, I.A., Kinnaird, J.W. & Patterson, I.S. 1980. The influence of polluted atmospheres on cuticle degradation in Scots pine (*Pinus sylvestris*). In: *Ecological impact of acid precipitation. Proceedings of an international conference*, edited by D. Drabløs and A. Tollan, 146, SNSF Project, Norway.

Fowler, D., Cape, J.N., Leith, I.D., Paterson, I.S., Kinnaird, J.W. and Nicholson, I.A. 1988. Effects of air filtration at small SO$_2$ and NO$_2$ concentrations on the yield of barley. *Environ. Pollut., (in press)*.

Fowler, D. & Unsworth, M.H. 1979. Turbulent transfer of SO$_2$ to a wheat crop. *Quat. J. Roy. Met. Soc.*, **105**, 767–83.

Frank, H. & Frank, W. 1985. Chlorophyll-bleaching by atmospheric pollutants and sunlight. *Naturwissenschaften*, **72**, 139–41.

Freer-Smith, P.H. 1984. The influence of gaseous SO$_2$ and NO$_2$ and their mixtures on the growth and physiology of conifers. In: *Air pollution and the Stability of Coniferous Forest Ecosystems. Brno*, edited by I.E. Klimo, Proceedings of the MAB/IUFRO Meeting, Ostravia, Czechoslovakia.

Freer-Smith, P.H. 1985. The influence of SO_2 and NO_2 on the growth, development and gas exchange of *Betula pendula* roth. *New Phytol.*, **99**, 417–30.

Freer-Smith, P.H. & Lucas, P. 1987. Application of a polymeric coating can protect coniferous trees from acute pollution injury. *Forest Ecol. & Manage.* (in press.)

Friedland, A-J., Gregory, R.A., Karenlampi, L. & Johnson, A.H. 1984. Winter damage to foliage as a factor in red spruce decline. *Can. J. of For. Res.*, **14**, 963–5.

Fry, G.L.A. & Cooke, A.S. 1984. *Focus on nature conservation no. 7, Acid deposition and its Implications for Nature Conservation in Britain.* Nature Conservancy Council, Peterborough.

Fuhrer, V.E. 1983. Industrial pollution and forest insect pests. *Allg. Forstz.*, **26/7**, 668–9.

Garsed, S.G. & Rutter, A.J. 1982. Relative performance of conifer populations in various tests for sensitivity to SO_2, and the implications for selecting trees for planting in polluted areas. *New Phytol.*, **92**, 349–67.

Garty, J., Ziv, O. & Eshel, A. 1985. The effect of coating polymers on accumulation of airborne heavy metals by lichens. *Environ. Pollut. Ser. A*, **38**, 213–20.

Gauslaa, Y. 1985. The ecology of *Lobarion pulmonariae* and *Parmelion caperate* in *Quercus*-dominated forests in south-west Norway. *Lichenologist*, **17**, 117–40.

Gignac, L.D. & Beckett, P.J. 1986. The effect of smelting operations on peatlands near Sudbury, Ontario, Canada. *Can. J. Bot.*, **64**, 1138–47.

Gilbert, O.L. 1965. Lichens as indicators of air pollution in the Tyne Valley. In: *Ecology and the Industrial Society* edited by G.T. Goodman, R.W. Edwards and J.M. Lambert, 35–49. 5th Symposium of the British Ecological Society. Blackwell, Oxford.

Gilbert, O.L. 1968. Bryophytes as indicators of air pollution in the Tyne Valley. *New Phytol.*, **69**, 629–34.

Gilbert, O.L. 1986. Field evidence for an acid rain effect on lichens. *Environ. Pollut. Ser. A*, **40**, 227–31.

Grant, I.F., Bancroft, K. & Alexander, M. 1979. Sulphur dioxide and nitrogen dioxide effects on microbial activity in an acid forest soil. *Microbial Ecol.*, **5**, 85–9.

Grindon, L.H. 1859. *The Manchester Flora*, W. White, London.

Grodzinski, W., Weiner, J. & Maycock, P.F. 1984. (eds). *Forest Ecosystems in Industrial Regions.* Springer-Verlag, Berlin.

Grzywacz, A. & Wazny, J. 1973. The impact of industrial air pollutants on several important pathogenic fungi. *Eur. J. Forest Pathol.*, **3**, 129–41.

Guderian, R. 1985. (ed). *Air Pollution by Photochemical Oxidants.* Springer-Verlag, Berlin.

Guerrero, M.G., Vega, J.M. & Losada, M. 1981. The assimilatory nitrate reducing system and its regulation. *Ann. Rev. Pl. Physiol.*, **32**, 168–204.

Hallbäcken, L. and Tamm, C.O. 1986. Charges in soil acidity from 1927 to 1982–1984 in a forest area of South-West Sweden. *Scand. J. For Res.*, **1**, 219–232.

Hällgren, J-E. & Gezelius, K. 1982. Effects of SO_2 on photosynthesis and ribulose bisphosphate carboxylase in pine tree seedlings. *Physiologia Pl.*, **54**, 153–61.

Hällgren, J-E. 1984. Photosynthetic gas exchange in leaves affected by pollutants. In: *Gaseous Air Pollutants and Plant Metabolism*, edited by M.J. Koziol and F.R. Whatley, 147–60. Butterworths, London.

Harter, R.D. 1983. Effect of soil pH on adsorption of lead, copper, zinc and nickel. *Soil Sci. Soc. Am. J.*, **47**, 47–51.

van Haut, H. & Stratmann, H. 1970. *Farbtafelatlas über Schwefeldioxid-Wirkungen an Pflanzen* Essen: W. Giradet.

Havas, P.J. 1971. Injury to pines growing in the vicinity of a chemical processing plant in northern Finland. *Acta for. fenn.*, **121**, 1–21.

Havas, P.J. & Huttunen, S. 1972. The effect of air pollution on the radial growth of Scots pine (*Pinus sylvestris* L.). *Biol. Conserv.*, **4**, 361–8.

Havas, P.J. & Huttunen, S. 1980. Some special features of the ecophysiological effects of air pollution of coniferous forests during the winter. In: *Effects of Acid Precipitation on Terrestrial Ecosystems*, edited by T.C. Hutchinson and M. Havas, 123–32. Plenum Publishing Corporation.

Hawksworth, D.L. & Rose, F. 1970. Qualititative scale for estimating sulphur dioxide air pollution in England and Wales using epiphytic lichens. *Nature, Lond.*, **227**, 145–8.

Hawksworth, D.L. & Rose, F. 1976. *Lichens as Pollution Monitors.* Studies in Biology (66), Edward Arnold, London.

Heagle, A.S. 1973. Interactions between air pollutants and plant parasites. *Ann. Rev. Phytopathol.*, **11**, 365–88.

Heagle, A.S. 1977. Effect of ozone on parasitism of corn by *Helminthosporium maydis*. *Phytopathology*, **67**, 616–8.

Heagle, A.S. 1982. Interactions between air pollutants and parasitic plant diseases. In: *Effects of Gaseous Air Pollution in Agriculture and Horticulture*, edited by M.H. Unsworth and D.P. Ormrod, 333–48. Butterworths, London.

Heagle, A.S. & Letchworth, M.B. 1982. Relationships among injury, growth and yield responses of soybean cultivars exposed to ozone at different light intensities. *J. environ. Qual.*, **11**, 690–4.

Heck, W.W., Taylor, O.C., Adams, R., Bingham, G., Miller, J., Preston, E. & Weinstein, L. 1982. Assessment of crop loss from ozone. *J. Air Pollut. Control Assoc.*, **32**, 353–61.

Heck, W.W., Adams, R.M., Cure, W.W., Heagle, A.S., Heggestad, H.E., Kohut, R.J., Kress, L.W., Rawlings, I.O. & Taylor, O.C. 1983. A reassessment of crop loss from ozone. *Environ. Sci. Tech.*, **17**, 573–81A.

Heggested, H.E. 1980. Field assessment of air pollution impacts on growth and productivity of crop species. Presentation at APCA meeting, Montreal.

Heggestad, H.E. & Bennett, J.H. 1981. Photochemical oxidants potential yield losses in snap beans attributable to SO_2. *Science*, **213**, 1008–10.

Heggestad, H.E., Gish, T.J., Lee, E.H., Bennett, J.H. & Douglas, L.W. 1985. Interaction of soil moisture stress and ambient zone on growth and yield and yields of soybeans. *Phytopathology*, **75**, 472–7.

Heggestad, H.E., Heagle, A.S., Bennett, J.H. & Koch, E.J. 1980. The effects of photochemical oxidants on the yield of snap bean. *Atmos. Environ.*, **14**, 317–26.

Hibben, C.R. & Stotzky, G. 1969. Effects of ozone on the germination of fungus spores. *Can. J. Microbiol.*, **15**, 1187–96.

Hibben, C.R. & Taylor, M.P. 1975. Ozone and sulphur dioxide effects on the lilac powdery mildew fungus. *Environ. Pollut. Ser. A*, **9**, 107–14.

Hill, A.C. & Bennett, J.H. 1970. Inhibition of apparent photosynthesis by nitrogen oxides. *Atmos. Environ.*, **4**, 341–8.

Hillman, R.C. 1972. *Biological Effects of Air Pollution on Insects, Emphasising the Reactions of Honeybee (Apis mellifera L.) to Sulfur Dioxide.* Ph.D. thesis, The Pennsylvannia State University, University Park, Pa.

Hoffman, W.A., Lindberg, S.E. & Turner, R.R. 1980. Precipitation acidity: the role of the forest canopy in acid exchange. *J. environ. Qual.*, **9**, 95–100.

Hofstra, G., Tonneijck, A.E.G. & Allen, O.B. 1985. Cumulative effects of low levels of SO_2 on O_3 sensitivity in bean and cucumber. *Atmos. Environ.*, **19**, 195–8.

Horntvedt, R., Dollard, G.J. & Joranger, E. 1980. Effects of acid precipitation on soil and forest. 2. Atmosphere–vegetation interactions. In: *Ecological Impact of Acid Precipitation*, edited by D. Drabløs and N. Tollan, 192–3, SNSF Project, Norway.

Horsman, D.C., Nicholls, A.O. & Calder, D.M. 1980. Growth responses of *Dactylis glomerata*, *Lolium perenne* and *Phalaris aquatica* to chronic ozone exposure. *Aust. J. Pl. Physiol.*, **7**, 511–7.

Horsman, D.C., Roberts, T.M. & Bradshaw, A.D. 1979. Studies on the effects of sulphur dioxide on perennial ryegrass. II. Evolution of sulfur dioxide tolerance. *J. exp. Bot.*, **30**, 495–501.

House of Commons. 1984. *Acid Rain.* Fourth Report of the Environment Committee. HC 446, HMSO 1984.

House of Lords. 1984. *Air Pollution.* Twenty-second Report of the Select Committee on the European Countries. HL 265, HMSO 1984.

Houston, D.B. 1974. Response of selected *Pinus strobus* L. clones to fumigation with sulphur dioxide and ozone. *Can. J. For. Res.*, **4**, 65–8.

Hughes, P.R., Chiment, J.S. & Dickie, A.I. 1985. Effect of pollutant dose on the response of Mexican bean beetle (*Coleoptera: Coccinellidae*) to SO_2-induced changes in soybean. *Environ. Ent.*, **14**, 718–21.

Hughes, P.R., Dickie, A.I. & Pentan, M.A. 1983. Increased success of the Mexican bean beetle on field-grown soybeans exposed to SO_2. *J. environ. Qual.*, **12**, 565–8.

Hughes, P.R., Potter, J.E. & Weinstein, L.H. 1981. Effects of air pollutants on plant–insect interactions: reactions of the Mexican bean beetle to SO_2-fumigated pinto plants. *Environ. Ent.*, **10**, 741–4.

Hughes, P.R., Potter, J.E. & Weinstein, L.H. 1982. Effects of air pollution on plant–insect interactions: increased susceptibility of greenhouse-grown soybeans to Mexican bean beetle after plant exposure to SO_2. *Environ. Ent.*, **11**, 173–6.

Hughes, P.R., Weinstein, L.H., Johnson, L.M. & Braun, A.R. 1985. Fluoride transfer in the environment: accumulation and effects on cabbage looper *Trichoplusia ni* of fluoride from water soluble salts and HF-fumigated leaves. *Environ. Pollut. Ser. A*, **37**, 175–92.

Hutterman, A. 1982. Fruhdiagnose von Immisionsschäden im Burzelbereich von Waldbaumer. *LOLF-Mitteilunger, Landesanstalt fur Okologie, Landschaft sentwicklung und Forstplanung Nordrhein-Westfalen*, 26–31.

Huttl, R. 1986. 'Neuartige' Waldshäden und Nahrelementversorgung von Fichtenbestanden (*Picea abies* Karst.) in Sudwestdeutschland. Freiburger Bodenkunlche Abhandlungen Heft 16, ISBN 0344–2691.

Huttunen, S. 1973. Studies on tree damage due to air pollution in Oulu. *Aguilo Ser. Bot.,* **12**, 1–11.

Huttunen, S. 1974. Apreliminary monitoring survey on a test field near a chemical processing plant. *Aquilo Ser. Bot.,* **13**, 23–24.

Huttunen, S. 1975. The influence of air pollution on the forest vegetation around Oulu. *Acta Univ. Oulu,* **33A**, Biol. 2.

Huttunen, S. 1978. Effects of air pollution on provenances of Scots pine and Norway spruce in northern Finland. *Silva fenn.,* **12**, 1–16.

Huttunen, S., Havas, P.J. & Laine, K. 1981. Effects of air pollutants on the wintertime water economy of the Scots pine (*Pinus sylvestris*). *Holarctic Ecol.,* **4**, 94–101.

Huttunen, S., Karenlampi, L. & Kolari, K. 1981. Changes in osmotic potential and some related physiological variables in needles of polluted Norway spruce (*Picea abies*). *Ann. Bot. Fenn.,* **18**, 63–71.

Huttunen, S., Karhu, M. & Laine, K. 1983. Air pollution induced stress and its effects on the photosynthesis of *Pinus sylvestris* in Oulu. *Aquilo Ser. Bot.,* **19**, 275–82.

Huttunen, S. and Laine, K. 1981. Effects of air-borne pollutants on the surface wax structure of *Pinus sylvestris* needles. *Ann. Bot. Fenn.,* **20**, 79–86.

Ineson, P. & Gray, T.R.G. 1980. Monitoring the effects of acid rain and sulphur dioxide on soil micro-organisms. *Soc. appl. Bacteriol. Techn. Ser.,* **15**, 21–6.

Ineson, P. 1983. *The Effect of Airborne Sulphur Pollutants upon Decomposition and Nutrient Release in Forest Soils.* Unpublished Ph.D., University of Liverpool.

Innes, J.L. 1987. *Air Pollution and Forestry.* Forestry Commission Bulletin 70, HMSO London.

Innes, J.L. & Boswell, R.C. 1987. *Forest Health Surveys Part I: Results.* Forestry Commission Bulletin 74, HMSO London.

Innes, J.L., Boswell, R.C., Binns, W.O. & Redfern, D.B. 1986. *Forest Health and Air Pollution, 1986 survey.* Res and Dev. Paper No. 150, Forestry Commission, Edinburgh.

Irving, P.M. 1983. Acidic precipitation effects on crops: a review and analysis of research. *J. environ. Qual.,* **12**, 442–53.

Irving, P.M. 1985. Modelling the response of greenhouse grown radish plants to acidic rain. *Environ. & Exp. Bot.,* **25**, 327–38.

Irving, P.M. 1986. Report on the Crop Response Workshop of the National Acid Precipitation Assessment Program. Chicago, Illinois.

Jacobson, J.S. 1982. Ozone and the growth and productivity of agricultural crops. In: *Effects of Gaseous Air Pollution in Agriculture and Horticulture*, edited by M.H. Unsworth and D.P. Ormrod, 293–304. Butterworths, London.

Jacobson, J.S. 1984. Effects of acidic aerosol, fog, mist and rain on crops and trees. *Phil. Trans. R. Soc. Lond. Ser. B,* **305**, 327–38.

Jacobson, J.S., Troiano, J. & Heller, L. 1985. Stage of development response and recovery of radish plants from episodic exposure to simulated acidic rain. *J. exp. Bot.,* **36**, 159–67.

James, R.L., Cobb, F.W., Miller, P.R. & Parmeter, J.R. 1980. Effects of oxidant air pollution on susceptibility of pine roots to *Fomes annosus. Phytopathology,* **80**, 560–3.

Jeffords, M.R. & Endress, A.G. 1984. Possible role of ozone in tree defoliation by the gypsy moth (*Lepidoptera: Lymantriidae*). *Environ. Ent.,* **13**, 1249–52.

Jensen, K.F. 1981. Growth analysis of hybrid poplar cuttings fumigated with ozone and sulphur dioxide. *Environ. Pollut. Ser. A,* **26**, 243–50.

Jones, T. & Mansfield, T.A. 1982a. Studies on dry matter partitioning and distribution of ^{14}C-labelled assimilates in plants of *Phleum pratense* exposed to SO_2 pollution. *Environ. Pollut. Ser. A*, **28**, 199–207.

Jones, T. & Mansfield, T.A. 1982b. The effect of SO_2 on growth and development of seedlings of *Phleum pratense* under different light and temperature environments. *Environ. Pollut. Ser. A*, **27**, 57–71.

Johannes, A.H., Altwicker, E.R. & Clesceri, N.L. 1981. Characterisation of acidic precipitation in the Adirondack region. EPRI Report EA-1826, Research project 1155–1. Renselaer Polytechnic Institute, Troy, N.Y.

Johnson, D.W. & Henderson, G.S. 1979. Sulfate adsorption and sulfur fractions in a highly weathered soil under a mixed deciduous forest. *Soil Sci.*, **128**, 34–40.

Johnson, A.H., Friedland, A.J. & Dushoff, J.G. 1986. Recent and historic red spruce mortality: Evidence of climatic influence. *Wat. Air & Soil Pollut.*, **30**, 319–30.

Johnson, A.H. & Siccama, T.G. 1983. Acid deposition and forest decline. *Environ. Sci. Technol.*, **17**, 294–305.

Johnson, A.H. & Siccama, T.G. 1984. Decline of red spruce in the northern Appalachians: assessing the possible role of acid deposition. *Tappi J.*, **67**, 68–72.

Johnson, A.H., Siccama, T.G., Wang, D., Turner, R.S. & Barringer, T.H. 1981. Recent changes in patterns of tree growth rates in the New Jersey pinelands: a possible effect of acid rain. *J. environ. Qual.*, **10**, 427.

Johnston, A.E., Goulding, K.W.T. & Poulton, P.R. 1986. Soil acidification during more than 100 years under permanent grassland and woodland at Rothamsted. *Soil Use & Manage.*, **2**, 3–10.

Jordan, S. & Bonner, F.T. 1973. Nitrogen and oxygen exchange between nitric oxide and aqueous solutions of nitric acid. *Ing. Chem.*, **12**, 1369–73.

Karnosky, D.F. 1977. Evidence for genetic control of response to SO_2 and O_3 in *Populus tremuloides*. *Can. J. For. Res.*, **7**, 437–40.

Karnosky, D.F. 1985. Genetic variability in growth responses to SO_2. In: *Sulphur dioxide and Vegetation*, edited by W.E. Winner, H.A. Mooney and R.A. Goldstein, 346–56, Stanford University Press, California, USA.

Kay, C.E., Tourangeau, P.C. & Gordon, C.C. 1975a. Fluoride levels in indigenous animals and plants collected from uncontaminated ecosystems. *Fluoride*, **8**, 125–33.

Kay, C.E., Tourangeau, P.C. & Gordon, C.C. 1975b. Industrial fluorosis in wild mule and whitetail deer from western Montana. *Fluoride*, **8**, 182–91.

Keller, T. 1976. Auswirkungen niedriger SO_2-Konzentrationen auf junge Fichten. *Schweiz. Z. Forstwes.*, **127**, 237–51.

Keller, T. 1978a. Einfluss neidriger SO_2-Konzentrationen auf die CO_2-Aufnahme von Fichte und Tanne. *Photosynthetica*, **12**, 316–22.

Keller, T. 1978b. Winter time atmospheric pollutants – do they affect the performance of deciduous trees in the ensuing growing season? *Environ. Pollut.*, **16**, 243–7.

Keller, T. 1978c. Frostschaden als Folge einer 'latenten' Immissionsschadigung. *Staub.*, **38**, 24–6.

Keller, T. 1981. Winter uptake of airborne SO_2 by shoots of deciduous species. *Environ. Pollut. Ser. A*, **26**, 313–7.

Keller, T. 1984. Direct effects of sulphur dioxide on trees. *Phil. Trans. R. Soc. Lond. Ser. B*, **305**, 317–26.

Keller, T. & Bucher, J. 1976. Zur SO_2 – Empfindlichkeit der Laubbaumarten. Schweiz. Z. Forstwes, **127**, 476–484.

Killham, K. & Firestone, M.K. 1982. Evaluation of accelerated H^+ applications in predicting soil chemical and microbial changes due to acid rain. *Communs. Soil Sci. & Pl. Analysis*, **13**, 995–1001.

Killham, K. & Wainwright, M. 1984. Chemical and microbiological changes in soil following exposure to heavy atmospheric pollution. *Environ. Pollut. Ser. A*, **33**, 121–31.

Köck, G. 1935. Eichenmehltau und Rauchgasschäden. *Z. Pflkrankh.*, **45**, 44–5.

Konda, N., Akiyama, Y., Fujiwara, M. & Sugahara, K. 1980. Sulfite-oxidising activities in plants. In: *Research Report from the National Institute for Environmental Studies, Japan*, **11**, 137–50.

Koskela, V. 1970. Occurrence of frost damage in Norway spruce, Scots pine, silver birch and Siberian larch in the forest fertilisation experiment area at Kivisvo. *Folia Forestalia*, **28**, 1–25.

Koziol, M.J. & Jordan, C.F. 1978. Changes in carbohydrate levels in red kidney bean (*Phaseolus vulgaris* L) exposed to sulphur dioxide. *J. exp. Bot.*, **29**, 1037–43.

Kozlowski, T.T. & Pallardy, S.S. 1979. Effects of low temperature on leaf-diffusion resistance of *Ulmus americana* and *Fraxinus pennsylvanica* seedlings. *Can. J. Bot.*, **57**, 2466–70.

Knabe, W. 1970. Kiefernwaldbreitung und Schwefeldioxid-Immissionen im Ruhrgebiet. *Staub-Reinhalt. Luft*, **39**, 32–5.

Krause, G.H.M., Jung, K–D. & Prinz, B. 1985. Experimentelle Untersuchungen zur Aufklärung der neuartigen Waldschäden in der Bundesrepublik Deutschland. In: *Waldschäden-Einflussfaktonen und ihre Bewertung* VDI-Berichte 560 Goslar.

Krause, C.R. & Weidensaul, T.C. 1978. Ultrastructural effects of ozone on the host–parasite relationship of *Botrytis cinerea* and *Pelargonium hortorum*. *Phytopathology*, **68**, 301–7.

Kress, L.W., Irving, P.M., Prepejchal, W. & Smith, H.J. 1986. Effects of ozone and water stress on soybeans. In: *Environmental Research Division Technical Progress Report Jan 1984 – Dec 1985*. Argonne National Laboratory, Illinois, USA.

Kress, L.W., Miller, J.E. & Smith, H.J. 1986. Impact of O_3 and SO_2 on soybean yield. *Environ. Pollut. Ser. A.* **41**, 105–23.

Kress, L.W. & Skelly, J.M. 1982. Response of several eastern forest trees to low doses of ozone and nitrogen oxide. *Pl. Dis.*, **66**, 1149–52.

Kress, L.W., Skelly, J.M. & Hinkelmann, K.H. 1982a. Growth impact of O_3, NO_2 and/or SO_2 on *Pinus taeda*. *Environ. Monit. and Assessm.*, **1**, 229–39.

Kress, L.W., Skelly, J.M. & Hinkelmann, K.H. 1982b. Growth impact of O_3, NO_2 and/or SO_2 on *Platanus occidentalis. Agric. Environ.*, **7**, 265–74.

Kruse, M., Apsimon, H.M. & Bell, J.N.B. 1986. An emissions inventory for ammonia arising from agriculture in Great Britain. London. Imperial College Centre for Enviromental Technology.

Kvist, K. 1985. Fungal pathogens interacting with air pollutants in agricultural crop production. In: *How are the Effects of Air Pollution on Agricultural Crops Influenced by the Interaction with Other Limiting Factors?* 67–78. Proceedings of CEC/COST workshop Risø and Copenhagen, (XII/ENV/32/86 EAD.46.86) March 1986. CEC, Brussels.

Lane, P.I. 1983. *Ambient Levels of Sulphur and Nitrogen Oxides in the UK and their Effects on Crop Growth*. Ph.D. thesis, University of London.

Lane, P.I. & Bell, J.N.B. 1984. The effects of simulated urban air pollution on grass yield: Part 2 – Performance of *Lolium perenne, Phleum pratense* and *Dactylis glomerata* fumigated with SO_2, NO_2 and/or NO. *Environ. Pollut. Ser. A*, **35**, 97–124.

Lang, A. 1970. Gibberellins: structure and metabolism. *A. Rev. Pl. Physiol.*, **21**, 537–70.

Larson, B.R. 1985. Effects of simulated acid rain and (+)-2-(2,4-Dichlorophenoxyl) propanoic acid on selected crops. *Ecotox. Environ. Safety*, **10**, 228–38.

Last, F.T. 1982. Effects of atmospheric sulphur compounds on natural and man-made terrestrial and aquatic ecosystems. *Agric. Environ.*, **7**, 299–387.

Laurence, J.A. & Aluisio, A.L. 1981. Effects of sulfur dioxide on expansion of lesions caused by *Corynebacterium nebraskense* in Maize and by *Xanthomonas phaseoli* var. *sojensis* in soybean. *Phytopathology*, **71**, 445–8.

Laurence, J.A., Aluisio, A.L., Weinstein, L.H. & McCune, D.C. 1981. Effects of sulphur dioxide on southern bean mosaic and maize dwarf virus. *Environ. Pollut. Ser. A*, **24**, 185–91.

Laurence, J.A., Hughes, P.R., Weinstein, L.H., Geballe, G.J. & Smith, W.H. 1983. Impact of air pollution on plant–insect interactions: implications of current research and strategies for future studies. ERC Report No. 20. Ecosystems Research Centre, Ithaca, NY.

Laurence, J.A. & Reynolds, K.L. 1982. Effects of concentrations of sulfur dioxide and other characteristics of exposure on the development of lesions caused by *Xanthemonas phaseoli* in red kidney bean. *Phytopathology*, **72**, 1243–6.

Laurence, J.A., Weinstein, L.H., McCune, D.C. & Aluisio, A.L. 1979. Effects of sulfur dioxide on southern corn leaf blight of maize and stem rust of wheat. *Pl. Dis. Reptr.*, **63**, 975–8.

Law, R.M. & Mansfield, T.A. 1982. Oxides of nitrogen and the greenhouse atmosphere. In: *Effects of Gaseous Air Pollution in Agriculture and Horticulture*, edited by M.H. Unsworth and D.P. Ormrod, 93–112, Butterworths, London.

Lawton, J.H. & McNeill, S. 1979. Between the devil and the deep blue sea: on the problem of being a herbivore. In: *Population Dynamics*, edited by R.M. Anderson, B.D. Turner & L.R. Taylor, 223–44, Blackwell, Oxford.

Lea, P.J. & Miflin, B.J. 1974. Alternative route for nitrogen assimilation in higher plants. *Nature, Lond.*, **251**, 614–6.

Lee, J.A., Press, M.C., Studholme, C. & Woodin, S.J. 1988. Effects of acidic deposition on wetlands. In: *Acid Rain and Britain's Natural Ecosystems*, edited by M.R. Ashmore, J.N.B. Bell and C. Garretty. Imperial College, Centre for Environmental Technology, London.

Lee, J.J. & Weber, D.E. 1979. The effect of simulated acid rain on seedling emergence and growth of eleven woody species. *Forest Sci.*, **25**, 393–8.

Lee, R., Bache, E.M., Wilson, M.J. & Sharp, G.S. 1985. Aluminium release in relation to the determination of cation exchange capacity of some podzolised New Zealand soils. *J. Soil Sci.*, **36**, 239–53.

Leetham, J.L., Lauenroth, W.K., Milchunas, D.G., Kirchner, T. & Yorks, T.P. 1984. Responses of heterotrophs. In: *The Effects of SO₂ on a Grassland*, edited by W.K. Lauenroth and E.M. Preston, 137–59. Springer-Verlag, New York.

Leetham, J.W., McNary, T.J., Dodd, J.L. & Lauenroth, W.K. 1982. Response of soil nematodes, rotifers and tardigrades to three levels of season-long sulfur dioxide exposures. *Wat. Air & Soil Pollut.*, **17**, 343–56.

Lefohn, A.S. & Ormrod, D.P. 1984. A Review and Assessment of the Effects of Pollutant Mixtures on Vegetation. EPA–600/3–84–037. US–EPA, Corvallis, USA.

Lendzian, K.J. 1984. Permeability of plant cuticles to gaseous pollutants. In: *Gaseous Air Pollutants and Plant Metabolism*, edited by M.J. Koziol and E.R. Whatley, 77–81, Butterworths, London.

Lettle, A. 1983. Effect of industrial SO₂ immissions on the epiphytic microflora of spruce. *Folia Microbiol.*, **28**, 187–94.

Levy, R., Chiu, Y.J. & Cromroy, H.L. 1972. Effects of ozone on three species of Diptera. *Environ. Ent.*, **1**, 608–11.

Libera, W., Zeigler, I. & Zeigler, H. 1975. The action of sulfite on the HCO_3^--fixation and the fixation pattern of isolated chloroplasts and leaf tissue slices. *Z. Pflanzenphysiol.*, **74**, 420–33.

Linder, S. 1972. Seasonal variation in pigments in needles. A study of Scots pine and Norway spruce seedlings grown under different nursery conditions. *Studia Forestalia Suecica*, **100**, 1–37.

Lines, R. 1984. Species and seed origin trials in the industrial Pennines. *Q. J. For.*, **78**, 9–23.

Lokke, H. 1984. Effects of 2,4-dichlorophenoxyacetic acid in artificial acid rain on *Brassica napus* and *Sinapis alba*. *Ecototox. Environ. Safety*, **8**, 328–38.

Lonsdale, D. 1986a. *Beech health study, 1985.* Res. and Dev. Paper No. 146, Forestry Commission, Edinburgh.

Lonsdale, D. 1986b. *Beech health study, 1986.* Res. and Dev. Paper No. 149, Forestry Commission, Edinburgh.

Lovett, G.M., Reiners, W.R. & Olson, R.K. 1982. Cloud droplet deposition in a subalpine balsam fir forest: hydrological and chemical inputs. *Science*, **218**, 1303.

McClenahen, J.R. & Dochinger, L.S. 1985. Tree ring response of White Oak to climate and air pollution near the Ohio river valley. *J. Enviorn. Qual.*, **14**, 274–280.

McKenzie, R.M. 1980. The adsorption of lead and other heavy metals on oxides of manganese and iron. *Aust. J. Soil Res.*, **18**, 61–73.

McLaughlin, S.B. 1985. Effects of air pollution on forests. *J. Air Pollut. Control Assoc.*, **35**, 512–34.

McLaughlin, S.B. & McConathy, R.K. 1983. Effects of SO₂ and O₃ on allocation of ¹⁴C-labelled photosynthate in *Phaseolus vulgaris*. *Pl. Physiol.*, **73**, 630–5.

McLaughlin, S.B., Shriner, D.S., McConathy, R.K. & Mann, L.K. 1979. The effects of SO₂ dosage kinetics and exposure frequency on photosynthesis and transpiration of kidney beans (*Phaseolus vulgaris* L.) *Environ. & Exp. Bot.*, **19**, 179–91.

McLaughlin, S.B. & Taylor, G.E. 1985. Effects on Dicot. Crops: Some issues mechanisms and indicators. In: *Sulfur Dioxide and Vegetation*, edited by W.E. Winner, H.A. Mooney and R.A. Goldstein, 227–49, Stanford University Press, California, USA.

McLeod, A.R. 1987. Effects of open-air fumigation with sulphur dioxide on the occurrence of fungal pathogens in winter cereals. *Phytopathology*, (in press).

McLeod, A.R., Alexander, K. & Cribb, D.M. 1986. Effects of open-air fumigation with sulphur dioxide on the growth of cereals. CEGB Lab. Report, TPRD/L/3071/R86. CERL (Leatherhead).

Macqueen, J.F. 1985. Sulphur dioxide and crop yield – A statistical analysis of dose-response relations. CEGB Lab. Report, TPRD/L/AP 0160/M85. CERL (Leatherhead).

McNary, T.J., Milchunas, D.G., Leetham, J.W., Lauenroth, W.K. & Dodd, J.L. 1981. Effects of controlled low levels of SO₂ on grasshopper densities on a northern mixed-grass prairie. *J. Econ. Ent.*, **74**, 91–3.

McNeill, S., Bell, J.N.B., Aminu-Kano, M. & Mansfield, P. 1986. SO_2 plant, insect and pathogen interactions. In: *How are the Effects of Air Pollution on Agricultural Crops Influenced by Interaction with Other Limiting Factors?* 108–15. Proceedings of CEC/COST workshop, Risø and Copenhagen, March 1986. (XII/ENV/32/86 EAD.46.86) CEC, Brussels.

Majernik, O. & Mansfield, T.A. 1971. Effects of SO_2 pollution on stomatal movements in *Vicia faba. Phytopath. Z.,* **71,** 123–8.

Manning, W.J. 1975. Interactions between air pollutants and fungal, bacterial and viral plant pathogens. *Environ. Pollut.,* **9,** 87–90.

Manning, W.J., Feder, W.A., Perkins, I. & Glickman, M. 1969. Ozone injury and infection of potato leaves by *Botrytis cinerea. Pl. Dis. Reptr.,* **53,** 691–3.

Mansfield, T.A., Davies, W.J. & Whitmore, M.E. 1986. Interaction between the responses of plants to air pollution and other environmental factors such as drought, light and temperature. In: *How are the Effects of Air Pollutants on Agricultural Crops Influenced by the Interaction with Other Limiting Factors?* 2–15. Proceedings of CEC/COST Workshop, Risø and Copenhagen, March 1986. (XII/ENV/ 32/86 EAD.46.86) CEC Brussels.

Mansfield, T.A. & Freer-Smith, P.H. 1981. Effects of urban air pollution on plant growth. *Biol. Rev.,* **56,** 343–68.

Mansfield, T.A. & Freer-Smith, P.H. 1984. The role of stomata in resistance mechanisms. In: *Gaseous Air Pollutants and Plant Metabolism,* edited by M.J. Koziol and F.R. Whatley, 131–46, Butterworths, London.

Mansfield, T.A. & Jones, T. 1985. Growth/environment interactions in SO_2 responses of grasses. In: *Sulfur Dioxide and Vegetation,* edited by W.E. Winner, H.A. Mooney and R.A. Goldstein, 332–45, Stanford University Press, California, USA.

Martin, M.H. & Coughtrey, P.J. 1987. Cycling and fate of heavy metals in a contaminated woodland ecosystem. In: *Pollutant Transport and Fate in Ecosystems,* edited by P.J. Coughtrey, M.H. Martin and M.H. Unsworth, Blackwell, Oxford (in press).

Martin, M.H., Campbell, C.L. & Bruck, P.I. 1985. Infectivity of *Phytopthora infestans* in simulated acid rain solutions. *Phytopathology,* **75,** 501.

Materna, J. 1973. Relationship between SO_2 concentration and damage to forest trees in the Slavkov forest region. *Prace. Vulhm.,* **43,** 169–77.

Materna, J. 1974. Einfluss der SO_2 – Immissionen auf fichten-pflanzen in Wintermonaten. IXth Int. Tanugn uber Luftverunreinigung und Forstwirtschaft. Czechoslavakia.

Materna, J. & Kohout, R. 1963. Die Absorption des Schwefeldioxide durch die Fichte. *Naturwissenschaften,* **50,** 407–8.

Matsuoka, Y. 1978. Experimental studies of sulphur dioxide injury on rice plant and its mechanism. Special Bulletin of the Chiba-Ken Agricultural Experiment Station, **7,** 1–63.

Matthews, P. 1981. *Some Effects of Air Pollution on Plant Growth in South East Northumberland.* MSc Thesis, University of Newcastle Upon Tyne, UK.

Mehlhorn, A. & Wellburn, A.R. 1987. Stress ethylene determines plant sensitivity to ozone. *Nature, Lond.* (in press).

Menser, H.A., Heggestad, H.E., Street, O.E. & Jeffrey, R.N. 1963. Responses of plants to air pollutants. I. Effects of ozone on tobacco plants preconditioned by light and temperature. *Pl. Physiol.,* **38,** 605–9.

Mies, V.E. & Zöttl, H.W. 1985. Zeitliche Änderung der Chlorophyll-und Elementgehalte in den Nadeln eines gelb-chlorotishen Fichtenbestandes. Forstwiss Centbl., **104,** 1–8 (CEGB Translation T17100).

Miflin, B.J. & Lea, P.J. 1976. The pathway of nitrogen assimilation in plants. *Phytochemistry,* **15,** 585–95.

Miller, J.E. & Xerikos, P. 1979. Residence time for sulfite in SO_2 'sensitive' and 'tolerant' soybean cultivars. *Environ. Pollut.,* **18,** 259–64.

Miller, P.R., Taylor, O.C. & Wilhour, R.G. 1982. Oxidant air pollution effects on a western coniferous forest ecosystem. EPA-600/D-82–276 Environmental Protection Agency, USA.

Mitchell, B.D. & Jarvis, R.A. 1956. *The Soils of the Country Round Kilmarnock,* Memoirs of the Soil Survey of Great Britain, Scotland, HMSO, Edinburgh.

Mooi, J. 1980. Influence of ozone on growth of two poplar cultivars. *Pl. Dis.,* **64,** 772–3.

Mooi, J. 1981. Influence of ozone and sulphur dioxide on defoliation and growth of poplar. *Mitt. Forst. Bundesversuchsanst Wien,* **137,** 47–51.

Mooi, J. 1983. Responses of some poplar species to mixtures of SO_2, NO_2 and O_3. *Aquilo Ser. Bot.,* **19,** 189–96.

Mooi, J. 1984. Wirkungen von SO$_2$, NO$_2$, O$_3$ und ihrer Mischungen auf Pappeln und einige andere Pflanzenarten. In: *Der Forst-Und Holzwirt*, edited by M. & H. Schaper, 438–44. Hannover.

Mooi, J. 1985. Wirkungen von SO$_2$, NO$_2$, O$_3$ und ihrer Mischungen auf Pappeln und einige andere Pflanzenarten. *Die Holzzucht*, **1/2**, 8–12.

Montes, R.A., Blum, U. & Heagle, A.S. 1982. The effects of ozone and nitrogen fertiliser on tall fescue, ladino clover, and a fescue clover mixture. I. Growth, regrowth, and forage production. *Can. J. Bot.*, **60**, 2745–52.

Morrison, I.K. 1984. Acid rain: a review of literature on acid deposition effects in forest ecosystems. *For. Abstr.*, **45**, 483–506.

Mudd, J.B. 1982. Effects of oxidants on metabolic function. In: *Effects of gaseous air pollutants in agriculture and horticulture*, edited by M.H. Unsworth and D.P. Ormrod, 189–294, Butterworths, London.

Mudd, J.B., Banerjee, S.K., Dooley, M.M. & Knight, K.L. 1984. Pollutants and plant cells: effects on membranes. In: *Gaseous air pollutants and plant metabolism*, edited by M.J. Koziol and F.R. Whatley, 105–16, Butterworths, London.

Murdy, W.H. & Ragsdale, H.L. 1980. The influence of relative humidity on direct sulfur dioxide damage to plant sexual reproduction. *J. environ. Qual.*, **9**, 493–6.

Murphy, M.D. 1978. Responses to sulphur in Irish grassland. In: *Sulphur in Forages*, edited by J.C. Brogan, 95–109, An Foras Taluntais, Dublin.

Murphy, M.D. 1979. Much Irish grassland is deficient in sulphur. *Farm & Food Res.*, **10**, 190–2.

NAS. 1974. *Effects of fluorides on animals.* Subcommittee on fluorosis, National Research Council. National Academy of Sciences. Washington DC. 70 pages.

Naturi, T. & Totsuka. 1984. Effects of mixed gas on transpiration rate of several woody plants. 1. Interspecific difference in the effects of mixed gas on transpiration rate. Research Report of the National Institute for Environmental Studies, Ibaraki, Japan, No. 15, 1984.

Navara, J., Horvath, I. & Kaleta, M. 1978. Contribution to the determination of limiting values of sulphur dioxide for vegetation in the region of Bratislava. *Environ. Pollut.*, **16**, 263–75.

Newman, J.R. & Schreiber, R.K. 1984. Animals as indicators of ecosystem responses to air emissions. *Environ. Manage.*, **8**, 309–24.

Nicholson, I.A., Cape, J.N., Fowler, D., Kinnaird, J.N. & Paterson, I.S. 1980. Effects of a Scots pine *(Pinus sylvestris* L.*)* canopy on the chemical composition and deposition pattern of precipitation. In: *Ecological Impact of Acid Precipitation*, Proceedings of an International Conference, edited by D. Drabl ø and A. Tollan, 148–9, SNSF Project, Norway.

Nielsen, D.G., Terrell, L.E. & Weidensaul, T.C. 1977. Phytotoxicity of ozone and sulphur dioxide to laboratory-fumigated Scotch pine. *Pl. Dis. Reptr.*, **61**, 699–703.

Niemann, B.L. 1984. Analysis of wind and precipitation data for assessments of transboundary transport and acid deposition between Canada and the United States. In: *Meteorological Aspects of Acid Rain*, edited by C. Bhumralkar, 57–92 (Acid Precipitation Series, Volume 1). Butterworth Publications, Woburn.

Nobel, P.S. 1970. *Plant Cell Physiology*, W.H. Freeman & Co., San Francisco.

Norby, R.J. & Kozlowski, T.T. 1981. Response of SO$_2$-fumigated *Pinus resinosa* seedlings to post-fumigation temperature. *Can. J. Bot.*, **59**, 470–5.

Norby, R.J. & Kozlowski, T.T. 1982. The role of stomata in sensitivity of *Betula papyrifera* Marsh. seedlings to SO$_2$ at different humidities. *Oecologia (Berl.)*, **53**, 34–9.

Norby, R.J. & Kozlowski, T.T. 1983. Flooding and SO$_2$ stress interaction in *Betula papyrifera* and *B. nigra* seedlings. *For. Sci.*, **29**, 739–50.

Noyes, R.D. 1980. The comparative effects of sulphur dioxide on photosynthesis and translocation in bean. *Physiol. Pl. Pathol.*, **16**, 73–9.

Olszyk, D.M. & Tibbitts, T.W. 1981. Stomatal response and leaf injury of *Pisum sativum* L. with SO$_2$ and O$_3$ exposures, II Influence of moisture stress and time of exposure. *Pl. Physiol.*, **67**, 545–9.

Ordin, L., Garber, M.J. & Kindinger, J.I. 1972. Effect of 2,4-dichlorophenoxyacetic acid on growth and on B-glucan synthases of peroxyacetyl nitrate pretreated *Avena* coleoptile sections. *Physiologia Pl.*, **26**, 17–23.

Ormrod, D.P. 1982. Air pollutant interactions in mixtures. In: *Effects of Gaseous Air Pollutants in Agriculture and Horticulture*, edited by M.H. Unsworth and D.P. Ormrod, 307–32, Butterworths, London.

Oshima, R.J.. 1978. The impact of sulphur dioxide on vegetation; a SO_2/O_3 response model. California Air Resources Board, Final Report, Agreement A6–162–30.

Oshima, R.J., Braegelman, P.K., Flagler, R.B. & Teso, R.R. 1979. The effects of ozone on the growth, yield and partitioning of dry matter in cotton. *J. environ. Qual.*, **8**, 474–9.

Paces, T. 1985. Sources of acidification in Central Europe estimated from elemental budgets in small basins. *Nature, Lond.*, **315**, 31–6.

Pande, P.C. 1985. Responses of spring barley to SO_2 and NO_2 pollution. *Environ. Pollut. Ser. A*, **38**, 87–97.

Pande, P.C. & Mansfield, T.A. 1985a. Responses of spring barley to SO_2 and NO_2 pollution. *Environ. Pollut. Ser. A*, **38**, 87–97.

Pande, P.C. & Mansfield, T.A. 1985b. Responses of winter barley to SO_2 and NO_2 alone and in combination. *Environ. Pollut. Ser. A*, **39**, 281–91.

Parry, M.A.J. & Gutteridge, S. 1983. The effects of SO_3^{2-} and SO_4^{2-} ions on the reactions of ribulose bisphosphate carboxylase. *J. exp. Bot.*, **35**, 157–68.

Peiser, G.D. & Yang, S.F. 1979. Ethylene and ethane production from SO_2-injured plants. *Pl. Physiol.*, **63**, 1142–5.

Peiser, G. & Yang, S.F. 1985. Biochemical and physiological effects of SO_2 on nonphotosynthetic processes in plant. In: *Sulfur Dioxide and Vegetation*, edited by W.E. Winner, H.A. Mooney and R.A. Goldstein, 148–61, Stanford University Press, California, USA.

Pell, E.J. & Brennan, E. 1973. Changes in respiration, photosynthesis, adenosine 5′-triphosphate, and total adenylate content of ozonated pinto bean foliage as they relate to symptom expression. *Pl. Physiol.*, **51**, 378–81.

Pemadasa, M.A. 1979. Stomatal response to two herbicidal auxins. *J. exp. Bot.*, **30**, 267–74.

Percy, K. 1986. The effects of simulated acid rain on germinative capacity, growth and morphology of forest tree seedlings. *New Phytol.*, **104**, 473–84.

Percy, K.E. & Riding, R.T. 1981. Histology and histochemistry of elongating needles of *Pinus strobus* subjected to a long-duration, low-concentration exposure of sulphur dioxide. *Can. J. Bot.*, **59**, 2558–67.

Perrin, D.A. 1987. Sulphur deposition in the United Kingdom – A comparison of model results with measurements for 1986. In: *Proceedings International Conference, Acid Rain, Lisbon* September 1987 (in press).

Pitcairn, C.E.R. & Grace, J. 1985. Wind and surface damage, In: *Effects of Shelter on the Physiology of Plants and Animals*, edited by J. Grace, 115–26, (Progress in Biometeorology Volume 2) Swets & Zeitlinger B.V., Lisse.

Pollanschutz, J., Kilian, W., Neumann, M. & Seigal, G. 1985. Instruktion fur die Feldarbeit die Waldzustandsinvertur nach bundeseinheitlichen Richtlinien, 1984–88. *Forst. Bundesversuchsans.*, Wien.

Port, G.R. 1981. Auchenorrhyncha on roadside verges. A preliminary survey. *Acta ent. fenn.*, **38**, 29.

Port, G.R. & Thompson, J.R. 1980. Outbreaks of insect herbivores on plants along motorways in the United Kingdom. *J. appl. Ecol.*, **17**, 649–56.

Posthumus, A.C. & Tonneijck, A.E.G. 1984. Annual Report of the Research Institute for Plant Protection, Wageningen, Holland.

Prinz, B., Krause, G.H.M. & Jung, K–D. 1985. Untersuchungen der landesanstalt für Immissions-schutz des Landes NRW zur Problematik der Waldschäden. Symposium der Schwaben AG, *Waldschäden 85- Theorie und Praxis auf der Suche nach. Antworten* Stuttgart-Hohenheim.

Prinz, B., Krause, G.H.M. & Jung, K–D. 1985. Responses of German forests in recent years: causes for concern elsewhere? In: *Effects of Acid Deposition on Forests, Wetlands and Agricultural Ecosystems*. Proceedings of NATO advanced research workshop, Toronto, May 1985. Springer-Verlag.

Press, M.C., Ferguson, P. & Lee, J.A. 1983. Two hundred years of acid rain. *Naturalist*, **108**, 125–9.

Press, M.C., Henderson, J. & Lee, J.A. 1985. Arylsulphatase activity in peat in relation to acidic deposition. *Soil Biol. & Biochem.*, **17**, 99–103.

Press, M.C., Woodin, S.J. & Lee, J.A. 1986. The potential importance of an increased atmospheric nitrogen supply to the growth of ombrotrophic *Sphagnum* species. *New Phytol.*, **103**, 45–55.

Przybylski, Z. 1979. The effects of automobile exhaust gases on the arthropods of cultivated plants, meadows and orchards. *Environ. Pollut.*, **19**, 157–61.

Puckett. L.J. 1982. Acid rain, air pollution and tree growth in Southeastern New York. *J. environ. Qual.*, **11**, 376–81.

Puckett, K.J., Nieboer, E., Flora, W.P. & Richardson, D.H.S. 1973. Sulphur dioxide: its effect on photosynthetic ^{14}C fixation in lichens and suggested mechanisms of toxicity. *New Phytol.*, **72**, 141–54.

Raschke, K. 1975. Simultaneous requirement of CO_2 and abscisic acid for stomatal closing. *Planta*, **125**, 243–59.

Raynor, G.S. & Hayes, J.V. 1982. Variation in chemical wet deposition with meteorological conditions. *Atmos. Environ.*, **16**, 1647–56.

Rebbeck, J. & Brennan, E. 1984. The effect of simulated acid rain and ozone on the yield and quality of glasshouse-grown alfalfa. *Environ. Pollut. Ser. A*, **36**, 7–16.

Rehfuess, K.E. 1986. Perceptions on forest diseases in Central Europe. Paper presented at a meeting of the Foundation for Science and Technology at the Royal Society of London.

Rehfuess, K.E. & Bosch, C. 1986. Experimentelle Untersuchungen zur Erkrankung der Fichte (*Picea abies* (L.) Karst.) auf sauren Boden der Hochlagen: Arbeitshypothese and Versuchsplan. *Fortwiss Centbl.*, **105**, 202–6.

Reid, J.M. 1979. *Geochemical Balances in Glendye, an Upland Catchment in Grampian Region*, Ph.D. Thesis, University of Aberdeen.

Reich, P.B. & Amundson, R.G. 1984. Low level O_3 and/or SO_2 exposure causes a linear decline in soybean yield. *Environ. Pollut. Ser. A*, **34**, 345–55.

Reich, P.B. & Amundson, R.G. 1985. Ambient levels of ozone reduce net photosynthesis in tree and crop species. *Science*, **230**, 566–70.

Reich, P.B., Schoettle, A.W. & Amundson, R.G. 1986. Effects of O_3 and acidic rain on photosynthesis and growth in Sugar maple and Northern red oak seedlings. *Environ. Pollut. Ser. A*, **40**, 1–15.

Reinert, R.A. & Gray, T.N. 1981. The response of radish to NO_2, SO_2 and O_3 alone and in combination. *J. environ. Qual.*, **10**, 240–3.

Reinert, R.A., Heagle, A.S. & Heck, W.W. 1975. Plant response to pollutant combinations. In: *Responses of Plants to Air Pollution*, edited by J.B. Mudd & T.T. Kozlowski, 159–77. Academic Press, New York.

Reinert, R.A. & Sanders, J.S. 1982. Growth of radish and marigold following repeated exposure to NO_2, SO_2 and O_3. *Pl. Dis.*, **66**, 122–4.

Reiter, R. & Kanter, H-J. 1982. Time behaviour of CO_2 and O_3 in the lower troposphere based on recordings from neighbouring mountain stations between 0.7 and 3.0 km ASL including the effects of meteorological parameters. *Arch. Met. Geoph. Biokl. Ser. B*, **30**, 191–225.

Reuss, J.O. 1983. Implications of the calcium–aluminium exchange system for the effect of acid precipitation on soils. *J. environ. Qual.*, **12**, 591–5.

Rich, S. & Turner, N.C. 1972. Importance of moisture on stomatal behaviour of plants subjected to ozone. *J. Air Poll. Contr. Assoc.*, **22**, 718–21.

Roberts, T.M. 1984. Long term effects of sulphur dioxide on crops: an analysis of dose-response functions. *Phil. Trans. R. Soc., London. Ser. B*, **305**, 299–316.

Roberts, T.M., Bell, R., Horsman, D.C. & Colvill, K. 1983. The use of open-top chambers to study the effects of air pollutants in particular SO_2 on the growth of ryegrass *Lolium perenne* L. *Environ. Pollut. Ser. A*, **31**, 9–33.

Roberts, T.M., Darrall, N.M. & Lane, P. 1983. Effects of gaseous air pollutants on agriculture and forestry in the UK. *Adv. appl. Biol.*, **9**, 1–141.

Rodhe, H. & Rood, M.J. 1986. Temporal evolution of nitrogen compounds in Swedish precipitation since 1955.

Roeloffs, J.G.M., Kempers, A.J., Houdijk, A.L.F.M. & Jansen, J. 1985. The effect of airborne ammonium sulphate on *Pinus nigra* var *maritima* in The Netherlands. *Pl. Soil*, **84**, 45–56.

Roose, M.L., Bradshaw, A.D. & Roberts, T.M. 1982. Evolution of resistance to gaseous air pollutants. In: *Effects of Gaseous Air Pollution in Agriculture and Horticulture*, edited by M.H. Unsworth and D.P. Ormrod, 379–410. Butterworths, London.

Rose, C. & Neville, M. 1985. Final Report Tree Dieback Survey. Friends of the Earth Ltd, London.

Rosen, P.M. & Runeckles, U.C. 1976. Interaction of ozone and greenhouse whitefly in plant injury. *Environ. Conserv.*, **3**, 70–71.

Rosenberg, C.R., Hutnik, R.J. & Davis, D.D. 1979. Forest composition at varying distances from a coal-burning power plant. *Environ. Pollut.*, **19**, 307–17.

Rowland, A., Murray, A.J.S. & Wellburn, A.R. 1987. Oxides of nitrogen and their impact on vegetation. *Reviews on Environmental Health* (in press).

Rutter, A.J. 1975. The hydrological cycle in vegetation. In: *Vegetation and the atmosphere. 1. Principles*, edited by J.L. Monteith, 111–54, London, Academic Press.

Ryskova, L. 1978. The influence of low doses of SO_2 on spruce (*Picea abies*) and pine (*Pinus sylvestris*) plants. *Prace Vulhm.*, **52**, 115–25.

Saunders, P.J.W. 1966. The toxicity of sulphur dioxide to *Diplocarpon rosae* Wolf causing blackspot of roses. *Ann. appl. Biol.*, **58**, 103–14.

Saunders, P.J.W. 1973. Effects of atmospheric pollution on leaf surface microflora. *Pesticide Sci.*, **4**, 589–95.

Saxe, H. 1983. Long-term effects of low levels of SO_2 on bean plants (*Phaseolus vulgaris*). Immission-response pattern of net photosynthesis and transpiration during life-long continuous measurement. *Physiologia Pl.*, **57**, 101–7.

Saxe, H. 1986. Effects of NO, NO_2 and CO_2 on net photosynthesis, dark respiration and transpiration of pot plants. *New Phytol.*, **103**, 185–97.

Scheffer, T.C. & Hedgecock, G.G. 1955. Injury to northwestern forest trees by sulfur dioxide from smelters. US Department of Agriculture, Technical Bulletin No. 1117.

Scherbatskoy, T. & Klein, R.M. 1983. Response of spruce and birch foliage to leaching by acidic mists. *J. environ. Qual.*, **12**, 189–95.

Schopfer, W. 1985. Waldschadenssituation 1985 in Baden-Wurttemberg. *Allg. Forstz.* **51/52**: 1381–4.

Seaward, M.R.D. 1982. Lichen ecology of changing urban environments. In: *Urban Ecology*, edited by R. Bornkamm, J.A. Lee and M.R.D. Seaward, 181–9, Blackwell Scientific Publications, Oxford.

Sekiya, J.L., Wilson, L. & Filner, P. 1982. Resistance to injury by SO_2: correlation with its reduction to, and emission of, hydrogen sulfide in Cucurbitaceae. *Pl. Physiol.*, **70**, 437–41.

Shafer, S.R., Bruck, R.I. & Heagle, A.S. 1985. Influence of simulated acidic rain on *Phytophthora cinnamoni* and phytophthora root rot of blue lupine. *Phytopathology*, **75**, 996–1003.

Shaner, D.L. & Lyon, J.L. 1979. Stomatal cycling in *Phaseolus vulgaris* L. in response to glyphosate. *Pl. Sci. Lett.*, **15**, 83–7.

Sherwood, C.H. & Rolph, C.D. 1970. Ozone protects plants from air pollution with 2,4-D. *Hort. Sci.*, **5**, 190.

Shew, B.B., Reinert, R.A. & Barker, K.R. 1982. Response of tomatoes to ozone, sulfur dioxide, and infection by *Pratylenchus penetrans*. *Phytopathology*, **72**, 822–6.

Shriner, D.S. 1978. Effects of simulated acidic rain on host–parasite interactions in plant diseases. *Phytopathology*, **68**, 213–7.

Shriner, D.S. 1980. Vegetation surfaces: a platform for pollutant/parasite interactions. In: *Polluted Rain*, edited by M.W. Toribara, M.W. Miller and P.E. Morrow, 259–72. Plenum Publishing Corporation.

Shupe, J.L., Peterson, H.B. & Leone, N.C. 1983. *Fluorides: Effects on Vegetation, Animals and Humans.* Paragon Press, Salt Lake City, 370.

Skeffington, R.A. & Roberts, T.M. 1985. The effects of ozone and acid mist on Scots pine seedlings. *Oecologia*, **65**, 201–6.

Skelly, J.M., Yang, Y-S., Chevone, B.I., Long, S.J., Nellessen, J.E. & Winner, W.E. 1983. Ozone concentrations and their influence on forest species in the Blue Ridge Mountains of Virginia. In: *Air Pollution and the Productivity of the Forest*, edited by D.D. Davis, A.A. Miller and L. Dochinger, 143–60. Isaac Walton League of America.

Smith, R.A. 1872. *Air and rain. The Beginnings of a Chemical Climatology.* Longmans, Green & Co., London.

Smith, W.H. 1976. Air pollution-effects on the structure and function of plant surface microbial ecosystems. In: *Microbiology of Aerial Plant Surfaces*, edited by C.H. Dickinson & T.F. Preece, 75–105. Academic Press.

Snaith, P.J. & Mansfield, T.A. 1982. Control of the CO_2 response of stomata by IAA and ABA. *J. exp. Bot.*, **33**, 360–5.

Soikkeli, S. & Karenlampi, L. 1984. The effect of nitrogen fertilization on the ultrastructure of mesophyll cells of conifer needles in northern Finland. Quoted by Friedland *et al.*, 1984.

Spotts, R.A., Lukezie, F.L. & Lacasse, N.L. 1975. The effect of benzinidazole, chloresterol and a steroil inhibitor on leaf sterols and ozone resistance of bean. *Phytopathology*, **65**, 45–9.

Strivastava, H.S., Jolliffe, P.A. & Runeckles, V.C. 1975. The effects of environmental conditions on the inhibition of leaf gas exchange by NO_2. *Can. J. Bot.*, **53**, 475–82.

Starkey, T.E., Davis, D.D., Pell, E.J. & Merrill, W. 1981. Influence of peroxyacetyl nitrate (PAN) on water stress in bean. *Pl. Hort. Sci.*, **16**, 547–8.

Steubing, von L., Fangmeier, A., Fischer, A. & Grittke, J. 1986. Immissionssituation der Waldbodenvegetation: Sensitivität genenüber SO$_2$ am natürlichen Standort. Allg. Forstz. **21**, 526–8.

Suttle, N.F. 1974. Effects of organic and inorganic sulphur on the availability of dietary copper to sheep. Br. J. Nutr., **32**, 559–68.

Szerszén, J. 1981. Comparative study of phyto-pathogenic fungal microflora in three regions differing in the degree of pollution with industrial emissions. Polish Ecol. Stud., **7**, 107–16.

Takemoto, B.K. & Noble, R.D. 1982. The effects of short-term SO$_2$ fumigation on photosynthesis and respiration in soybean (Glycine max). Environ. Pollut. Ser. A, **28**, 67–74.

Tallis, J.H. 1964. Studies on southern Pennine blanket peat. III. The behaviour of Sphagnum. J. Ecol., **52**, 345–53.

Tallis, J.H. 1987. Fire and flood at Holme Moss. J. Ecol., (in press).

Tamm, C.O. 1976. Acid precipitation: biological effects in soil and on forest vegetation. Ambio, **5**, 235–8.

Tamm, C.O., Wiklander, L. & Popovic, B. 1977. Effects of application of sulphuric acid to poor pine forests. Wat. Air & Soil Pollut., **8**, 75–87.

Taylor, G.E., Tingey, G.T. & Gunderson, C.A. 1986. Photosynthesis, carbon allocation and growth of sulphur dioxide ecotypes of Geranium carolinium L. Oecologia (Berlin), **68**, 350–7.

Thomas, M.D. 1961. Effects of Air Pollution on Plants. Air Pollution: WHO Monograph Ser 46, 233–78. World Health Organisation, Geneva.

Thompson, T.R.E. & Loveland, P.J. 1985. The acidity of Welsh soils. Soil Use & Manage., **1**, 21–4.

Thor, E. & Gall, W.R. 1978. Variation in air-pollution tolerance and growth rate among progenies of southern Appalachian white pine. In: Proceedings of the first conference of the Metropolitan Tree Improvement Alliance (METRIA), Lanham, Maryland, **1**, 80–6.

Tingey, D.T., Heck, W.W. & Reinert, R.A. 1971. Effects of low concentrations of ozone and sulphur dioxide on foliage, growth and yield of radish. J. Amer. Soc. Hort. Sci., **96**, 364–71.

Tingey, D.T. & Olszyk, D.M. 1985. Intraspecies variability in metabolic responses to SO$_2$. In: Sulfur Dioxide and Vegetation edited by W.E. Winner, H.A. Mooney and R.A. Goldstein, 178–205, Stanford University Press, California, USA.

Tingey, D.T. & Taylor, G.E. 1982. Variation in plant response to ozone: a conceptual model of physiological events. In: Effects of Gaseous Air Pollutants in Agriculture and Horticulture, edited by M.H. Unsworth and D.P. Ormrod, 113–38, Butterworths, London.

Tranquillini, W. 1982. Frost-drought and its ecological significance. In: Encyclopedia of Plant Physiology, New Series, 12B. Physiological Plant Ecology II, edited by O.L. Lange, P.S. Nobel, C.B. Osmond, and H. Ziegler. Springer-Verlag.

Treshaw, M. 1970. Environment and Plant Response. McGraw–Hill.

Troiano, J., Colavito, L., Heller, L., McCune, D.C. & Jacobson, J.S. 1983. Effects of acidity of simulated rain and its joint action with ambient ozone on measures of biomass and yield in soybean. Environ. Expt. Bot., **23**, 113–9.

Tveite, B. 1980. Foliar nutrient levels in field experiments. In: Ecological Impact of Acid Precipitation, Proceedings of an International Conference, edited by D. Drabløs and A. Tollan, 204–5, SNSF Project, Norway.

Ulrich, B., Mayer, R. & Khanna, P.K. 1980. Chemical changes due to acid precipitation in a loess-derived soil in central Europe. Soil Sci., **130**, 193–9.

UK PORG 1987. Ozone in the United Kingdom. UK Photochemical Oxidants Review Group Interim Report. Harwell Laboratory.

UK RGAR 1987. Acid Deposition in the United Kingdom 1981–85. UK Review Group on Acid Rain. Second Report. Warren Spring Laboratory, Stevenage.

Unsworth, M.H., Biscoe, P.V. & Pinckney, H.R. 1972. Stomatal responses to sulphur dioxide. Nature, Lond., **239**, 458–9.

Usher, S.M. 1984. The Effects of London Air Pollution on Vegetation. Ph.D. Thesis, University of London.

Vargo, R.H., Pell, E.J. & Smith, S.H. 1978. Induced resistance to ozone injury of soybean by tobacco ringspot virus. Phytopathology, **68**, 715–9.

Villemant, C. 1981. Influence de la pollution atmospherique sur les populations d'aphides du pin sylvestre en Fôret de Roumare (Seine-Maritime). *Environ. Pollut. Ser. A*, **24**, 245–62.

Wachter, A. 1978. German literature on Silver fir decline (1830–1978). *J. Pl. Dis. & Prot.*, **85**, 361–81.

Wallsgrove, R.M., Lea, P.J. & Miflin, B.J. 1979. The distribution of the enzymes of nitrogen assimilation within the pea leaf cell. *Pl. Physiol.*, **63**, 323–6.

Walmsley, L., Ashmore, M.R. & Bell, J.N.B. 1980. Adaptation of radish (*Raphanus sativus* L.) in response to continuous exposure to ozone. *Environ. Pollut. Ser. A*, **23**, 165–77.

Walton, K.C. 1984. Fluoride in fox bone near an aluminium reduction plant in Anglesey, Wales, and elsewhere in the United Kingdom. *Environ. Pollut. Ser. B*, **7**, 273–80.

Walton, K.C. 1985. Fluoride in bones of small rodents near an aluminium reduction plant. *Wat., Soil & Air Pollut.*, **26**, 65–70.

Walton, K.C. 1986. Fluoride in moles, shrews and earthworms near an aluminium reduction plant. *Environ. Pollut. Ser. A*, **42**, 361–71.

Walton, K.C. 1987. Tooth damage in field voles, wood mice and moles in areas polluted by fluoride from an aluminium reduction plant. *Sci. Total Environ.*, (in press).

Warren Spring Laboratory 1986. *The Investigation of Air Pollution: National Survey of Smoke and SO₂*. Annual Publication by the Warren Spring Laboratory, Stevenage.

Warrington, S. 1987. Relationship between SO_2 dose and growth of the pea aphid *Acyrthosiphon pisum*, on peas. *Environ. Pollut. Ser. A* (in press).

Webber, J. 1981. Trace elements in agriculture. In: *Effects of Heavy Metals on Plants, Vol. 2. Metals in the Environment*, edited by N.W. Lepp, 159–84, Applied Science Publishers, London and New Jersey.

Weber, D.E., Reinert, R.A. & Barker, K.R. 1979. Ozone and sulfur dioxide effects on reproduction and host–parasite relationships of selected plant–parasitic nematodes. *Phytopathology*, **69**, 624–8.

Weidensaul, T.C. & Darling, S.L. 1979. Effects of ozone and sulfur dioxide on the host–pathogen relationship of Scots pine and *Scirrhia acicola*. *Phytopathology*, **69**, 939–41.

Weinstein, C.H., McCune, D.C., Aluisio, A.L. & Van Leuken, P. 1975. The effect of sulphur dioxide on the incidence and severity of bean rust and early blight of tomato. *Environ. Pollut.*, **9**, 145–55.

Wellburn, A.R. 1985a. SO_2 effects on stromal and thylakoid function. In: *Sulfur Dioxide and Vegetation* edited by W.E. Winner, H.A. Mooney and R.A. Goldstein, 133–47, Stanford Univ. Press, California, USA.

Wellburn, A.R. 1985b. Ion chromatographic determination of levels of anions in plastids from fumigated and non-fumigated barley seedlings. *New Phytol.*, **100**, 329–39.

Wellburn, A.R. 1982. Effects of SO_2 and NO_2 on metabolic function. In: *Effects of Gaseous Air Pollution in Agriculture and Horticulture*, edited by M.H. Unsworth and D.P. Ormrod, 169–88, Butterworths, London.

Wellburn, A.R., Capron, T.M., Chan, H-S. & Horsman, D.C. 1976. Biochemical effects of air pollutants on plants. In: *Effects of Air Pollutants on Plants*, edited by T.A. Mansfield, 105–14. Cambridge University Press.

Wellburn, A.R., Higginson, C., Robinson, D. & Walmsley, C. 1981. Biochemical explanations of more than additive inhibitory effects of low atmospheric levels of SO_2 plus NO_2 on plants. *New Phytol.*, **88**, 223–37.

Wellburn, A.R., Majernik, O. & Wellburn, F.A.M. 1972. Effects of SO_2 and NO_2 polluted air upon the ultrastructure of chloroplasts. *Environ. Pollut.*, **3**, 37–49.

Wellburn, A.R., Wilson, J. & Aldridge, P.H. 1980. Biochemical responses of plants to nitric oxide polluted atmospheres. *Environ. Pollut.*, **22**, 219–28.

Wentzel, K.F. 1965. Insekten als Immissionsfolgeschädinge. *Naturwissenschaften*, **52**, 113.

Wheeler, S.M. & Fell, L.R. 1983. Fluorides in cattle nutrition. Commonwealth Bureau of Nutrition. *Nutr. Abstr. Rev. Ser. B*, **53**, 741–67.

White, K.L., Hill, A.C. & Bennett, J.H. 1974. Synergistic inhibition of apparent photosynthesis rate of alfalfa by combination of sulphur dioxide and nitrogen oxide. *Environ. Sci. Technol.*, **8**, 574–6.

Whitmore, M.E. 1985. Effects of SO_2 and NO_x on plant growth. In: *Sulphur Dioxide and Vegetation*, edited by Winner, W.E., Mooney, H.A. and Goldstein, R.A., 264–80, Stanford Univ. Press, California, USA.

Whitmore, M.E. & Mansfield, T.A. 1983. Effects of long-term exposures to SO_2 and NO_2 on *Poa pratensis* and other grasses. *Environ. Pollut. Ser. A*, **31**, 217–35.

Whitmore, M.E. & Freer-Smith, P.H. 1982. Growth effects of SO_2 and/or NO_2 on woody plants and grasses during spring and summer. *Nature, Lond.*, **300**, 55–7.

WHO. 1984. *Fluorine and Fluorides.* Experimental Health Criteria 36. World Health Organisation, Geneva.

Wiackowski, W. 1978. Impact of industrial air pollution upon parasites of pine bud moth (*Exoteleia dodecella*), aphid predators, and certain other insects occurring on pine in the vicinity of Tomaszou Maz. *Folia Forest. Polonica, Ser. A*, **23**, 175–87.

Wigley, T.M.L., Jones, P.D. & Briffa, K.R. 1986. Detecting the effects of acidic deposition and CO_2-fertilisation on tree growth. In: *Methods of dendrochronology: East/ West Approaches.* (IIASA/Polish Academy of Sciences) (in press).

Wilson, G.B. & Bell, J.N.B. 1985. Studies on the tolerances to sulphur dioxide of grass populations in polluted areas. III. Investigations on the rate of development of tolerance. *New Phytol.*, **100**, 63–77.

Winner, W.E. & Mooney, H.A. 1980a. Ecology of SO_2 resistance: III. Metabolic changes in C_3 and C_4 *Atriplex* species due to SO_2 fumigation. *Oecologia (Berlin)*, **46**, 49–54.

Winner, W.E. & Mooney, H.A. 1980b. Ecology of SO_2 resistance. II. Photosynthetic changes of shrubs in relation to SO_2 absorption and stomatal behaviour. *Oecologia (Berlin)*, **44**, 296–302.

Winner, W.E. & Mooney, H.A. 1980c. Ecology of SO_2 resistance. I. Effects of fumigations on gas exchange of deciduous and evergreen shrubs. *Oecologia (Berlin)*, **44**, 290–5.

Wolting, H.G. 1983, 1984 and 1985. In: Annual Reports of the Research Institute for Plant Protection, Wageningen, Holland.

Wood, T. & Bormann, F.H. 1977. Short term effects of a simulated acid rain upon the growth and nutrient relations of *Pinus strobus*, L., *Wat. Air & Soil Pollut.*, **7**, 479–88.

Woodin, S.J. 1986. *Ecophysiological Effects of Atmospheric Nitrogen Deposition on Ombrotrophic **Sphagnum** species.* Ph.D. Thesis, University of Manchester.

Woodin, S.J., Press, M.C. & Lee, J.A. 1985. Nitrate reductase activity in *Sphagnum fusum* in relation to wet deposition of nitrate from the atmosphere. *New Phytol.*, **99**, 381–8.

Woodin, S.J. & Lee, J.A. 1987. The fate of some components of acidic deposition in ombrotrophic mires. *Environ. Pollut.*, **45**, 61–72.

Wright, D.A., Davison, A.W. & Johnson, M.S. 1978. Fluoride accumulation by long-tailed field mice (*Apodemus sylvaticus* L.) field voles (*Microtus agrestis* L.) from polluted environments. *Environ. Pollut.*, **17**, 303–10.

Wright, E.A., Lucas, P.W., Cottam, D.A. & Mansfield, T.A. 1988. Physiological responses of plants to SO_2, NO_2 and O_3: Implications for drought resistance. In: *Direct Effects of Dry and Wet Deposition on Forest Ecosystems – in particular Canopy Interactions.* Proceedings of CEC/ COST Workshop, Lokeberg, Sweden. October 1986, (EAD. 62/87) CEC Brussels.

Yang, Y.S., Skelly, J.M. & Chevone, B.I. 1983. Effects of pollutant combinations at low doses on growth of forest trees. *Aquilo Ser. Bot.*, **19**, 406–418.

Young, J.E. & Matthews, P. 1981. Pollution injury in south east Northumberland: the analysis of field data using canonical correlation analysis. *Environ. Pollut. Ser. B*, **2**, 353–65.

Zeigler, I. 1972. The effect of SO_3^{2-} on the activity of ribulose-1,5-diphosphate carboxylase in isolated spinach chloroplasts. *Planta*, **103**, 155–63.

Zeevaart, A.J. 1976. Some effects of fumigating plants for short periods with NO_2. *Environ. Pollut.*, **11**, 97–108.

GLOSSARY

This glossary covers scientific terms specific to pollution science and others which may be difficult to locate in dictionaries. Terms not appearing in the glossary can be found in the following: Penguin Dictionary of Botany (1985) Penguin Books Ltd, 1985; Penguin Dictionary of Chemistry (1985) Penguin Books Ltd, 1985; Chambers Dictionary of Science and Technology (1983) Chaucer Press, Suffolk.

Bulk precipitation

The total input of wet and dry deposition measured by a horizontal gauge.

Clone

A population of genetically identical individuals commonly produced by vegetation propagation.

Cultivar

A variety or strain of a plant produced by horticultural or agricultural techniques and not normally found in natural populations; a *culti*vated *vari*ety.

Dry deposition

The direct transfer of gaseous and particulate material from the atmosphere to the surface, ie. excluding the indirect input in aqueous solution or suspension (wet deposition).

Episode

Short periods of large concentrations of gaseous pollutants (which may occur when there are nearby sources of pollutants or if the weather favours the build up of secondary pollutants).

Horizon

A layer of soil which may differ in colour, texture and composition from other layers lying above or below.

Minerotrophic

Receiving nutrients from the soil.

Mycorrhiza

A symbiotic association between a fungus and the roots of a higher plant.

Mineralization

Production of inorganic ions in the soil by the oxidation of organic compounds.

Nitrification

Oxidation of ammonia to nitrites and of nitrites to nitrates, as by action of bacteria.

Occult deposition

The turbulent transfer of cloud, mist or fog droplets, containing large concentrations of pollutants, to vegetation.

Ombrotrophic

Receiving nutrients from rain-fall.

pH

A logarithmic index for the hydrogen ion concentration in an aqueous solution. Used as a measure of acidity of a solution. Given by $pH - \log_{10}[H^+]$ where $[H^+]$ is taken as the hydrogen ion concentration. A pH below 7 denotes acidity and one above 7 denotes alkalinity.

Podzol

A soil type in which there is a surface layer of acid humus and below this a severely leached mineral layer; typically found under coniferous forest and heathland.

Pollution climate

A phrase used to describe the mixtures of pollutants that occur on a regional scale.

Soil acidification

This may be defined in 2 ways. i) A process causing a decrease in soil solution pH. ii) A process which reduces the acid-neutralising capacity of the soil. The former definition is the one adopted in this report.

Stemflow

Water that reaches the ground by flowing down the surfaces of stems.

Stratosphere

The earth's atmosphere above the troposphere extending for up to 50 km.

Throughflow

Water that (i) drips from plant surfaces (crown drip) and (ii) falls uninterrupted through gaps in the canopy (direct penetration).

Wet Deposition

The transfer of an element or substance from the atmosphere in rain or snow.

APPENDIX

APPENDIX **2**

UNITS AND CONVERSION FACTORS

The concentrations of pollutant gases in this report are expressed in parts per billion by volume (ppb) where a billion is defined as 10^9. Concentrations may also be given in microgrammes per cubic metre (g m^{-3}) and conversion factors (calculated at standard temperature, 20 C (293 K) and pressure, 101.3 k Pa) are given in Table 1.

Table 1 Calculated conversion factors

Gas	Molecular weight (g mol^{-1})	Boiling point (°C)	Density (kg m^{-3})	Diffusivity in air (mm^2s^{-1})	To convert from ppb to μg m^3, multiply ppb by	To convert from μg m^{-3} to ppb, multiply μg m^3 by
Ammonia NH_3	17.0	−33.4	0.72	25	0.71	1.414
Chlorine Cl_2	70.9	−34.6	2.99	12	2.95	0.339
Ethylene C_2H_4	28.0	−103.8	1.17	19	1.16	0.859
Fluorine F_2	38.0	−187.0	1.58	16	1.58	0.633
Hydrogen chloride HCl	36.5	−85.0	1.53	17	1.52	0.659
Hydrogen fluoride HF	20.0	19.4	0.83	23	0.83	1.202
Hydrogen sulphide H_2S	34.1	−59.6	1.43	18	1.42	0.705
Nitric oxide NO	30.0	−151.0	1.25	18	1.25	0.801
Nitrogen dioxide NO_2	46.0	21.3	1.88*	15	1.91	0.523
Ozone O_3	48.0	−112.0	1.99	15	2.00	0.501
Peroxyacetyl nitrate (PAN) CH_3COONO_2	105.0	**	**	10	4.37	0.229
Sulphur dioxide SO_2	64.1	−10.0	2.73	12	2.67	0.375

* At 25°C, 101.3 k Pa (note boiling point 21.3°C)

** Values not known

Table 2 Conversion of pH values to Microequivalents Hydrogen Ion per Litre

μeq $H^+ l^{-1}$ = antilog (6.0 − pH)

pH	μeq $H^+ l^{-1}$	pH	μeq $H^+ l^{-1}$	pH	μeq $H^+ l^{-1}$
3.0	1000	4.0	100	5.0	10
3.1	794	4.1	79	5.1	8
3.2	631	4.2	63	5.2	6
3.3	501	4.3	50	5.3	5
3.4	398	4.4	40	5.4	4
3.5	316	4.5	32	5.5	3
3.6	251	4.6	25	5.6	3
3.7	200	4.7	20	5.7	2
3.8	158	4.8	16	5.8	2
3.9	126	4.9	13	5.9	1

APPENDIX

3

MEMBERSHIP OF TERRESTRIAL EFFECTS REVIEW GROUP

Professor M.H. Unsworth *Chairman*
University of Nottingham
School of Agriculture
Sutton Bonington
Loughborough
Leics
LE12 5RD

Dr J.N. Bell
Department of Pure and Applied Biology
Imperial College at Silwood Park
Ascot
Berks
SL5 7PY

Dr V.J. Black
Department of Human Sciences
Loughborough University of Technology
Loughborough
Leics
LE11 3TU

Dr M.S. Cresser
Department of Soil Science
University of Aberdeen
Meston Walk
Aberdeen
AB9 2UE

Dr N.M. Darrall
C.E.R.L.
Kelvin Avenue
Leatherhead
Surrey
KT22 7SE

Dr A.W. Davison
Department of Plant Biology
Ridley Building
University of Newcastle-Upon-Tyne
Newcastle-Upon-Tyne
NE1 7RU

Dr P.H. Freer-Smith
Forestry Commission Research Station
Alice Holt Lodge
Wrecclesham
Farnham
Surrey
GU10 4LH

Dr P. Ineson
Institute of Terrestrial Ecology
Merlewood Research Station
Grange-over-Sands
Cumbria
LA11 6JU

Dr J.A. Lee
Department of Environmental Biology
University of Manchester
Manchester
M13 9PL

Prof. F.T. Last
Department of Soil Science
University of Newcastle
Newcastle-Upon-Tyne
NE1 7RU

Prof. T.A. Mansfield
Department of Biological Sciences
University of Lancaster
Lancaster
Lancs
LA1 4YQ

Dr M.H. Martin
Department of Botany
University of Bristol
Woodland Road
Bristol
BS8 7UG

Prof. H.G. Miller
Department of Forestry
University of Aberdeen
St. Machair Drive
Aberdeen
AB9 2UU

Dr T.M. Roberts
C.E.R.L.
Kelvin Avenue
Leatherhead
Surrey
KT22 7SE

Dr C.E.R. Pitcairn *Technical Secretary*
Department of the Environment
c/o Institute of Terrestrial Ecology
Edinburgh Research Station
Bush Estate
Penicuik
Midlothian
EH26 0QB

Mr R.B. Wilson *Technical Secretary*
Department of the Environment
Room B352
Romney House
43 Marsham Street
London
SW1P 3PY

APPENDIX 4

REPORTS PREPARED AT THE REQUEST OF THE DEPARTMENT OF THE ENVIRONMENT

Acid Deposition in the United Kingdom

UK Review Group on Acid Rain, December 1983.

Acid Deposition in the United Kingdom 1981–1985

UK Review Group on Acid Rain. August 1987

Copies of both available from

Warren Spring Laboratory
Gunnels Wood Road
Stevenage
Herts
SG1 2BX

Price £10.00 each.

Acidity in United Kingdom Fresh Waters

UK Acid Waters Review Group, April 1986.

Ozone in the United Kingdom

UK Photochemical Oxidants Review Group, February 1987.

Copies of both available from

DOE/DTP Publications Sales Unit
Building 1
Victoria Road
South Ruislip
Middlesex
HA4 0NZ

Price £10.00 each.

Stratospheric Ozone

UK Stratospheric Ozone Review Group, August 1987

Copies available from HMSO (ISBN 0 11 752018 7) Price £9.95 each

Building Effects Review Group Report. Not yet published. To be available from HMSO.

Printed in the United Kingdom for Her Majesty's Stationery Office
Dd 240133   7/88   C15   443   59471